VOICE-
OVERS

SUNY series in
Latin American and Iberian Thought and Culture

Jorge J. E. Gracia, editor

VOICE-OVERS

Translation and
Latin American Literature

DANIEL BALDERSTON and MARCY SCHWARTZ

editors

*para Marisol
con el canto de
Daniel
Iowa City, octubre de 2002*

STATE UNIVERSITY OF NEW YORK PRESS

Published by

State University of New York Press

Albany

© 2002 State University of New York

For information, address
State University of New York Press,
90 State Street, Suite 700, Albany, NY 12207

Production, Laurie Searl
Marketing, Patrick Durocher

Library of Congress Cataloging-in-Publication Data

Voice-overs : translation and Latin American literature / Daniel Balderston and Marcy
Schwartz, editors.
        p. cm. — (SUNY series in Latin American and Iberian thought and culture)
Includes bibliographical references and index.
ISBN 0-7914-5529-7 (alk. paper) — ISBN 0-7914-5530-0 (pbk. : alk. paper)
        1. Latin American literature—20th century—Translations into English—History and
criticism. 2. Latin American literature—20th century—History and criticism. 3.
Translating and interpreting. I. Balderston, Daniel, 1952– II. Schwartz, Marcy E., 1958–
III. Series.

PQ7081 .V65 2002
860.9'98—dc21

                                                                          2002075885

10   9   8   7   6   5   4   3   2   1

Contents

Acknowledgments   ix

Introduction   1
    Daniel Balderston and Marcy Schwartz

PART I
WRITERS ON TRANSLATION

The Homeric Versions   15
    Jorge Luis Borges

Translate, Traduire, Tradurre: Traducir   21
    Julio Cortázar

The Desire to Translate   23
    Gabriel García Márquez

Gender and Translation   26
    Diana Bellessi

Where Do Words Come From?   30
    Luisa Futoransky

On Destiny, Language, and Translation,
    or, Ophelia Adrift in the C. & O. Canal   32
    Rosario Ferré

Language, Violence, and Resistance   42
    Junot Díaz

Translation as Restoration   45
    Cristina García

Language and Change   49
    Rolando Hinojosa-Smith

Metamorphosis   52
    Nélida Piñon

Resisting Hybridity   55
    Ariel Dorfman

A Translator in Search of an Author   58
    Cristina Peri Rossi

Trauma and Precision in Translation   61
    Tomás Eloy Martínez

Writing and Translation   64
    Ricardo Piglia

PART II
TRANSLATING LATIN AMERICA

A Conversation on Translation
    with Margaret Sayers Peden   71
    Margaret Sayers Peden

Words Cannot Express . . .
    The Translation of Cultures   84
    Gregory Rabassa

Infante's Inferno   92
    Suzanne Jill Levine

The Draw of the Other   100
    James Hoggard

Anonymous Sources:
    A Talk on Translators and Translation   104
        Eliot Weinberger

Can Verse Come Across into Verse?   119
        John Felstiner

PART III
CRITICAL APPROACHES

Reading Latin American Literature Abroad:
    Agency and Canon Formation
    in the Sixties and Seventies   129
        María Eugenia Mudrovcic

How the West Was Won: Translations of Spanish
    American Fiction in Europe and the United States   144
        Maarten Steenmeijer

Translating García Márquez,
    or, The Impossible Dream   156
        Gerald Martin

Translating Vowels, or, The Defeat of Sounds:
    The Case of Huidobro   164
        José Quiroga

The Indigenist Writer as a (Mis)Translator of
    Cultures: The Case of Alcides Arguedas   170
        Edmundo Paz-Soldán

Borges, the Original of the Translation   182
        Walter Carlos Costa

Puga's Fictions of Equivalence:
The Tasks of the Novelist as Translator   194
Vicky Unruh

Translation in Post-Dictatorship Brazil: A Weave
of Metaphysical Voices in the Tropics   204
Else Ribeiro Pires Vieira

Bodies in Transit: Travel, Translation, and Gender   213
Francine Masiello

De-facing Cuba: Translating and Transfiguring
Cristina García's *The Agüero Sisters*   224
Israel Reyes

Translation and Teaching: The Dangers of
Representing Latin America for
Students in the United States   235
Steven F. White

Bibliography   245

List of Contributors   257

Index   263

Acknowledgments

We gratefully acknowledge the following publishers and agents for assisting in the publication of the first edition of *Voice-Overs* by according us the right to reprint the following:

Bellessi, Diana: "Gender and Translation," translated for this anthology by Daniel Balderston and Marcy Schwartz, was published in Spanish as "Género y traducción," in *Lo propio y lo ajeno,* 1996. Reprinted by permission of Feminaria.

Borges, Jorge Luis: "The Homeric Versions," translated by Eliot Weinberger, from *Selected Non-Fictions,* edited by Eliot Weinberger, (c) 1999 by Maria Kodama; translation (c) 1999 by Penguin Putnam, Inc. Used by permission of Viking Penguin, a division of Penguin Putnam Inc. and The Wylie Agency (UK) Ltd. Permission also granted by Eliot Weinberger for one-time use only and to be used solely in the printing of this edition and reprints of the same.

Cortázar, Julio: "Translate, traduire, tradurre: traducir," translated for this anthology by Daniel Balderston and Marcy Schwartz, was published in *Grandes Firmas. Antología de artículos hispanoamericanos y españoles,* 1987. Reprinted by permission of Carmen Balcells.

Felstiner, John: "Can Verse Come Across into Verse," is reprinted from *Translating Neruda: The Way to Macchu Picchu,* by John Felstiner, 1980. Reprinted by permission of Stanford University Press.

Ferré, Rosario: "On Destiny, Language, and Translation; or, Ophelia Adrift in the C & O Canal" is reprinted from *The Youngest Doll,* 1991. Reprinted by permission of Susan Bergholz.

Garcia Márquez, Gabriel: "The Desire to Translate," translated for this anthology by Daniel Balderston and Marcy Schwartz, was published in Spanish as "Los pobres traductores buenos" in *GGM: Notas de prensa (1980–1984),* 1991. Reprinted by permission of Carmen Balcells.

Hahn, Oscar: "Why Do You Write," translated from the Spanish by James Hoggard, is reprinted from *Stolen Verses and Other Poems,* 2000. Reprinted by permission of Northwestern University Press.

Levine, Suzanne Jill: "Infante's Inferno," is reprinted from *The Subversive Scribe: Translating Latin American Fiction,* by Suzanne Jill Levine, 1991. Reprinted by permission of Graywolf Press.

The essays of José Quiroga ("Translating Vowels and the Defeat of Sounds: The Case of Huidobro," *Translation Perspectives 6* [1991]), Gregory Rabassa, ("Words Cannot Express . . . The Translation of Cultures,"

Translation Perspectives 9 [1996], as well as "A Conversation on Translation with Margaret Sayers Peden," *Translation Perspectives 4* [1986–87], are published here with the kind permission of the Research Foundation of the State of New York which holds the copyright.

We gratefully acknowledge the Research Council of Rutgers University for a generous grant.

Introduction

Daniel Balderston and Marcy E. Schwartz

—¿Por qué tú no escribes?—le pregunté de pronto.
—¿Por qué no te preguntas mejor por qué no traduzco?
—No. Creo que podrías escribir. Si quisieras . . .

—Guillermo Cabrera Infante, *Tres tristes tigres*

Translation has become both a mechanism and a metaphor for contemporary transnational cultures in the Americas. Literature in the United States, for example, is filled with "marks" of difference—words, concepts, practices—that have served with increasing frequency and ever greater intensity to define the nation's complex "multiculture," and similar phenomena are present in the contemporary literature of Canada, Britain, and many of the countries of Western Europe. Readers of these texts encounter concepts that are to some extent already translated, but not fully, as elements of estrangement or differentiation in the text signal other languages, other cultures, other experiences. Thus, when the anthropologist James Clifford, in his book *Routes: Travel and Translation in the Late Twentieth Century,* speaks of translation as a symptom of our modernity or postmodernity, he considers translation as part of a cluster of cultural practices that define and characterize contemporary experience. Similarly, Beatriz Sarlo, in her recent book *La máquina cultural,* regards translation as a function of a cultural "machine" that has constructed Argentine culture, and Latin American culture in general. Translation continues to be one of the main tools, and defining images, of Latin American culture in its relation to world cultures.

The history of translation in Latin America is anchored in the region's colonial past and its post-Independence process of developing and redefining cultural identities. The twenty-odd Latin American countries have as their official languages those of the European powers that colonized them, Spanish and Portuguese. (Brazil, though the only Portuguese-speaking country in the region, has a population equal to that of all the Spanish-speaking countries of the hemisphere combined.) As with Europe in the Renaissance, at the time of the colonization of the

1

Americas the language of learning was Latin, with an extensive industry of scholars involved in the translation of documents to and from that language, as well as from Arabic and Hebrew (including Arabic translations of the Greek classics) in the famous translation school in Toledo and in the universities. Commerce, and the penetration into the region of England, France, and the Netherlands, meant that there was a considerable circulation of texts among the various European languages. The enormous task of communication between the Europeans and the indigenous peoples, who spoke hundreds of languages, sometimes resulted in the European use of indigenous languages. In particular, in Jesuit Paraguay and southern Brazil, Tupi-Guarani was spoken; in central Mexico many Europeans learned Nahuatl; and Quechua and Aymara were spoken in the Andean region. Eventually, colonialism established widespread use of the Roman alphabet to transcribe native languages early in the colonial period (see Braga-Pinto). The linguistic diversity throughout the region (especially in the Caribbean region, with its wealth of creole languages) has made translation a central characteristic of New World identities. The role of the lettered class, therefore, regardless of race, incorporated translation as a practice and as a method of analysis. The Inca Garcilaso de la Vega and Guaman Poma de Ayala present mestizo and indigenous examples of cultural "interpreters" of the colonial experience. Through their own strategies and methods, they consciously provided bridges for the texts and practices of their "hybridized" identities and communities. Afro-Latin American experience later contributes to this multicultural expression in the literary texts associated with negritude and negrismo.[1]

Independence, which came early in the nineteenth century in most of Spanish America and near the close of the century in Brazil and Cuba, meant something of a cultural realignment with considerable repercussions for the linguistic situation. As most of the new republics adopted the Napoleonic code for their legal systems, so most of the elite groups of the Latin American countries adopted French as the language of learning and culture, and the French educational system as a model. A few Latin American writers of the nineteenth century and well into the twentieth wrote in French (Lautréamont, the Countess of Merlin, Jules Supervielle, Victoria Ocampo, César Moro, Héctor Bianciotti) while countless others read more in French than in any local language. English became dominant as the language of international commerce with the building of railroads and modern ports, and with the power of the British Empire. As Jorge Luis Borges notes in his famous essay "The Argentine Writer and Tradition," by the middle of the twentieth century the contemporary writing of Spain was something of an acquired taste for Spanish American writers. The emerging Latin American nations' cultural, political, and economic connections with France and England, and later the United States, created a complex geopolitics with Europe and North America that recent literary trends continue to evidence (see Schwartz).

The contests over language and cultural identity that still rage in contemporary writing derive from these early nation-building struggles. Whether post-Independence Latin America truly represents a postcolonial situation, or whether its pattern of a resettled and transplanted European culture determined by *criollo* élites warrants some other defining term, is a continuing debate in colonial studies.[2] Nevertheless, Latin American writing and literary movements have always revealed a conscious reflection upon the many languages of the Americas and have directly incorporated that awareness into their texts. Translation is central to the process of self-identification in the throes of cultural and linguistic differences, in Latin America's "constant production of differential sites of enunciation" (Mignolo "Occidentalización" 32, our translation).

Whether or not one considers Latin America to have been "colonial" or "postcolonial" or neither, its literature exhibits many of the characteristics of "postcolonial" writing that theorists have studied in writing from India and Africa (see Bhabha, Tiffin et al.). The intersection of languages is a hallmark of postcolonial literature, according to William Ashcroft, and Latin American writing clearly demonstrates this distinguishing feature. Translation and language variance are symptoms of "a writing which actually *installs* distance and absence in the interstices of the text" (Ashcroft 61). The projection onto other cultures and literatures results in conflicting identifications, such as that of Europe as a figure of a former colonizer from which the new nations need to be freed as well as a source of "high" culture or "civilization" with which to identify. This straddling and overlapping of cultural associations and relationships is what marks the literature of the Americas. As Ashcroft notes, foreign terms, neologisms, ethno-rhythmic prose, transcription of dialects, and syntactic fusion are the discursive markers of postcolonial writing before it is even translated. These markers are what Homi Bhabha considers a text's "unhomely moments," or the rites of "extra-territorial and cross-cultural initiation" (9) . This book has chosen to highlight those moments, historically and textually, to unveil the story of translation embedded in Latin American texts in the multilingual otherness inherent in their original Spanish, Portuguese, and most recently, English.

It is not surprising, then, that the task of translation itself has been of central cultural importance in Latin America for a long time. Many Latin American intellectuals have worked as translators for important periods of their lives, making translation a part of their intellectual practice, and a reflection on it a central part of their systems of thought. The names of Borges, Julio Cortázar, Octavio Paz, and Haroldo de Campos, for instance, are inseparably associated with their work as translators, their overseeing the translations of their own works, and their theorizing of translation as an integral part of communication and intellectual life. Perhaps only Russia could be posited as a comparable situation, in that cultural life there was integrally involved with the translation of texts and with the circulation of foreign texts in the original languages among multilingual intellectuals in the nineteenth and twentieth centuries. Britain, France, and the United States were for a long time somewhat isolated from this sort of circulation of languages in the space of everyday life, though that isolation is now coming to an end with the large displacements of populations, and the movement back and forth of those populations to other countries, at the close of the twentieth and the beginning of the twenty-first centuries.

Despite extensive borders shared between Brazil and many of the Spanish-speaking countries, and the growth of a lingua franca, "Portuñol," in some of these border areas, the cultural histories of Brazil and Spanish America have developed largely independently from one another. However, some Latin American intellectuals on both sides of that linguistic divide promoted the cultural integration of the two halves of Iberian America through translation. Intellectuals such as Alfonso Reyes, Angel Rama, Emir Rodríguez Monegal, Haroldo de Campos, Antonio Cândido, Jorge Schwartz, Davi Arrigucci, and Raúl Antelo have worked to bridge the cultural gaps between Brazil and Spanish America, and in that process to reconnect Latin America with world literature.

The best-known Brazilian theorist of translation, Haroldo de Campos, has not only translated but also written extensively on translation as re-creation such as in his essay "Mephistofaustian Transluciferation (Contributions to the Semiotics of Poetic Translation)." In that essay, de Campos calls "the translator of poetry . . . a choreographer of the internal dance of language" and opposes the "straight ahead goal of a word-to-word competition, the Pavlovian bell of the conditioned feedback" (183) to what he advocates: "to hear the beating of the 'wild heart' of the art of translation, regarded as a 'form': poetic translation, 'transcreation,' hypertranslation" (184). In a section of the essay that purports to give instruction to translators, de Campos argues that

> in operational terms a creative translating practice [means] to go over the configurative road of the poetic function again, recognizing it in the source-text and re-inserting it, as a device for textual engendering, in the translator's language, in order to arrive at the transcreated poem as an isomorphic re-project of the original's design. (183)

De Campos's approach has influenced many scholars of translation in Brazil, especially at the University of Minas Gerais and at the Pontifícia Universidade Católica de São Paulo, largely devoted to explicating his ideas (see articles by Vieira). A bold example of a method of translation and commentary inspired by de Campos is Vera Mascarenhas do Campo's *Borges & Guimarães*. This project presents a "translation" of Borges's famous story "Hombre de la esquina rosada" into a Portuguese inflected by the personal idiom of João Guimarães Rosa, and then uses that translation as the point of departure for a fascinating literary commentary on the two authors. John Felstiner's *Translating Neruda,* an excerpt of which is reprinted in this volume, is a somewhat parallel example in English, without the influence of de Campos but with a similar concern for translinguistic re-creation.

Brazil is not the only Latin American country to institutionalize translation as a discipline. Alongside many Latin American universities, nonacademic publishing in literary magazines and the cultural supplements of newspapers has long maintained a tradition of translation. Translation was central to Victoria Ocampo's magazine *Sur,* part of whose mission was to bring the latest ideas and literary texts of Europe and the United States to Argentina (and thus to Latin America in general) (see King and Sarlo).

During the earlier part of the twentieth century, translation was a major concern of writers as diverse as Alfonso Reyes (Mexican essayist), Jorge Luis Borges (Argentine poet, essayist, and short story writer), and José María Arguedas (Peruvian anthropologist, novelist, and short story writer). While many critics have considered Borges a "cosmopolitan" intellectual disassociated from his national and regional surroundings, his interest in translation actually pertains to an intense effort to establish connections between Argentine and world literature. Recent studies have pointed out that his fascination with British and North American literature, Dante and the classics, Biblical translations, *The Arabian Nights,* and variations of Homer (see the reprinted Borges essay as well as Costa's discussion in this volume) rather than alienating him from the regional concerns of Latin America, actually demonstrates an extremely *local* preoccupation with belonging and place in a heterogeneous, postcolonial society (see Sarlo, Balderston, and Molloy). He even privileges the translated text over the original as a site of transnational nexus between the periphery and the "center." In his famous essay on Beckford's *Vathek* (1943), he complains ironically that "the original is unfaithful to the translation" (in this case, the English translation of Beckford's French original, a translation in which the author was involved) (Borges 732).

In an analogous spirit of cultural soul-searching, Arguedas made his Spanish-Quechua bilingualism an esthetic nucleus of his literary production, and asserted this hybrid, bicultural consciousness as a mark of Andean cultural identity. His prose is known for not only frequent codeswitching between Spanish and Quechua, but also incorporating Quechua syntax into his narration in Spanish. In his essay, "The Novel and the Problem of Literary Expression in Peru" (1950), he explains that Spanish, particularly what he calls "the most correct and literary Spanish" (xvii), could not adequately recount the struggle of Andean indigenous communities. He considers Spanish "spurious" because it reveals "an apparently contrived world—marrowless and bloodless" (xvii). Therefore, Spanish must be modified to reflect this interlingual and intercultural reality:

> Could I perhaps be advocating the Indianization of Spanish? No. But there is a case, a real case, in which the man from those regions, feeling ill at ease with the Spanish he has inherited, sees the need to use it as a raw material that he may modify, taking from and adding to it, until he transforms it into his own means of expression. . . . I solved the problem by creating . . . a special Spanish language, which has since been used with horrible exaggeration in the work of others. But the Indians do not speak that Spanish, not with Spanish speakers, and much less among themselves. It is a fiction. (xvii, xix)

Augusto Roa Bastos's incorporation of Guaraní into the Spanish of his 1974 novel *Yo el Supremo* provides another example of language convergence in the contemporary Latin American novel.

In more recent decades, many literary movements in Latin America have extended this tradition of translation as a practice and a cultural perspective. Octavio Paz wrote on translation and poetry. His interest in "translating" the experience of the avant garde across languages perpetuates an earlier concern of the Chilean poet Vicente Huidobro, who declared his intention of writing poetry that could be translated (see Balderston). Paz defends the translatability of poetry in his 1971 essay, "Translation: Literature and Letters." He begins with a reference to the confusion of Babel, and laments the loss of language's role in human and spiritual universality when modern translation tendencies served to point out foreignness rather than confirm similarities. According to Paz, difference and conflict only inspired more translation:

> Thanks to translation, we become aware that our neighbors do not speak and think as we do. On the one hand, the world is presented to us as a collection of similarities; on the other, as a growing heap of texts, each slightly different from the one that came before it: translations of translations of translations. Each text is unique, yet at the same time it is the translation of another text. No text can be completely original because language itself, in its very essence, is already a translation—first from the nonverbal world, and then, because each sign and each phrase is a translation of another sign, another phrase. (154)

From this philosophy of language and difference, Paz enters into a discussion of poetic translation and its challenges. He praises "the interdependence between creation and imitation, translation and original work" (161) in the process from the original poem to a new, original translation:

> The poet, immersed in the movement of language, in constant verbal preoccupation, chooses a few words—or is chosen by them. As he combines them, he constructs his poem: a verbal object made of irreplace-

able and immovable characters. The translator's starting point is not the language in movement that provides the poet's raw material but the fixed language of the poem. A language congealed, yet living. His procedure is the inverse of the poet's: he is not constructing an unalterable text from mobile characters; instead, he is dismantling the elements of the text, freeing the signs into circulation, then returning them to language. . . . The second phase of the translator's activity is parallel to the poet's, with this essential difference: as he writes, the poet does not know where his poem will lead him; as he translates, the translator knows that his completed effort must reproduce the poem he has before him. The two phases of translation, therefore, are an inverted parallel of poetic creation. The result is a reproduction of the original poem in another poem that is . . . less a copy than a transmutation. (159–160)

Paz honors the process of translation as a different but still "original" creative activity. His engagement with poetry internationally, from his own work translating neighboring U.S. poets into Spanish to participating in Japanese *rengas,* further demonstrates his contribution to translation's possibilities and results.

The multilingual texture of writing from areas with strong indigenous presence, as Edmundo Paz-Soldán's contribution to this volume elaborates, complicates the issues of language and regional identity. More recently, the complex role of the translator/interviewer in testimonial writing further demonstrates the wide arena in which translation plays a crucial role in Latin American discursive practice (see Gugelberger). As Steven White discusses in his essay in this volume, testimonial writing, whose best-known example is Rigoberta Menchu's and Elizabeth Burgos's book, is already a sort of translation that poses further challenges in marketing and teaching translations into English and other languages for readers distant from the complex linguistic, geographical, and cultural contexts of these mediated projects.

The displacement of thousands of intellectuals and writers from Cuba after the 1959 revolution and from Brazil and the Southern Cone in the 1970s and 1980s due to political exile gave the project of translation a new international purpose. In order to flee repressive regimes, many writers "returned" to Europe, providing an ironic twist to Latin America's complicated relationship with European literary traditions that projects in translation had been attempting to resolve. Not only did writers produce fiction, poetry, and journalism abroad denouncing the human rights violations at home; this recent chapter in Latin American writing also recorded the bombardment of "foreign" cultures in the Spanish of exiled writers facing linguistic and cultural alienation in Western Europe and North America (see Masiello in this volume).[3]

Since the 1960s, Latin American literature has been celebrated internationally in large part due to and in translation. The explosion of experimental fiction of the 1960s and 1970s, which included works by

Mario Vargas Llosa, Gabriel García Márquez, Julio Cortázar, and Carlos Fuentes, has been coined the "Boom." This period of unprecedented massive distribution, extensive media coverage, and academic interest coincided with an enormous surge in translations in the United States, Europe, and Asia (see Mudrovcic and Steenmeijer in this volume). Therefore, the long tradition of translation already established, even institutionalized, in Latin America acquired a new dimension in the reception of that literature abroad. Latin American writing is now often read in translation, whether in community book clubs or in college courses in American studies, English, or Latin American studies. One of the aims of this book is to contextualize this multifaceted tradition of translation for Anglo-American readers of Latin American literature (see White here).

The burgeoning field of Latino/a literature, usually in English, prompts a rethinking of many of the conventional approaches to language and cultural identity in the United States. Translation is at the core of these texts that recreate a hybridized language ("Spanglish") with extensive code-switching and cross-cultural plays on words and social behaviors. There is also a growing phenomenon of the translation of this literature into Spanish—Juan Bruce-Novoa, for instance, has published an anthology of the Chicano short story in Mexico, in Spanish translation. This new wave of translation projects from English into Spanish has highlighted how Spanish varies considerably throughout the region. The Dominican-U.S. writer Julia Alvarez found inadequate the Argentine translation of her best-known novel *How the García Girls Lost Their Accents,* and a second translation into Dominican Spanish was subsequently published. Cristina García recounts a similar disorder in the translation of her first novel, *Dreaming in Cuban,* in her essay for this volume. In Yolanda Martínez-San Miguel's convincing analysis of language and translation in writers such as García, Alvarez, and Sandra Cisneros, she highlights the difficulties and losses in translation from English into Spanish, and even suggests the *impossibility* of translation into only one language because of the multilingual registers in the original texts:

> It seems that what is lost in translation is precisely the bilingualism of the original episode, or the contact between languages that enriches the nuances of the narration. . . . [T]his "untranslatability" of the text is paradoxical, since Latino/a writing is based on a continuous practice of translation, displacements and exchanges, both cultural and linguistic. (21, 23, our translation)

Israel Reyes's essay here broaches the complexities of García's second novel, *The Agüero Sisters,* as it crosses into Spanish in translation, while Junot Díaz and Rolando Hinojosa-Smith offer insights into the production and negotiation of language(s) and place(s) inherent in translation. In these and other Latino/a writers, family sagas, generational dynamics, and geopolitical identification are all bound up with linguistic belonging and hybridity. David Johnson elaborates on the interconnected nature of place and language for U.S. Latino/a writers, exemplifying the "law" of Hinojosa-Smith's novelistic series: "everything will be in its place and every place will be determined by language, even if by 'language' is meant the mixture of tongues, a certain babel" (Johnson 150). Poetry by Latino/a writers capitalizes on both the musicality and the politics of multiple languages. In Nuyorican and Chicano literary circles, writers such as Miguel Algarín, Gloria Anzaldúa, and Francisco Alarcón use language combatively, in their often militant pedagogy of cultural consciousness raising. The growing Hispanic population in the United States, and the dynamic literary activity of this community in both English and Spanish in this country and abroad, are testaments to the expansion, geographically and linguistically, of Latin American literature.

This book, besides considerations of the economy and politics of translation, dramatizes the integral role that translation has played in the evolution of Latin American letters. This collaborative examination situates translation and its politics at the core of literary and intellectual identification in Latin America's postcolonial context. As the anthropologist James Clifford states, place and identity must be interpreted "as an itinerary rather than a bounded site—a series of encounters and translations" (11). While statistical analyses of the marketing and publishing of Latin American writing, and extensive bibliographies of translated titles, may provide concrete data, this project moves beyond numbers and lists to help account for *how* and *why* the phenomenon of translation has flourished as such a dynamic process in the Americas. *Voice-Overs* attempts to fill several gaps in this significant arena of literary history. Key essays that we have included in English by major Latin American writers on translation (by Borges, Cortázar, García Márquez, Ferré) access some of the foundations of translation's practice in Latin America, and demonstrate its importance for their own reading, writing and thinking. The short pieces from contemporary writers and translators included in the volume offer candid portraits of the relationship between individuals, texts, and languages within the dual challenge of creation and recreation represented by translation. Whether a means of livelihood, a source of communication and friendship, a frustrating impasse, or a step toward resolving linguistic and cultural identity, translation persists as a relevant and unavoidable ritual in American letters.

This book is an invitation to reflect on multiple and intersecting circuits of cultural production. We hope it will be pertinent to readers of Latin American literature and students of translation who participate in these very networks. *Voice-Overs* proposes that translation is integral not only to the distribution and circulation of printed literature but more fundamentally to the constitution of contemporary culture itself in the Americas.

NOTES

1. Nicolás Guillén in Cuba and Nicomedes Santa Cruz in Peru are examples of poets who develop their own versions of Afro-Latin American Spanish and use the black experience in Caribbean and coastal regions to examine the complexities of cultural identity in their work. See studies by Prescott, Jackson, and Lewis.

2. The anthropologist J. Jorge Klor de Alva has argued with the term *post-colonial* because according to him Latin America never had a truly colonial past but rather transplanted European society in a new place. Walter Mignolo considers Latin America as "post-Occidental," in terms of its contradictory impulses that resist Westernized globalization while at the same time continually redefine its relationship to Western culture.

3. Many examples of narrative and poetry in exile employ translation as a metaphor for the displacement and alienation of the exile experience. In José Donoso's principal novel of exile, *El jardín de al lado,* for example, the protagonists are professional translators and frustrated novelists. Cristina Peri Rossi and Luisa Futoransky, in their poetry and fiction, explore the transnational semiotics of urban life in exile through images of Babelic linguistic chaos and dictionary definitions. Literature of the Cuban exile experience also highlights linguistic hybridity, such as in Cristina García's novels (see her short essay in this volume).

WORKS CITED

Alvarez, Julia. *How the García Girls Lost Their Accents.* Chapel Hill: Algonquin, 1991.

Arguedas, José María. "The Novel and the Problem of Literary Expression in Peru." *Yawar Fiesta.* Trans. Frances Horning Barraclough. Austin : U Texas P, 1985. xiii–xxi.

Ashcroft, W. D. "Constitutive Graphonomy: A Post-Colonial Theory of Literary Writing." *After Europe: Critical Theory and Post-Colonial Writing.* Ed. Stephen Slemon and Helen Tiffin. Sydney, Australia; Dangaroo, 1989. 58–73.

Balderston, Daniel. "Borges: The Argentine Writer and the 'Western' Tradition." *Borges and Europe Revisited.* Ed. Evelyn Fishburn. London: Institute of Latin American Studies, University of London, 1998. 37–48.

———. "Huidobro and the Notion of Translatability." *Fragmentos* (Florianópolis, Brazil) 3.1 (1990): 59–74.

Bhabha, Homi. *The Location of Culture.* London and New York: Routledge, 1994.

Borges, Jorge Luis. *Obras completas.* Buenos Aires: Emecé, 1974.

Braga-Pinto, César. "Translating, Meaning and the Community of Languages." *Studies in the Humanities* 22.1–2 (1995): 33–49.

Bruce-Novoa, Juan, and Guillermo Saavedra, eds. *Antología retrospectiva del cuento chicano.* Mexico City: Consejo Nacional de Población, 1988.

Campos, Haroldo de. "Mephistofaustian Transluciferation (Contribution to the Semiotics of Poetic Translation)." Trans. Gabriela Suzanna Wilder and the author. *Dispositio* 7.19–20 (1982): 181–87.

Clifford, James. *Routes: Travel and Translation in the Late Twentieth Century.* Cambridge: Harvard UP, 1997.

Donoso, José. *El jardín de al lado.* 1981. Santiago: Alfaguara, 1996.

Felstiner, John. *Translating Neruda: The Way to Macchu Picchu.* Stanford: Stanford UP, 1980.

García, Cristina. *The Agüero Sisters.* New York: Random House, 1997.

———. *Dreaming in Cuban.* New York: Random House, 1992.

Gugelberger, Georg, ed. *The Real Thing : Testimonial Discourse and Latin America.* Durham : Duke UP, 1996.

Jackson, Richard. *The Black Image in Latin America.* Albuquerque: U New Mexico P, 1976.

Johnson, David E. "The Time of Translation: The Border of American Literature." In *Border Theory. The Limits of Cultural Politics.* Ed. Scott Michaelsen and David E. Johnson. Minneapolis: U Minnesota P, 1997. 129–65.

Klor de Alva, J. Jorge. "Colonialism and Postcolonialism as (Latin) American Mirages." *Colonial Latin American Review* 1.2 (1992): 3–23.

Lewis, Marvin. *Afro-Argentine Discourse: Another Dimension of the Black Diaspora.* Columbia: U Missouri P, 1996.

———. *Afro-Hispanic Poetry, 1940–1980: From Slavery to Negritud in South American Verse.* Columbia: U Missouri P, 1983.

———. *Ethnicity and Identity in Contemporary Afro-Venezuelan Literature: A Culturalist Approach.* Columbia: U Missouri P, 1992.

———. *Treading the Ebony Path: Ideology and Violence in Contemporary Afro-Colombian Prose Fiction.* Columbia: U Missouri P, 1987.

Martínez-San Miguel, Yolanda. "Bitextualidad y bilingüismo: reflexiones sobre el lenguaje en la escritura latina contemporánea." *Centro Journal* 12.1 (2000): 19–34.

Mascarenhas do Campo, Vera. *Borges & Guimarães na esquina rosada do grande sertão.* São Paulo, Perspectiva, 1988.

Mignolo, Walter. "Occidentalización, imperialismo, globalización: herencias coloniales y teorías postcoloniales." *Revista Iberoamericana* 170–71 (1995): 27–41.

———. "Posoccidentalismo: las epistemologías fronterizas y el dilema de los estudios (latinoamericanos) de área." *Revista Iberoamericana* 176–77 (1996): 679–96.

Molloy, Sylvia. "Lost in Translation: Borges, the Western Tradition and Fictions of Latin America." In *Borges and Europe Revisited.* Ed. Evelyn Fishburn. London: Institute of Latin American Studies, University of London, 1998. 8–20.

Paz, Octavio. *Traducción: literatura y literalidad.* (1971). Barcelona: Tusquets, 1980.

————. "Translation: Literature and Letters." Trans. Irene del Corral. *Theories of Translation. An Anthology of Essays from Dryden to Derrida.* Ed. Rainer Schulte and John Biguenet. Chicago: U Chicago P, 1992. 152–62.

Peri Rossi, Cristina. *La tarde del dinosaurio.* Barcelona: Plaza y Janés, 1984.

Prescott, Laurence. *Candelario Obeso y la iniciación de la poesía negra en Colombia.* Bogotá: Instituto Caro y Cuervo, 1985.

Roa Bastos, Augusto. *Yo el Supremo.* Buenos Aires: Siglo XXI, 1974.

Sarlo, Beatriz. *La máquina cultural.* Buenos Aires: Planeta, 1998.

————. *Jorge Luis Borges: A Writer on the Edge.* London: Verso, 1993.

Schwartz, Marcy. *Writing Paris: Urban Topographies of Desire in Contemporary Latin American Fiction.* Albany: SUNY P, 1999.

Vieira, Else Ribeiro Pires. "A Postmodern Translational Aesthetics in Brazil." *Translation Studies: An Interdiscipline.* Ed. Mary Snell Hornby, Franz Pöchhacker, and Klaus Kaindl. Amsterdam/Philadelphia: John Benjamins, 1992. 65–72.

————. "Liberating Calibans: Readings of *Antropofagia* and Haroldo de Campos' Poetics of Transcreation." *Post-colonial Translation: Theory and Practice.* Ed. Susan Bassnett and Harish Trivedi. London: Routledge, 1999. 95–113.

I

Writers on Translation

The Homeric Versions

Jorge Luis Borges

No problem is as consubstantial to literature and its modest mystery as the one posed by translation. The forgetfulness induced by vanity, the fear of confessing mental processes that may be divined as dangerously commonplace, the endeavor to maintain, central and intact, an incalculable reserve of obscurity: all watch over the various forms of direct writing. Translation, in contrast, seems destined to illustrate aesthetic debate. The model to be imitated is a visible text, not an immeasurable labyrinth of former projects or a submission to the momentary temptation of fluency. Bertrand Russell defines an external object as a circular system radiating possible impressions; the same may be said of a text, given the incalculable repercussions of words. Translations are a partial and precious documentation of the changes the text suffers. Are not the many versions of the *Illiad*—from Chapman to Magnien—merely different perspectives on a mutable fact, a long experimental game of chance played with omissions and emphases? (There is no essential necessity to change languages; this intentional game of attention is possible within a single literature.) To assume that every recombination of elements is necessarily inferior to its original form is to assume that draft nine is necessarily inferior to draft H—for there can only be drafts. The concept of the "definitive text" corresponds only to religion or exhaustion.

The superstition about the inferiority of translations—coined by the well-known Italian adage—is the result of absentmindedness. There is no good text that does not seem invariable and definitive if we have turned to it a sufficient number of times. Hume identified the habitual idea of causality with that of temporal succession. Thus a good film, seen a second time, seems even better; we tend to take as necessity that which is no more than repetition. With famous books, the first time is actually the second, for we begin them already knowing them. The prudent common phrase "rereading the classics" is the result of an unwitting truth. I do not know if the statement "In a place in La Mancha, whose name I don't wish to recall, there lived not long ago a nobleman who kept a lance and shield, a greyhound and a skinny old nag" would be considered good by an impartial divinity; I only know that any modification would be sacrilegious and that I cannot conceive of any other beginning for the *Quixote*. Cervantes, I think, ignored this slight superstition and perhaps never noted that particular paragraph. I, in contrast, can only reject any divergence. The *Quixote*, due to my congenital practice of Spanish, is a uniform monument, with no other variations except those provided by the publisher, the bookbinder, and the typesetter; the *Odyssey*, thanks to my opportune ignorance of Greek, is an international bookstore of works in prose and verse, from Chapman's couplets to Andrew Lang's "Authorized Version" or Bérard's classic French drama or Morris's vigorous *saga* or Butler's ironic bourgeois novel. I abound in the mention of English names because English literature has always been amicable toward this epic of the sea, and the series of its versions of the *Odyssey* would be enough to illustrate the course of its centuries. That heterogenous and even contradictory richness is not attributable solely to the evolution of the English language, or to the mere length of the original, or to the deviations or diverse capacities of the translators, but rather to a circumstance that is particular to Homer: the difficult category of knowing what pertains to the poet and what pertains to the language. To that fortunate difficulty we owe the possibility of so many versions, all of them sincere, genuine, and divergent.

I know of no better example than that of the Homeric adjectives. The divine Patroclus, the nourishing earth, the wine-dark sea, the solid-hoofed horses, the damp waves, the black ship, the black blood, the beloved knees, are recurrent expressions, inopportunely moving. In one place, he speaks of the "rich noblemen who drink of the black waters of the Aesopos"; in another, of a tragic king who, "wretched in delightful Thebes, governed the Cadmeans by the gods' fatal decree." Alexander Pope (whose lavish translation we shall scrutinize later) believed that these irremovable epithets were liturgical in character. Rémy de Gourmont, in his long essay on style, writes that at one time they must have been incantatory, although they no longer are so. I have preferred to suspect that these faithful epithets were what prepositions still are: modest and obligatory sounds that usage adds to certain words and upon which no originality may be exercised. We know that it is correct to go "on foot" and not "with foot." The rhapsodist knew that the correct adjective for Patroclus was "divine." Neither case is an aesthetic proposition. I offer these speculations without enthusiasm; the only certainty is the impossibility of separating what pertains to the author from what pertains to the language. When we read, in Agustín Moreto (if we must read Agustín Moreto):

> *Pues en casa tan compuestas*
> *¿Qué hacen todo el santo dia?*

> [At home so elegant/What do they do the whole blessed day?]

we know that the holiness of the day is an instance of the Spanish language, and not of the writer. With Homer, in contrast, we remain infinitely ignorant of the emphases.

For a lyric or elegiac poet, our uncertainty about his intentions could be devastating, but not for a reliable expositor of vast plots. The events of the *Iliad* and the *Odyssey* amply survive, even though Achilles and Odysseus, what Homer meant by naming them, and what he actually thought of them have all disappeared. The present state of his works is like a complex equation that represents the precise relations of unknown quantities. There is no possible greater richness for the translator. Browning's most famous book consists of ten detailed accounts of a single crime by each of those implicated in it. All of the contrast derives from the characters, not from the events, and it is almost as intense and unfathomable as that of ten legitimate versions of Homer.

The beautiful Newman-Arnold debate (1861–62), more important than either of its participants, extensively argued the two basic methods of translation. Newman defended the literal mode, the retention of all verbal singularities; Arnold, the strict elimination of details that distract or detain the reader, the subordination of the Homer who is irregular in every line to the essential or conventional Homer, one composed of a syntactical simplicity, a simplicity of ideas, a flowing rapidity, and loftiness. The latter method provides the pleasures of uniformity and nobility; the former, of continuous and small surprises.

I would like to consider the various fates of a single passage from Homer. These are the events recounted by Odysseus to the ghost of Achilles in the city of the Cimmerians, on the night without end, and they concern Achilles' son Neoptolemus (*Odyssey* XI). Here is Buckley's literal version:

> But when we had sacked the lofty city of Priam, having his share and excellent reward, he embarked unhurt on a ship, neither stricken with the sharp brass, nor wounded in fighting hand to hand, as oftentimes happens in war; for Mars confusedly raves.

That of the equally literal but archaicizing Butcher and Lang:

> But after we had sacked the steep city of Priam, he embarked unscathed with his share of the spoil, and with a noble prize; he was not smitten with the sharp spear, and got no wound in close fight: and many such chances there be in war, for Ares rageth confusedly.

Cowper in 1791:

> At length when we had sack'd the lofty town
> Of Priam, laden with abundant spoils

He safe embark'd, neither by spear of shaft
Aught hurt, or in close fight by faulchion's edge
As oft in war befalls, where wounds are dealt
Promiscuous, at the will of fiery Mars.

Pope's 1725 version:

And when the Gods our arms with conquest crown'd
When Troy's proud bulwarks smok'd upon the ground,
Greece to reward her soldier's gallant toils
Heap'd high his navy with unnumber'd spoils.
Thus great in glory from the din of war
Safe he return'd, without one hostile scar;
Tho'spears in the iron tempests rain'd around,
Yet innocent they play'd and guiltless of a wound.

George Chapman in 1614:

. . . In the event,
High Troy depopulate, he made ascent
To his fair ship, with prise and treasure store
Safe; and no touch away with him he bore
Of far-off-hurl'd lance, or of close-fought sword,
Whose wounds for favours and war doth oft afford,
Which he (though sought) missd in war's closest wage.
In close fights Mars doth never fight, but rage.

And Butler in 1900:

Yet when we had sacked the city of Priam he got his handsome share
of the prize money and went on board (such is the fortune of war)
without a wound upon him, neither from a thrown spear nor in close
combat, for the rage of Mars is a matter of great chance.

The first two versions—the literal ones—may be moving for a variety of reasons: the reverential mention of the sacking of the city, the ingenuous statement that one is often injured in war, the sudden juncture of the infinite disorders of battle in a single god, the fact of madness in a god. Other, lesser pleasures are also at work: in one of the texts I've copied, the excellent pleonasm of "embarked on a ship"; in another, the use of a copulative conjunction for the causal in "and many such chances there be in war."[1] The third version, Cowper's, is the most innocuous of all: it is as literal as the requirements of Miltonic stresses permit. Pope's is extraordinary. His luxuriant language (like that of Góngora) may be defined by its unconsidered and mechanical use of superlatives. For example: the hero's single black ship is multiplied into a fleet. Always subject to this law of amplification, all of his lines fall into two large classes: the purely oratorical ("And when the Gods our arms with conquest crown'd") or the visual ("When Troy's proud bulwarks smok'd upon the ground"). Speeches and spectacles: that is Pope. The passionate Chapman is also spectacular, but his mode is the lyric, not oratory. Butler, in contrast, demonstrates his determination to avoid all visual opportunities and to turn Homer's text into a series of sedate news items.

Which of these many translations is faithful? my reader will want to know. I repeat: none or all of them. If fidelity refers to Homer's imaginations and the irrecoverable men and days that he portrayed, none of them are faithful for us, but all of them would be for a tenth-century Greek. If it refers to his intentions, then any one of the many I have transcribed would suffice, except for the literal versions, whose virtue lies entirely in their contrast to contemporary practices. It is not impossible that Butler's unruffled version is the most faithful.

Translated by Eliot Weinberger

NOTE

1. Another of Homer's habits is the fine abuse of adversative conjunctions. Here are some examples:

"Die, but I shall receive my own destiny wherever Zeus and the other immortal gods desire" (*Iliad* XXII).

"Astyokhe, daughter of Aktor: a modest virgin when she ascended to the upper rooms of her father's dwelling, but secretly the god Ares lay beside her" (*Iliad* II).

" [The Myrmidons] were like wolves carnivorous and fierce and tireless, who rend a great stag on a mountainside and feed on him, but their jaws are reddened with blood" (*Iliad* XVI).

"Zeus of Dodona, god of Pelasgians, O god whose home lies far! Ruler of wintry harsh Dodona! But your ministers, the Selloi, live with feet unwashed, and sleep on the hard ground" (*Iliad* XVI).

"Be happy, lady, in this love, and when the year passes you will bear glorious children, for the couplings of the immortals are not without issue. But you must look after them, and raise them. Go home now and hold your peace and tell nobody my name, but I tell it to you; I am the Earthshaker Poseidon" (*Odyssey* XI).

"After him I was aware of powerful Herakles; his image, that is, but he himself among the immortal gods enjoys their festivals, married to sweet-stepping Hebe, child of great Zeus and Hera of the golden sandals" (*Odyssey* XI).

I shall add the flamboyant translation that George Chapman did of this last passage:

> Down with these was thrust
> The idol of the force of Hercules,
> But his firm self did no such fate oppress.

He feasting lives amongst th'immortal States
White-ankled Hebe and himself made mates
In heav'nly nuptials. Hebe, Jove's dear race
And Juno's whom the golden sandals grace.

Translate, Traduire, Tradurre: Traducir

Julio Cortázar

Author's royalties may or may not arrive, but if they do arrive it's always late, reason enough for a writer who is not the son of an oil sheik or of Henry Ford III to spend much of his life making do as best he can. Since I never expected royalties (and perhaps because of that I received them, unsolicited advice to any anxious young writers), I spent the greater part of my already long life translating books, birth certificates, patents, consular receipts and reports from the General Director of UNESCO, these last in collaboration with a diverse and good-humored crew of Catalan, Ecuadoran, Argentine, Basque and Galician colleagues. Silent interpreter in my youth, I spent many delightful hours translating works such as Marguerite Yourcenar's *Mémoires d'Adrien* or André Gide's *L'Immoraliste*. Years later I paid for it with horrifically boring days translating United Nations' documents in what they described as the fields of sociology/literacy/irrigation/mass communication/library science/heavy water atomic reactors, etc., with their usually well-deserved name of *"informes"* ("reports"), but understood by its secondary meaning: "formless."

All this has left me with an appreciation for the subtle transmigrations and transgressions that take place in the translation of any text when its meaning goes beyond the bridges of language. . . . Not to mention the more subtle distortion that historical and cultural distance imposes; Borges showed this better than anyone in "Pierre Menard, Author of *Don Quixote*," where it isn't even a question of translation but instead a literal reproduction that, nevertheless, comes out completely different from the original text.

Finally I was given a well-deserved promotion from translator to editor for international organizations, and revising other people's work provided me with some unforgettable moments. One legendary example consists of the following text in French: *Comme disait feu le président Roosevelt, rien n'est à craindre hormis la crainte elle-même* [As President Roosevelt said, we have nothing to fear but fear itself], which was delightfully translated as: *Como decía con ardor el presidente Roosevelt, el miedo a las hormigas lo crean ellas mismas* [As President Roosevelt

21

said so ardently, the fear of ants is created by the ants themselves].
Undoubtedly the Spanish version is much richer and more metaphysical
than the original, something equally notable in the case of a report on
scholarships awarded by the United States to Mexican students, in
which the word *scholarship* was understood as "a ship full of students"
left drifting freely for pages and pages. . . .

Few activities are as uncertain and constrained as translation, something
that gives the calling a kind of charming madness when it is practiced
with good-natured humor. I shudder rereading fragments of my old literary versions, as in the case of the celebrated but forgotten treatise by
Abbot Brémond on prayer and poetry, where I misunderstood *esprit* in
the sense of wit or genius and translated it simply as "espíritu," ruining
the passage by the good abbot. Even worse, Borges translating a poem
by Francis Ponge translated *sol* as *sol* (sun) instead of *suelo* (soil), but
we know that such things happen in the best of families, even to Saint
Jerome. I have been translated memorably at times, as when my short
short story "Continuidad de los parques" (Continuity of Parks)
appeared in France as "Continuité des Parques" (Continuity of the Par-
cae), which enriched it considerably thanks to the unexpected arrival of
Clotho, Lachesis and Atropos. It sometimes happens that when you put
your foot in your mouth you encounter buried treasure, but I wouldn't
recommend this as a general practice.

Translated by Daniel Balderston and Marcy Schwartz

The Desire to Translate

Gabriel García Márquez

Someone said that translating is the best kind of reading. I think that it is also the most difficult, the least recognized and the worst paid. *Traduttore, traditore,* says the well-known Italian tag, taking it for granted that they who translate us betray us. Maurice-Edgar Coindreau, one of the most intelligent and generous translators in France, revealed in his oral memoirs some secrets that lead us to the contrary. "The translator apes the novelist," he said, paraphrasing Mauriac, meaning that the translator should gesture and pose exactly as the writer does, whether he or she likes it or not. His translations into French of U.S. novelists, who were young and unknown at the time—Faulkner, Dos Passos, Hemingway, Steinbeck—are not only masterly recreations, they introduced a historic generation in France, whose influence on their European contemporaries—including Sartre and Camus—is more than evident. Which implies that Coindreau was not a traitor, but quite the opposite: a brilliant accomplice. All great translators throughout time have made enormous contributions to their translated works, contributions that usually go unnoticed, while readers harp on their defects.

When we read authors in languages that are not theirs we feel a natural desire to translate them. This is understandable, because one of the pleasures of reading—and of music—is the possibility of sharing it with friends. Perhaps that explains why Proust died without realizing one of his recurring desires, which was to translate from English someone as strange as he was himself, John Ruskin. Two of the writers I would have liked to translate for the sheer pleasure of the task are André Malraux and Antoine de Saint-Exupéry, both of whom, it should be said, do not enjoy the highest reputation among their compatriots today. But I have never pursued it. On the other hand, I have been translating bit by bit the *Cantos* of Giacomo Leopardi, but I do that on the sly and in my few free hours, in full knowledge that that will not be the path to glory for Leopardi or for me. I do it only as one of those pastimes that the Jesuit fathers call solitary pleasures. But the attempt itself has persuaded me how difficult, and how unselfish, is the task of the translator.

It is unlikely that a writer would ever be satisfied with the translation of any of his or her works. In every word, in every phrase, in every emphasis of a novel there is almost always a secret implied meaning that only the author knows. That is why it is no doubt beneficial for a writer to participate in the translation to the extent possible. One notable experience in this sense is the exceptional French translation of Joyce's *Ulysses*. The original first draft was done completely and solely by August Morell, who later worked toward the final version with Valery Larbaud and with Joyce himself. The result is a masterpiece, hardly surpassed—according to those who know—by Antonio Houaiss's translation into Brazilian Portuguese. The only translation that exists in Spanish is, however, almost nonexistent. But its story may explain it. The Argentine, J. Salas Subirat, who in real life was an expert in life insurance, took it on as a hobby. The publisher Santiago Rueda, in Buenos Aires, found out about it, unfortunately, and published it in the late 1940s. I met Salas Subirat a few years later in Caracas, perched on an impersonal desk in an insurance company, and we spent a wonderful afternoon talking about English novelists, whose work he knew almost by heart. The last time I saw him it was like a dream: he was dancing, by now quite old and more solitary than ever, in the mad crowds of the Barranquilla carnival. It was such a strange sight that I chose not to say hello.

Other important projects include the French translations by Gustav Jean-Aubry and Phillippe Neel of the novels of Joseph Conrad. This immortal writer—whose real name was Josef Teodor Konrad Korzeniowski—had been born in Poland, and his father was in fact a translator of English writers, including Shakespeare. Conrad's first language was Polish, but as a young child he learned French and English, and eventually became a writer in both those languages. Today we consider him, rightly or wrongly, one of the masters of the English novel. It is said that he made life impossible for his French translators trying to impose his own perfection on them, but he never chose to translate himself. It's odd, but there are few bilingual writers who do. The closest case to us is that of Jorge Semprún, who writes the same in Spanish as in French, though always without mixing them. He never translates himself. Stranger still is the case of the Irishman Samuel Beckett, Nobel Prize for Literature, who writes the same work twice in two languages, but insists that one is not the translation of the other, but instead that they are two distinct works in two different languages.

Some years ago, in the blazing summer of Pantelaria, I had an enigmatic experience as a translator. Count Enrico Cicogna, who was my Italian translator until he died, spent his vacation translating *Paradiso* by the Cuban writer José Lezama Lima. I am a devoted admirer of Lezama's poetry, and also of this rare individual, although I saw him only on a few occasions, and at the time I wanted to get better acquainted with his hermetic novel. So I helped Cicogna a bit, not so much with the translation as with the difficult business of making sense of the prose. That was when I understood that it is true that translating is the deepest kind of reading. Among other things, we came across a sentence the subject of which changed gender and number several times in less than ten lines, to the point that it was impossible to know for sure who it was, when, or where. Knowing Lezama Lima, it is possible that that confusion was deliberate, but only he could have said so, and we were never able to ask him. The question that Cicogna asked was whether the translator had to carry over into Italian all of those confusions of agreement or whether he should transform them with academic rigor. My opinion was that they should be preserved, so that the work would pass into the other language as it was, not only in its virtues but also in its defects. It was an act of loyalty to the reader in the other language.

For me there is nothing more boring than reading the translations of my novels in the three languages in which I am capable of doing so. I don't recognize myself in any language other than Spanish. But I have read some of the books that were translated into English by Gregory Rabassa and I have to admit that I found some passages that I liked better than in the Spanish. The impression that Rabassa's translations gives me is that he learns the whole book by heart in Spanish and then writes it all over again in English: his faithfulness is always more complex than simple literalness. He never inserts a footnote, which is the most lame but nevertheless most frequently exploited recourse of bad translators. In this sense, the most notable example is that of the Brazilian translator of one of my works, who explained the word *astromelia* in a footnote: imaginary flower invented by García Márquez. The worst thing about that is that I later read that *astromelias* not only exist, as everyone in the Caribbean knows, but that their name comes from the Portuguese.

Translated by Daniel Balderston and Marcy Schwartz

Gender and Translation

Diana Bellessi

The center of my life's work has been poetry writing. From the various metamorphoses or undertakings that branch off from this central nucleus, I can see three: teaching, reflective writing, and translation. Translation—and I speak strictly of the translation of poetry—is, perhaps, closest to the writing of poetry; it is carried out through a slow process of internalization and silence, weighing simultaneously the sonorous mass of a song, of speech, that has its origin in a language other than the mother tongue. It also demands being receptive to—through one's own emotions—the thoughts and emotions of another voice. The poet recognizes in his or her own writing, when, on saying "I," she feels both a close and a more distant voice at the same time. It means translating into one's own voice something that comes from distant reaches of time. Translating poetry requires the immediate precision of a craft that has been slowly honed over an entire lifetime of work.

If the poem appears first as rhythm, and only later unfolds meaning in its own way, then translation is above all an attempt at alterity. Alterity of the body, breathing the music of another language and of the utter uniqueness of a speaking voice. A double effort founded, no doubt, on love, that permits the translator to identify with the text on a variety of levels. Echo, instead of contesting as in the myth of Narcissus, is sustained by the possibilities and mysteries of the native language in which the translator rewrites her. Feeling the text like the body, alert at the same time to its meaning, so that something can find expression in a language in which it was not conceived. Something—always something other than that blossom full of meaning that the original offers. Perhaps because of this the translation of poetry is more intuitive and less derivative and logical than other kinds of translation.

Translation always provokes a meditation on one's own language—on its powers and limits—and on language itself. Since translation is the disarticulation of the original, it casts in doubt the certainty of the signifiers that surround us and affects how we relate to our original language, as Walter Benjamin and Paul de Man have shown.

This task requires sacrifices and tough choices, feelings of betrayal and at the same time the joy of reconstruction. Mimesis and rupture, that is to say, a nearly impossible task. It is a gesture that matures in a long phase of coexistence, of soulful intimacy where everything is written and rewritten: that sonorous carnality that hides in silences, that sequence of signs in empty space.

Sometimes translators have the chance to choose for whom they will speak—and it is this paradox that intercepts the usual function of ventriloquism. As long as they do not force the texts—a conflict that often besets male translators who are working on poems written by women—they will have the opportunity to construct an expansive region on which their very life depends.

Well, and what is my place in all of this? First of all, U.S. poetry. To be more specific: that of the twentieth century. And more precisely: women poets, and of a particular kind: contemporaries who are extremely talented and at the same time outlaws. In what sense? In their revision of the cultural world they have been given, in their striving to achieve their own full humanity and defend the human rights of others, those who are marginalized by visible or invisible centers of power. Voices that believe in the transformation of the world and of personal lives, through courses of action at opportune moments, but sustaining always a central path: poetry writing. Voices alert to the pulse of history, to the delicate humanity that unfolds in different cultural constructions, to the right of desire and of life, but never devoured by a prior assumption, by rational ideology put before all else, killing the adventure and mystery of writing, that is to say its fullest possible meaning. Thus, voices outside the law of canonical discourse.

With them, for many years now, I have constructed part of my lineage. A lineage conceived as a dialogue that puts up with and even embraces our differences.

Translating is also the broadening of that initial gesture: reading. And it is the accumulation of those readings throughout the poet's life, causing that lineage to be subject to perpetual transformation. In those roots, in that wake that accompanies us, that contextualizes us, I can render homage and declare a debt of love and wisdom to some of those U.S. women poets who have filled my days with reading and translation. I refer to Muriel Rukeyser, Ursula Le Guin, Denise Levertov, Adrienne Rich, Lucille Clifton, and also to some more recent voices such as June Jordan, Judy Grahn, Irene Klepfizs, Olga Brournas. Behind them all, the majestic echo of the work of H.D.

Lineage and genealogy. This is a preoccupation of contemporary women writers, given our late inscription in the history of literature and of written culture, due to the peculiar construction of male and female genders. This construction left the female enclosed in the limits of the domestic sphere as her only space of production, often exercising only the reproductive function that social structures demanded, and as a function of the object of the lone subject: the masculine subject. Our recent access to the category of *person* the remembering of which may seem excessively obvious here, but which I consider insufficiently discussed and acted upon in local [Argentine] reflections, brings the women writers of the last few decades to ask constantly about the construction of their own subjectivity as women, leaving behind binary patterns more and more. We lack an adequate gallery of mirrors in which to see ourselves, or in which to see reflected certain peculiar features of our way of looking at the world, so as to make possible the construction of what we could call a basic narcissism, that would allow us to recognize ourselves, to say *I, this woman who writes*. Gestures that open the mirror so that *others* can then be reflected in it.

And what does she write? What she thinks she sees and how she thinks she sees herself. The speaking subject seen as object and theme not only in her individual singularity but also in the singularity of gender. If we conceive language and its structuring of discourse as a primarily historical construction, this leads the producer of the original to explore in semantic and syntactic terms her place in it, with both approval and disapproval that imply a detailed process of resemanticization. *The translator is also implicated in this process, as she watches her language broken apart violently by the original that she translates.* From that derives perhaps the preference of many contemporary women writers for women translators, distrusting what might be misconstrued by gender difference, perhaps because gender as a social construction is still not sufficiently recognized. . . .

The creation of a genealogy of women writers, the discovery and reading of them, is a fundamental path toward the constitution of that productive self, as much in the reader as in the writer, as well as their later insertion in a heritage that is vaster still, and that beyond a doubt belongs to us and constitutes us. I would say that my work as a translator, in the process of selection that I have carried out, formed part of this need and also turned out to be part of that contribution. Alterity in some space of interiority: something that male translators exercised for centuries, in texts whose authors explored their multiple connections to the world, among others through the theme of masculine brotherhood, or of all kinds of relationships with women, or the paradigm of "the feminine," that is, the "written woman." This activity in language, in the field of writing, was finally reclaimed by women in the nineteenth century, except for some isolated earlier cases, and in a more massive way in the twentieth. Writing, critical reflection, and translation have produced small changes, to my way of thinking, but nevertheless have profoundly destabilized the earlier discursive canons and the very languages that sustained them. Behold the written woman writing herself, inscribing her look at the world in multiple details of connection, struggling body to body with words that no longer *contain* her—besides which they never did so completely, that I know, or that would do away with her writing—in symbolic spaces that are stormily, rapidly recodified. And at the same time, behold the woman reader, the woman translator. In 1984, the publishing house Ultimo Reino published the first edition of an anthology of contemporary U.S. women poets, which was characterized by its including only six writers, but with a large number of poems by each one of them, and with an essay by Barbara Deming on the theme of gender and writing. That book, later expanded, constitutes my *place* in translation. I would like to recall part of the brief preface that opens it:

> "Who will speak these days/ if not I/ if not you?" asks Muriel Rukeyser in one of the poems included in this selection. Who will struggle body to body with words and acts in the midst of life? Living memory—who will grasp it, if not I, if not you? These women do it. Linked to a literary current that has infused profoundly the rebel spirit of the great literature of the United States. A colloquial, powerful language, with open forms that give voice to irony, humor, ambiguity, and also to a passionate, naked impulse. Potent and extremely delicate at the same time.
>
> Incorporated in this poetry are the recent years of U.S. history. Events and the process of expanding individual consciousness that those events made possible.
>
> There is, however, an element that gives these poets their deepest ties and that we hope gives coherence to our selection. Something that may seem obvious: they are all women. The revealing essay by Barbara Deming included as an epilogue reflects on this fact. Few women appear in anthologies of poetry; as Deming says, perhaps this is because the anthologists and translators have almost always been male. . . .
>
> No more terror or dark rooms. No more suicides on spring days. The voice of these women, passionate and profound, makes us want to live, in a new way, our lives.

Ten years later, even if I could add many lines to this brief preface, I still agree with its force, and a similar impulse leads me to choose and rededicate myself to translation.

Translated by Daniel Balderston and Marcy Schwartz

Where Do Words Come From?

Luisa Futoransky

The languages of speech, writing, and thought sometimes reflect in a simple way, as in the latest astronomical discoveries of the "brown dwarves" (dark stars that constitute a large share of the universe), the strong power of the absent language. That is to say, what permits and yet impedes the acquisition of what the expatriate finds most difficult to access: internal residence.

On June 11, 1938, Freud wrote to the Swiss psychoanalyst Raymond de Saussure that emigrants suffer most from the loss of the language in which they lived and thought, which is irreplaceable. Freud took refuge not in German or English, but in a dead tongue, Latin, to define the irreversible: FINIS AUSTRIAE, two words that came to summarize the drama of emigration from one circle of hell to another.

Transterrado: landless, expatriated, in asylum, exiled, distanced, absent, colonized, in flight, because almost always, at the beginning, emigration is a swallow, a river overflowing its banks, without accounting for the missing pieces that go beyond the surface. Missing pieces that spring up at the first unspoken evocation. Eclipses that reappear in dreams that we quickly wipe away.

Many travelers take on the painful process of translation, to decant, to transfer one human landscape to another. Above all to build a bridge. Each person will establish with what means he or she has available, with flimsy ropes or with sophisticated works of engineering, to carry appropriate words across successfully, words that reveal the inner landscape, what since childhood traces with its peculiar tastes and bitterness the common denominator of that other shore, a transaction that is no doubt complicated by memory's lapses and falsified accounts. But almost always the transmutation has occurred by the time one suffers through the ravages of winter, both internal and external.

Exiles and refugees are stripped of their characteristics and all that is left to them sometimes for self-defense is to shield themselves with armor, a callus against otherness made of clumsy or painful irony and sometimes to wound those that they consider barbarians. That is to say, they begin to translate.

But what is translation and exile if not taking a random block of words, a planetary system of old ideas, phonemes, and illusions and transporting them into a new and unknown planetary system. Frequently the orbits are disrupted and many words and laws, generally the most important ones, the deepest and most secret are left floating like inert particles out of orbit. Translation and exile are always synonyms of loss.

To come from one language and write in another, sometimes thinking in a third and living in whichever one you can, has become a large part of the literary experience of the contemporary novel.

The answers vary, and the rules, sometimes pushed to their limits, establish excessive ties to things far away and the filigrees of nostalgia are revealed in the undercurrent of hatred and resentment. *Finnegans Wake* would be in this sense the great text of exile, but there are other alliances and negotiations that are almost as dramatic with language: Primo Levi, Kundera, Conrad, Singer, Nabokov, Kosinski, Beckett, Gombrowicz, Kafka, Cortázar. Or for examples closer to mine: Dujovne, Bianciotti. The relation to the country of origin where you no longer live emerges from the mere listing of their names, the dense jungle that exile has produced.

Each author in some way, in his or her own way, is a kind of traveling library, an atlas, which refers to and sends us back to the libraries where the unwritten and uncharted multiply endlessly.

We all participate in this great leap of communication, negotiating sometimes in an extreme way with language because the only inalienable weapon in the hands of the exile is sarcasm. Irony is capable of absorbing hatred and pity without poisoning its user too much. Out of this dispossession the world may become a chaos inhabited only by barbarians.

As I translate my theme of exile as it traverses and grows, almost like a Bermuda Triangle, translation being a synonym of marginalization and remainder, an image sticks in my mind: a detail from a painting by Bacon. From a chaotic circle of green lines emerges a massive tree, uprooted, defenseless. Without anesthesia. Like a wisdom tooth. Roots lying on the earth, disproportionate to the hapless trunk. I foresee that from them there will be some sprouts while others will perish. Over this shape there is a glow, something like a yellow point clearly tracing a path. Perhaps a man's head. An easel perhaps. The title of Bacon's painting announces: Portrait of Van Gogh.

Translated by Daniel Balderston and Marcy Schwartz

On Destiny, Language, and Translation, or, Ophelia Adrift in the C. & O. Canal

Rosario Ferré

Language is the most salient model of Heraclitean flux. . . .
So far as we experience and realize them in linear progression,
time and language are intimately related; they move and the
arrow is never in the same place.

—George Steiner,
After Babel

What is translation? On a platter
A poet's pale and glaring head,
A parrot's screech, a monkey's chatter,
And profanation of the dead.

—Nabokov,
"On Translating Eugene Onegin"

A few weeks ago, when I was in Puerto Rico, I had an unusual dream. I had decided, after agonizing over the decision for several months, to return to the island for good, ending my five-year stay in Washington, D.C. My return was not only to be proof that Thomas Wolfe had been wrong all along and that one *could* go home again; it was also an anguishedly mulled over decision, which had taken me at least a year to arrive at. I wanted to come in contact with my roots once again; to nurture those hidden springs of consciousness from which literary inspiration flows, and which undoubtedly are related to the world we see and dream of as infants, before we can formulate it into words.

In my dream I was still in Washington, but was about to leave it for good. I was traveling on the C. & O. Canal, where horse-towed barges full of tourists still journey picturesquely today, led by farmers dressed up in costumes of Colonial times. I had crossed the canal many times before, entering the placid green water, which came up to my waist: without any trouble, and coming out on the other side, where the bright green, African-daisy-covered turf suspiciously resembled the Puerto Rican countryside. This time, however, the canal crossing was to be

32

definitive. I didn't want my five professionally productive years in Washington to become a false paradise, a panacea where life was a pleasant limbo, far removed from the social and political problems of the island. I felt that this situation could not continue, and that in order to write competently about my world's conflicts, as war correspondents have experienced, one has to be able to live in the trenches and not on the pleasant hillocks that overlook the battlefield.

As I began to cross the canal, however, and waded into the middle of the trough, I heard a voice say loudly that all the precautions of language had to be taken, as the locks were soon to be opened and the water level was going to rise. Immediately after this someone opened the heavy wooden gates of the trough at my back and a swell of water began to travel down the canal, lifting me off my feet and sweeping me down current, so that it became impossible to reach either of the two shores. At first I struggled this way and that, as panic welled up in me and I tried unsuccessfully to grab onto the vegetation which grew on the banks, but I soon realized the current was much too powerful and I had no alternative but to let it take hold of me. After a while, as I floated face up like Ophelia over the green surface of the water, I began to feel strangely at ease and tranquil. I looked at the world as it slid by, carried by the slowly moving swell of cool water, and wondered at the double exposure on both shores, the shore of Washington on my right and the shore of San Juan on my left, perfectly fitted to each other and reflected on the canal's surface like on a traveling mirror on which I was magically being sustained.

The water of the canal reminded me then of the mirror on the door of my wardrobe when I was a child, whose beveled surface entranced me when I crawled up to it because, when one looked closely into its edge, left and right fell apart and at the same time melted into one. The canal had the same effect on me; in it blue sky and green water, north and south, earth and vegetation ceased to be objects or places and became passing states, images in motion. The water of words, the water in the C. & O. Canal where "all the precautions of language had to be taken," was my true habitat as a writer; neither Washington nor San Juan, neither past nor present, but the crevice in between. Being a writer, the dream was telling me, one has to learn to live by letting go, by renouncing the reaching of this or that shore, but to let oneself become the meeting place of both.

In a way all writing is a translation, a struggle to interpret the meaning of life, and in this sense the translator can be said to be a shaman, a person dedicated to deciphering conflicting human texts, searching for the final unity of meaning in speech. Translators of literary texts act like a writer's telescopic lens; they are dedicated to the pursuit of communication, of that universal understanding of original meaning which may one day perhaps make possible the harmony of the world. They struggle to bring together different cultures, striding over the barriers of those prejudices and misunderstandings that are the result of diverse ways of thinking and of cultural mores. They wrestle between two swinging axes, which have, since the beginning of mankind, caused wars to break out and civilizations to fail to understand each other: the utterance and the interpretation of meaning; the verbal sign (or form) and the essence (or spirit) of the word.

I believe that being both a Puerto Rican and a woman writer has given me the opportunity to experience translation (as well as writing itself) in a special way. Only a writer who has experienced the historical fabric, the inventory of felt moral and cultural existence embedded in a given language, can be said to be a bilingual writer, and being a Puerto Rican has enabled me to acquire a knowledge both of Spanish and English, of the Latin American and of the North American way of life. Translation is not only a literary but also a historical task; it includes an interpretation of internal history, of the changing proceedings of consciousness in a civilization. A poem by Góngora, written in the seventeenth century, can be translated literally, but it cannot be read without taking into account the complex cultural connotations that the Renaissance had in Spain. Language, in the words of George Steiner, is like a living membrane; it provides a constantly changing model of reality. Every civilization is imprisoned in a linguistic contour, which it must match and regenerate according to the changing landscape of facts and of time.

When I write in English I feel that the landscape of experience, the fields of idiomatic, symbolic, communal reference are not lost to me, but are relatively well within my reach, in spite of the fact that Spanish is still the language of my dreams. Writing in English, however, remains for me a cultural translation, as I believe it must be for such writers as Vladimir Nabokov and Vassily Aksyonov, who come from a country whose cultural matrix is also very different from that of the United States. Translating a literary work (even one's own) from one language to another curiously implies the same type of historical interpretation that is necessary in translating a poem of the seventeenth century, for example, as contemporary cultures often enclaved in different epochs of time coexist with each other. This is precisely what happens today with North American and Latin American literatures, where the description of technological, pragmatic, democratic modern states coexists with that of feudal, agrarian, and still basically totalitarian states. Translating literature from Spanish into English (and vice versa) in the twentieth century cannot but take into account very different views of the world, which are evident when one compares, for example, the type of novel produced today by Latin American writers such as Carlos Fuentes, Gabriel García Márquez, and Isabel Allende, who are all preoccupied by the processes of transformation and strife within totalitarian agrarian societies, and the novels of such North American writers as Saul Bellow, Philip Roth, and E. L. Doctorow, who are engrossed in the complicated unraveling of the human psyche within the dehumanized modern city-state.

Translating has taught me that it is ultimately impossible to transcribe one cultural identity into another. As I write in English I am inevitably translating a Latin American identity, still rooted in preindustrial traditions and mores, with very definite philosophical convictions and beliefs, into a North American context. As Richard Morse has so accurately pointed out in his book *El espejo de Próspero: un estudio de la dialéctica del Nuevo Mundo* (1982), Latin American society is still rooted in Thomistic, Aristotelian beliefs, which attempt to reconcile Christian thought with the truths of the natural universe and of faith. Spain (and Latin America) have never really undergone a scientific or an industrial revolution, and they have never produced the equivalent of a Hobbes or a Locke, so that theories such as that of pragmatism, individual liberty, and the social contract have been very difficult to implement.

Carlos Fuentes's novel *Terra Nostra,* for example, tries to point out this situation, as it analyzes the failure of the Latin American totalitarian state (the PRI in Mexico), founded both on the Spanish tradition of absolute power established by Philip II during the seventeenth century and on the blood-soaked Aztec Empire. Fuentes's case, however, as well as that of Alejo Carpentier, can be said to be exceptions to the rule in the Latin American literary landscape, as both writers make an effort in their novels to escape arbitrary descriptions of their worlds, and often integrate into their novels rationalistic analyses that delve into Latin American traditions from diverging points of view.

Translating my own work, I came directly in contact with this type of problem. In the first place, I discovered that the Spanish (and Latin American) literary tradition permits a much greater leeway for what may be called "play on words," which generally sound frivolous and innocuous in English. In Puerto Rico, as in Latin America, we are brought up as children on a constant juggling of words, which often has as its purpose the humorous defiance of apparent social meanings and established structures of power. In undermining the meaning of words, the Latin American child (as the Latin American writer) calls into question the social order, which he is obliged to accept without sharing in its processes. This defiance through humor has to do with a heroic stance ("el relajo," "la bachata," "la joda") often of anarchic origin which is a part of the Latin personality, but it also has to do with faith, with a Thomistic belief in supernatural values. It is faith in the possibility of Utopia, of the values asserted by a society ruled by Christian, absolute values rather than by pragmatic ends, which leads the Puerto Rican child to revel in puns such as "Tenemos mucho oro, del que cagó el loro" (We have a lot of gold, of the kind the parrot pukes) or "Tenemos mucha plata, de la que cagó la gata" (We have a lot of silver, of the kind the cat shits), which permit him to face, and at the same time defy, his island's poverty; or in popular Puerto Rican sayings of the blackest humor and unforgiving social judgment such as, "el día que la mierda valga algo, los pobres nacerán sin culo" (the day shit is worth any money, the poor will be born without assholes).

But faith in the magical power of the image, in the power to transform the world into a better place through what Lezama Lima calls the "súbito," is only one of the traditions that enable Latin American writers to revel in puns and wordplay; there is also a historical, geographic tradition which I believe helps to explain the elaboration of extremely intricate forms of expression. It is not casually or by expediency that the literary structures in Alejo Carpentier's *Los pasos perdidos* (The Lost Steps), Guimarães Rosa's *Grande Sertão: Veredas,* or Nélida Piñón's *Tebas do meu coração* often remind us of the baroque altarpieces of the churches of Brazil, Mexico, and Peru, where baroque art reached its maximum expression. When the Spanish conquerors reached the New World in the fifteenth and sixteenth centuries they brought the Spanish language and tradition with them, but that language and tradition, confronted by and superimposed on the complex realities of Indian cultures, as well as the convoluted forms of an equally diverse and till then unknown flora and fauna, began to change radically. In this sense Spanish literature in itself had received, by the time the seventeenth century had come around, considerable cultural influence from the Latin American continent. Don Luis de Góngora y Argote, for example, who never visited the Spanish colonies, would probably never have written the *Soledades* (a poem considered the apex of baroque literary expression) in which a shipwrecked traveler reaches the shores of a Utopian New World, if Spanish had not been the language in which Mexico and Peru were discovered and colonized. None has put it more clearly than José Lezama Lima, the Cuban poet, in an essay entitled "La curiosidad barroca." Lezama points out there how the baroque literary art of Góngora, as well as that of his nephew, the Mexican Don Carlos de Sigüenza y Góngora and of the Mexican nun Sor Juana Inés de la Cruz, evolves parallel to the carved altarpieces of Kondori, an Indian stonecarver from Peru, which represent "in an obscure and hieratic fashion the synthesis of Spanish and Indian, of Spanish theocracy with the solemn petrified order of the Inca Empire." Lezama's own novel, *Paradiso,* whose linguistic structure is as convoluted as the labyrinths of the Amazon jungle, remains today the most impressive testimony to the importance of baroque aesthetics in the contemporary Latin American novel.

A third characteristic that helps define Latin American tradition vis-à-vis North American tradition in literature today has often to do with magical occurrences and the world of the marvelously real ("lo real maravilloso"), which imply a given faith in the supernatural world which is very difficult to acquire when one is born in a country where technological knowledge and the pragmatics of reason reign supreme. We are here once again in the realm of how diverging cultural matrices determine to a certain extent the themes that preoccupy literature. In technologically developed countries such as the United States and England, for example, the marvelous often finds its most adequate expression in the novels of writers such as Ray Bradbury and Lord Dunsany, who prefer to place their fiction in extraterrestrial worlds where faith in magic can still operate and the skepticism inherent in inductive reasoning has not yet become dominant.

As I began to translate my novel, *Maldito Amor,* the issues I have just mentioned came to my attention. The first serious obstacle I encountered was the title. "Maldito Amor" in Spanish is an idiomatic expression that is impossible to render accurately in English. It is a love that is halfway between doomed and damned, and thus participates in both without being either. The fact that the adjective "maldito," furthermore, is placed before the noun "amor," gives it an exclamative nature which is very present to Spanish speakers, in spite of the fact that the exclamation point is missing. "Maldito Amor" is something very different from "Amor Maldito," which would clearly have the connotation of "devilish love." The title of the novel in Spanish is, in this sense, almost a benign form of swearing, or of complaining about the treacherous nature of love. In addition to all this, the title is also the title of a very famous danza written by Juan Morell Campos, Puerto Rico's most gifted composer in the nineteenth century, which describes in its verses the paradisiacal existence of the island's bourgeoisie at the time. As this complicated wordplay would have been totally lost in English, as well as the cultural reference to a musical composition which is only well known on the island, I decided to change the title altogether in my translation of the novel, substituting the much more specific "Sweet Diamond Dust." The new title refers to the sugar produced by the De Lavalle family, but it also touches on the dangers of a sugar that, like diamond dust, poisons those who sweeten their lives with it.

The inability to reproduce Spanish wordplay as anything but a mere juggling of words not only made me change the title; it also soon made me begin to prune my own sentences mercilessly like overgrown vines, because, I found, the sap was not running through them as it should. How did I know this? What made me arrive at this conclusion? As I faced sentence after sentence of what I had written in Spanish hardly two years before (when I was writing the novel), I realized that, in translating it into English, I had acquired a different instinct in my approach to a theme. I felt almost like a hunting dog that is forced to smell out the same prey, but one that has drastically changed its spoor. My faith in the power of the image, for example, was now untenable, and facts had become much more important. The dance of language had now to have a direction, a specific line of action. The possibility of Utopia, and the description of a world in which the marvelously real sustained the very fabric of existence, was still my goal, but it had to be reached by a different road. The language of technology and capitalism, I said to myself, must above all assure a dividend, and this dividend cannot be limited to philosophic contemplations, or to a feast of the senses and of the ear. Thus, I delved into a series of books on the history and sociology of the sugarcane industry in Puerto Rico, which gave me the opportunity to widen the scope of the novel, adding information and situating its events in a much more precise environment.

Is translation of a literary text possible, given the enormous differences in cultural tradition in which language is embedded? I asked myself this, seeing that as I translated I was forced to substitute, cancel, and rewrite constantly, now pruning, now widening the original text. In the philosophy of language and in reference to translation in general (not necessarily of a literary text) two radically opposed points of view can be and have been asserted. One declares that the underlying structure of language is universal and common to everyone. "To translate," in the words of George Steiner, "is to descend beneath the exterior disparities of two languages in order to bring into vital play their analogous and . . . common principles of being." The other one holds that "universal deep structures are either fathomless to logical and psychological investigation or of an order so abstract, so generalized as to be well-nigh trivial." This extreme, monadistic position asserts that real translation is impossible, as Steiner says, and that what passes for translation is a convention of approximate analogies, "a roughcast similitude, just tolerable when the two relevant languages or cultures are cognate . . ."

I lean rather more naturally to the second than to the first of these premises. Translating literature is a very different matter from translating everyday language, and I believe it could be evaluated on a changing spectrum. Poetry, where meaning can never be wholly separated from expressive form, is a mystery that can never be translated. It can only be transcribed, reproduced in a shape that will always be a sorry shadow of itself. That is why Robert Frost pronounced his famous dictum that "poetry is what gets lost in translation" and Ortega y Gasset evolved his theory on the melancholy of translation, in his *Miseria y esplendor de la traducción*. To one side of poetry one could place prose and poetic fiction, where symbolic expression may alternate with the language of analysis and communication. Here one could situate novels and prose poems that employ varying degrees of symbolic language and which are directed toward both an intuitive *and* an explanatory exposition of meaning. On the far side of the spectrum one could place literary texts of a historical, sociological, and political nature, such as the essays of Euclides da Cunha in Brazil, for example, and the work of Fernando Ortiz in Cuba or of Tomás Blanco in Puerto Rico. These texts, as well as those of literary critics who have been able to found their analytic theories on a powerfully poetic expression (such as Roland Barthes), are perhaps less difficult to translate, but even so the *lacunae* that arise from the missing cultural connotations in these essays are usually of the greatest magnitude.

Translating one's own literary work is, in short, a complex, disturbing occupation. It can be diabolic and obsessive: it is one of the few instances when one can be dishonest and feel good about it, rather like having a second chance at redressing one's fatal mistakes in life and living a different way. The writer becomes her own critical conscience; her superego leads her (perhaps treacherously) to believe that she can not only better but surpass herself, or at least surpass the writer she has been in the past. Popular lore has long equated translation with betrayal: "Traduttore-traditore" goes the popular Italian saying. "La traduction est comme la femme, plus qu'elle est belle, elle n'est pas fidèle; plus qu'elle est fidèle, elle n'est pas belle" goes the chauvinist French saying. But in translating one's own work it is only by betraying that one can better the original. There is, thus, a feeling of elation, of submerging oneself in sin, without having to pay the consequences. Instinct becomes the sole beacon. "The loyal translator will write what is correct," the devil whispers exultantly in one's ear, "but not necessarily what is right."

And yet translation, in spite of its considerable difficulties, is a necessary reality for me as a writer. As a Puerto Rican I have undergone exile as a way of life, and also as a style of life. Coming and going from south to north, from Spanish to English, without losing a sense of self can constitute an anguishing experience. It implies a constant recreation of divergent worlds, which often tend to appear greener on the other side. Many Puerto Ricans undergo this ordeal, although with different intensity, according to their economic situation in life. Those who come from a privileged class, who form a part of the more recent "brain drain" of engineers, architects, and doctors who emigrate today to the States in search of a higher standard of living, can afford to keep memory clean and well tended, visiting the site of the "Lares" with relative assiduity. Those who come fleeing from poverty and hunger, such as the taxi drivers, elevator operators, or seasonal grape and lettuce pickers who began to emigrate to these shores by the thousands in the forties, are often forced to be merciless with memory, as they struggle to integrate with and become indistinguishable from the mainstream. It is for these people that translation becomes of fundamental importance. Obliged to adapt in order to survive, the children of these Puerto Rican parents often refuse to learn to speak Spanish, and they grow up having lost the ability to read the literature and the history of their island. This cultural suicide constitutes an immense loss, as they become unable to learn about their roots, having lost the language that is the main road to their culture. I believe it is the duty of the Puerto Rican writer, who has been privileged enough to learn both languages, to try to alleviate this situation, making an effort either to translate some of her own work or to contribute to the translation of the work of other Puerto Rican writers. The melancholy of the Puerto Rican soul may perhaps this way one day be assuaged, and its perpetual hunger for a lost paradise be appeased. Memory, which so often erases the ache of the penury and destitution suffered on the island, after years of battling for survival in the drug-seared ghettos of Harlem and the Bronx, can, through translation, perhaps be reinstated to its true abode.

I would like now to talk a bit about the experience of being a woman writer from Latin America, and how I suspect being one has helped me to translate literary works. As a Latin American woman writer I feel a great responsibility in forming a part of, and perpetuating, a literary tradition that has only recently begun to flourish among us. I feel we must become aware that we belong to a community of countries that cannot afford to live at odds with each other; a community whose future, in fact, depends today on its ability to support and nurture itself, helping to solve each other's problems. A sense of belonging to a continental community, based on an identity that was first envisioned by Simón Bolívar, must rise above nationalistic passions and prejudices. In this respect, Brazilian women writers have always been at the forefront, for they were the first to write not solely for the women of Brazil, but for all those Latin American women who, like the feminine protagonists of Clarice Lispector and Nélida Piñón in stories such as "A Chicken" and "A Chocolate Cake," have suffered a stifling social repression.

As a woman writer who has lived both in Anglo America and Latin America I have had, like Ophelia drifting down the canal or the child that looks in the beveled mirror of her wardrobe, to be able to see left become right and right become left without feeling panic or losing my sense of direction. In other words, I have had to be able to let go of all shores, be both left-handed and right-handed, masculine and feminine, because my destiny was to live by the word. In fact, a woman writer (like a man writer), must live traveling constantly between two very different cultures (much more so than English and Spanish), two very different worlds which are often at each others' throats: the world of women and the world of men. In this respect, I have often asked myself whether translation of feminine into masculine is possible, or vice versa (here the perennial question of whether there is a feminine or a masculine writing crops up again). Is it possible to enter the mind of a man, to think, feel, dream like a man, being a woman writer? The idea seems preposterous at first, because deep down we feel that we cannot know anything but what we are, what we have experienced in our own flesh and bones. And yet the mind, and its exterior, audible expression, language or human speech, is mimetic by nature. Language, in Leibnitz's opinion, for example, was not only the vehicle of thought but its determining medium. Being matterless, language (thought) can enter and leave its object at will, can actually become that object, creating it and destroying it as it deems necessary. In this sense the cabalistic tradition speaks of a logos, or a word that makes speech meaningful and is like a hidden spring that underlies all human communication and makes it possible. This concept of the word as having a divine origin confers upon it a creative power which may perhaps justify the writer's attempt to enter into modes of being (masculine, Chinese, extraterrestrial?) in which she has not participated in the course of her own human existence.

I like to believe that in my work I have confronted language not as a revelation of a divine meaning or of an unalterable scheme of things, but as a form of creation, or recreation of my world. If writing made it possible for me to authorize (become the author of) my own life, why may it not also permit me to enter into and thus "create" (translate?) the lives of other characters, men, women, and children? These are questions I ask myself often, which I may never be able to answer, but I believe it is important to try to do so.

Language, Violence, and Resistance

Junot Díaz

In Patrick Chamoiseau's letter to his translators about his novel *Solibo Magnifique*,[1] he does not just explain to them this word is this, that word is that, but states the ethics of his writing vis-à-vis translation. He explains his use of language, how he grabs language from all over, that there's no word too archaic to be included in his texts, nor is there any word too recent not to be included. He tells his translators to cast the widest net possible, for indigenous terms to find some indigenous parallels. This wonderfully expansive mode of translation is how I would like my work translated.

The text I felt most responsible for, with *Drown,* was the English one. The other ones were really out of my hands. One of the things about writing in English is that there are certain members of my audience whom I clearly wanted to be able to read these texts but who didn't read in English so I always figured that they'd end up being translated informally by one of my family members. That's about as far as I originally thought about translation. The next time I want very strict controls over the Spanish translation. I want to make sure to resist the kind of Spanish people think will facilitate the reading, but rather to foster the kind that will facilitate the book. An edgier Spanish would have been better, a more mean-natured and expansive Spanish. The use of Spanish in *Drown* in the English version is more interesting than the use of Spanish in the translation. There's so little Spanish in the original, although people say there's a lot. The little bit that is there, interestingly, is not all Dominicanisms; it roams completely around the world. Any Spanish it can use for its purposes, it uses. My translator did a clean and clear but somehow also a sterile job. When the Spanish from the English texts gets translated, it's like throwing water on water. You lose the dissonance.

So many writers take the position that with translation you lose a lot. But really, how much do you lose? Do you lose more than when you speak any language? Isn't language already an act of compromise with reality? In the end everything is a translation but you do lose some of the aural energy, you lose some of the violence that languages inflict on each other. Spanish can be very violent inside of English the same way that

English was a very violent language onto my Spanish when I first arrived in the United States. You lose the playfulness and the energy in the language and so what remains is that the writing better be good, the characterizations, the story, because when people read the Spanish version they lose the inventiveness of the language. It's a sacrifice, but my goal is to communicate. It might not be perfect communication but many of my readers in the Dominican Republic said the Spanish translation was still powerful and moving.

I got a wide variety of reactions when the book came out in Spanish, and I felt there was a lot of support. Some of that comes from Dominican nationalism; they're really happy to see a young Dominican from the diaspora doing something positive. Some readers found it difficult: without the English-Spanish tension and violence, without the playfulness of the two languages, it seemed very brutal. There's the same amount of profanity in the English but the violence between the two languages eclipses the violence of the profanity. Caliban says, "You taught me your language but my only profit is to curse." Caliban taught that an imposed language is harsher than his cursing.

I enjoyed working with my translator. He is very smart and openminded. My English isn't very transparent. There's plenty of "urban" language, youth language, hiphop language, and a lot of "intellectual" language. To be able to juggle them all at once and get the valence of all of them as a translator is difficult. I found my interventions to be the most useful on the boundaries between all these areas. A lot of times the translator didn't get the nuances of the urban Englishes, and I had to explain some of the jokes to place them in their proper perspective. There were mistakes to correct. He corrected my Spanish, but I corrected his translations into Spanish. I trusted him in spite of the powerlessness one feels. It felt like a community enterprise. The Spanish translation was vetted by Silvio Torres Saillant and Frank Moya Pons. I was concerned about the Spanish (Castilian) nuances since my translator was from Spain, and we did a good job of eliminating most of them.

Being read outside the United States now doesn't change that my primary readership is still close to home. I don't have an internationalism running through me. I'm very U.S.-situated. I just hope to get it right in the local area. If it's right for here, hopefully it will resonate with some authority in the larger world. I don't want to roam too wide right now.

Everybody knows so much about the New York area that I tend to be writing about a lot of things that people have at least caught the edge or the perimeter of. Because it's got the rubric "it's New York," even though it's New Jersey, people will just skip over a lot they don't understand and they're willing to go through with it. If I was writing locally from Milwaukee, I don't know if that would be the case. The centrality of New York as a world city in the United States charges the text with a certain amount of literary world narrative.

I'm becoming more voracious at mixing varieties of languages and registers. This is nothing new, but just a specific variety coming out of the Dominican diasporic experience. Patrick Chamoiseau is completely voracious in his ability to use not only multiple languages and registers, but also anything and everything he can consolidate under the rubric of language. I find myself becoming more wide-ranging; where before I'd stick to Latino and black slang, I find myself now using South African slang because I find it sounds right. There's a larger community of words to steal from. When I wrote *Drown*, it was with the language I had available. The more I travel the more access I have to languages, traditions, conventions, to vernaculars and registers, and I begin to use as many of them as I can.

I have a multiplicity of identity sites, as one should. I love the fact that Toni Morrison always insisted that she was a "black woman writer" and after she won all these awards everyone called her "the great American writer" but she resisted that, and instead insisted that she was "the great black woman writer." I found that to be a really interesting act of resistance. People are desperately trying to define me with the speed of light, and so you need to define yourself at the speed of light too. It's a dance. First and foremost, I feel like I'm a Dominican writer. For many people I'm just a Latino writer but I feel like I'm a part of African diasporic tradition, the Caribbean tradition, I'm a writer from all these areas. There's strategic, rhetorical value to also being a Latino writer, being part of a larger group. I learned to write not from old Dominican texts, but from Cristina García, Sandra Cisneros, Oscar Hijuelos. I'm serious about being part of the African diasporic tradition. A lot of "traditional" black American writers formed who I am, they form my language family. It's an accident of history and blood that some of my language family also fits into my historical and blood family. A lot of times when I'm with just Latino or black writers, I'm considered very specifically a male writer because I do so much work on masculinity and male privilege that sometimes that is what comes to the foreground. There are multiple answers to the question of identity, because it depends on the context and on the political work that you want to do with that answer.

NOTES

This essay is based on a conversation with Marcy Schwartz in New Brunswick, N.J., on March 29, 1999.

1. Patrick Chamoiseau, *Solibo Magnifique* (Paris: Gallimard, 1988); in English: *Solibo Magnificent,* trans. Rose-Myriam Rejouis and Val Vinokurov (New York: Pantheon, 1998).

Translation as Restoration

Cristina García

Now that both *Dreaming in Cuban* and *The Agüero Sisters*[1] have been translated into Spanish it feels like a complete cycle. It feels incomplete to me in English; it almost needs to be translated in Spanish for me to feel like the process has been realized. For me to see the book in Spanish is more of a restoration than a translation, I feel like I'm the one who's the translator. I sense a porousness between the two languages, probably more Spanish into English. To me English doesn't really influence Spanish the same way Spanish influences written English. I think spoken English influences my spoken Spanish, because since I don't write in Spanish there's no influence there. Spoken and written Spanish definitely influences my written English but not my spoken English. The porousness I feel comes from Spanish into English and it's very palpable, maybe with every sentence I write, even if I'm not consciously thinking in Spanish or hearing a scene in Spanish, which sometimes happens, I feel that there's a cadence and a musicality and a sensibility that comes from Spanish that informs every line and I think that in one way or another, conscious or not, I'm trying to approximate Spanish in English, or trying to make English do things that it feels rather stiff about doing. I'm continuously massaging the English, limbering it up to accommodate the cadence and musicality of Spanish. It's a very interesting process of always having Spanish in the wings, in a way it's sort of a linguistic water table.

I've had some problems with the translations. *Dreaming in Cuban* was translated in Spain by a Puerto Rican woman who grew up in New York but who basically translates for the Spanish publishing houses and very much for the Spanish peninsular market. The result was too formal for my taste. There was no Cuban flavor or presence in the book; it was a very faithful and literal translation for the Spanish market but it didn't capture the Cuban seasoning. It's like putting a pork chop with salt and pepper in the oven versus the garlic and sour orange marination that goes on for three days, it just doesn't taste the same. With *The Agüero Sisters,* I just had a baby when the Spanish translation was proposed, and frankly my Spanish just isn't good enough; I cannot shepherd and oversee it in Spanish the way I do in English. My Spanish is not that evolved, it's not that sensitive, especially for the kinds of things I do in English. Ironically, the English does more for the Spanish flavor of the book than the Spanish. It feels more Cuban in English than it does in Spanish. It's a little bit alien in Spanish. The way I would envision it in Spanish is not how it's ever been rendered. It's in Cuba, from readers, writers, academics and translators, that I get the most bitter dismay about what's happened to the book in Spanish. They just don't get it. It seems like a stunted text.

With *The Agüero Sisters,* because of the dissatisfactions I had with *Dreaming in Cuban,* I was very particular about the translator, and really insisted that they get someone familiar with the Cuban and Cuban American idiom. They found a Cuban poet who grew up in Puerto Rico and is very bilingual and I think he did a pretty good job in capturing more of the seasoning. When the book was sent to Spain for consideration they told me they considered it substandard Spanish and that it would be unintelligible to a Spanish audience and even a broader South American audience, which I thought was pretty preposterous. So they actually retranslated certain passages and chapters to make it more to their taste. It was a big struggle. I'm still not fully satisfied. It came out almost simultaneously with the English edition for the domestic market and it came out the following winter in Spain for the Spanish and South American market, so there are actually two translations. It's frustrating to me because I feel that these books belong in Spanish as much as they belong in English, which is not to say that they belong there more than in English. To see them in somewhat diminished versions than the language that they normally take place in is a sadness for me. I don't have much say over what happens with the Finnish edition of *The Agüero Sisters,* but to me it's very important how it sounds and feels and smells in the Spanish edition. I wasn't consulted by the *Dreaming in Cuban* translator, but I was consulted by the *The Agüero Sisters* translator. Part of the frustration is my own frustration in having inadequate Spanish. I could never do what Rosario Ferré does, and I admire her very much. I suppose I could devote a couple of years to getting my Spanish into excellent shape so I can very carefully oversee these translations, but I'm not sure that's how I want to spend my time. The person who translated *The Agüero Sisters* is Cuban himself, and he got it. But ironically, he couldn't quite capture the freight of the English words, their nuance and implication in the Spanish. It's a pretty good literal and atmospheric rendition of *The Agüero Sisters* but it lacks a dimension and complexity and some of the finesse in the language of the English. Part of my frustration is not having solutions or suggestions for the translators. I can't fix it in Spanish. I can play with the dialogue, but I don't have a lyrical Spanish, I can't play with the language the way I do in English. There comes a point, when I've completed the book in English, even though it feels somehow still incomplete without having the Spanish version, I have to let it go. The Spanish edition is so critical, it's the one I really care about, and yet I feel a little helpless in making it sing the way I'd like it to. The anxiety over translation begins after the English version is done. The prospect of a translation, or writing something that I know will be complicated to translate, doesn't make me shy away from anything; I'm in it thick in the English and really don't worry about the Spanish translation until much later. But I do worry within the text about how to use Spanish and where I should translate. It's a question of spice for the English.

I'm having some trouble with the book that I'm working on now with an enormous number of idiomatic expressions about the Chinese in Cuba. For example, a Chinese street vendor might be selling toasted corn, and yelling out, "¡Maní tostado caliente para la vieja que no tiene dientes!" But when you translate this saying about toothless women it doesn't work! There's a whole joke about the Chinese peddlers, when the newcomers would come they would follow the ones who'd been there a while, with an identical basket, of, say, toasted corn, and say, "lo mismo," "the same," but when I translated it, it fell completely flat. Right now I have it in Spanish and in an English approximation and I'll have to resolve it later. There are all kinds of weird aphorisms such as, "En boca cerrada no entran moscas." How do you capture that? It's a Spanish expression, and I ended up making up a Chinese equivalent in translation, a proverb for my Chinese character that sounded like it, to acculturate it.

There are always those kinds of negotiations and decisions as you go along. It's complicated even more by point of view. The first half of the book is largely from the point of view of this foreigner in Cuba, someone from a radically different culture and language, looking at it all anew. His first impressions are of firecrackers going off, that's what the language sounds like to him, ratatatat. There's a lot of play with the idea of language in translation. It's set in the nineteenth century. He ends up on a sugar cane plantation with a lot of newly arrived slaves who are Asante and Carabalí and all of these different African tribes who are speaking their own languages. They are all negotiating that with the value of the whip and survival. My character gets whipped for telling a joke in Chinese that makes all of the Chinese workers laugh so hard they drop their machetes while they're cutting and it slows down production.

Complicating the stew of languages is music and all that that was fraught with for so long. There's a heavy musical theme in this book as well. There's a drumming throughout that begins in the slave days and continues through the present day with the great-grandson of the Chinese immigrant who is a conguero. It's a question of communicating in silences. Slaves could be shackled for two months for drumming. It was a very subversive act. To play a drum was akin to insurrection, it's another language.

Language is not for museums, it slips through the nets. You can take snapshots of it along the way, but you can't pin it like butterflies to the wall.

The last section in *Dreaming in Cuban* is called "Languages Lost." My Spanish is an oral "kitchen" Spanish from the 1950s. When I went back to Cuba, everyone found it very entertaining. There's a scene in *The Agüero Sisters* talking about Constancia's language and how it was from another era and it was there to describe another reality, and that Reina's Spanish reflects thirty years of a completely different existence. That's what so fascinates me about Miami and going to places like Café Nostalgia. They're attempting a kind of preservation in formaldehyde and I don't think you can do that with language. I was last in Cuba in 1996 in Oriente for a music festival and much to my astonishment there are Haitian communities in the easternmost province. I knew they existed but what I didn't know was that their Creole was more than two hundred years old and they had preserved it in a vacuum. There's a situation of a living museum, because they were so traumatized and displaced that at all cost they wanted to preserve what they had. It was fascinating historically because they had also done an extremely wonderful job of preserving dances from that period and music that was passed on from generation to generation.

It's not just about language; translating a culture is very hard, and that's what I found difficult to convey to the Spanish publisher. It's not just using this word over that word, these words are not in isolation, they're in a net and web of cultural context that you can't really get out of. The totality of that, to get that from one cultural language to another is very much the art of it. The struggle does inform the final decision, negotiation will underscore whatever decisions I make. Of the hundreds or thousands of pages that wind up on the floor, you're stealing from all of that. There's a way of surrounding an idea. I don't think it's exclusively a problem of translation; I see it as clusters of language approximating ideas rather than ideas themselves becoming crystalline centers. Sometimes you can't get it exactly right, and maybe that's the point. Even in *The Agüero Sisters*, you can finally know the "facts" of what happened, but you still don't know what happened. I'm not sure that Constancia or Reina finally knowing exactly what happened in the swamp brought them any closer to understanding *why* it happened. Although it was important for them to know the facts, it was only a springboard for speculation. At the center is Blanca, whiteness, the unknowable, and all you can hope to do is surround it and get close to the heat of it. In translation, getting as close as possible to the heart of the original is the most you can hope for.

NOTES

This essay is edited from an interview with Marcy Schwartz at Rutgers University on March 8, 1999.

1. *Las hermanas Agüero*, trans. Alan West (New York: Random House, 1997); *Soñar en cubano*, trans. Marisol Palés Castro (Madrid: Espasa Calpe, 1993).

Language and Change

Rolando Hinojosa-Smith

My first two novels, *Estampas del valle y otras obras* (1974) and *Klail City y sus alrededores* (1978), were translated into English by Gustavo Valadez and José Reyna, and by Rosaura Sánchez, respectively. I found them acceptable, although friends and colleagues and others who used them in either Spanish or Ethnic Studies classes did not. Later on, I discovered that many Mexican American college students were not fluent in Spanish. A matter of different generations, then.

This was particularly true of the urbanites and of many living in smaller communities. This dovetailed with my own plans: I wanted to write in several genres within the novel such as the epistolary, the fragmentary, reportage, and so on, and English fit the bill. I then decided to do my own translations, and *Estampas* came out as *The Valley* (1983), and *Klail City y sus alrededores* as *Klail City* (1987). In another novel, *Mi querido Rafa* (1981), some of the characters used English now and again; its translation, *Dear Rafe* (1985), had words and phrases in Spanish, as always because of the bilingualism in the Lower Rio Grande Valley of Texas. I found I liked doing my own translations, and since the work was engaging and challenging, this drove me on.

I don't know if Chicano/Mexican American literature is by definition a bilingual phenomenon. However, much of the early poetry by Alurista and Ricardo Sánchez employed such bilingualism. It looked easy to some less talented poets, but it certainly wasn't. One has to be proficient in both languages as well as in poetry, as is Angela de Hoyos. What the less able writers wrote was verse, not poetry.

It's not difficult to mix the languages when speaking, but unless one does it naturally, innately, the words sound forced and out of place. I'm no linguist, but I do know how language operates. I've been speaking both languages and mixing them as a matter of course since childhood. It happens that sometimes, even now, I may not think immediately of a noun I wish to use, and so I'll use its Spanish or English equivalent. But, there is a rule: one speaks this way when one knows that the other person will understand.

Here's something I've noticed as well: Two friends meet, one greets the other in Spanish, and the second replies in English. But here's the phenomenon: the first greeter, upon hearing the English, replies in that language, while the second may respond in Spanish. In seconds, a tacit agreement is made and the friends will use one or the other language or both. This happens quite frequently.

I first attempted the Tomás Rivera translation during my visiting professorship at UCLA in 1981 when I spent most of my weekends at his house in Riverside. I didn't get anywhere, but, in 1994, when he died, I decided to have another go at it. I went over the original manuscripts of *y no se lo tragó la tierra* and its variants, and the order of the chapters, which, not incidentally, is at variance with the original Quinto Sol publication. I then changed the order that appears in the original publication since the editors had changed Tomás's order. I further discovered that either Tomás or the editors had substituted the *Eva y Daniel* piece for another. One of Tomás's three handwritten title pages listed the months of the year, from *enero* to *diciembre*, sandwiched between *El año perdido* (The Lost Year) and *El año encontrado* (The Found Year). The point is that what the reader buys does not usually reflect the original or the rewrites of the writer's manuscript, or even editorial intervention.

Allan Cheuse on National Public Radio praised the work, as have other literary critics. There are at least two other translations on the market. Whatever their impact, the fact remains that Tomás Rivera's work set a high standard for contemporary Mexican American literature. As for the decisions made during the translation, although I can't remember them in detail, they were done with the view of reflecting the life and the language of the migrant farm laboring class.

Usually, my characters stay within one language or the other. Some five percent of their Spanish consists of regionalisms as well as slang of the period. It would be a fraud to have the rural folk speak as members of the professional classes. I also go to the Valley quite often for barbecues, weddings, baptisms, funerals, and so on. Some would call this research, but for me, they're nothing less than social gatherings and occasions. That I use the material is what writers do.

I've not conducted writing workshops in the context of translation. When I answer questions I offer the oldest advice a writer can give: read as much as possible, acquire as much language and language usage as possible, and start from there. A question I used to hear was, "What about the German translations of some of your work?" Will the Germans understand who we are, what we say, do, and so on?" I was fortunate to have the trilingually proficient Dr. Yolanda Julia Broyles do the work for *Klail City y sus alrededores* (Klail City und Umgebung). German is a synthetic language while Spanish is analytical, but nevertheless she did a fine job.

I think it only natural that Hispanic literature is being translated into English. Majority houses are in the business of making money, and if the translations reach a large number of book buyers, the houses will publish the works. However, most contemporary Latino writers write in English, particularly Puerto Rican and Cuban/Dominican American writers such as Nicholasa Mohr, Julia Alvarez, Gustavo Pérez Firmat, and Virgil Suárez. This goes for Mexican American writers as well. Caribbean Spanish usage differs from Central, South American, and Mexican Spanish usage. Not in the bulk of the language, no, but there are geographical and lexical differences in the Spanish spoken and used in Argentina, Puerto Rico, and Mexico, for three examples. The market may call for English, to be sure, but one has to be able to write in Spanish as well; the newer generation of Mexican American writers has not produced novels in that language for some time. Gary Soto, for one example, has his work translated into Spanish by professionals, and he is not alone in this regard. The writers previously mentioned have agents, and know that publishers want their material in English.

Textbooks for elementary and middle school students have been published in Spanish since the mid-eighties. Early on, the stories were English translations of Peninsular Spanish writers, but, more and more, works in English by U.S. Hispanic writers have become the order of the day. The elementary Spanish textbooks are a product of a market-driven reality: the increased migration of Spanish speakers to this country. My view is that, unlike the generations of the forties, thirties, twenties, and so on, acculturation and assimilation will occur at a more rapid pace.

Metamorphosis

Nélida Piñon

I don't always read or participate in the translations of my books, since they are often in languages I do not have easy access to. I was able to participate in, for example, Helen Lane's English translations and some of the short stories and long passages of *A República dos Sonhos* (The Republic of Dreams) into Spanish. Often the translation arrives from the publisher as a "fait accompli." In any case, I've learned a long time ago that a text is born within rules: aesthetic, grammatical rules, rules of the language itself. And from the moment a text crosses the boundaries—the limits or the lack of them in the Portuguese language—and visits another language, it takes on the role of a filter of another culture, almost of another civilization. It is impossible to imagine that a text, even when very well translated, can remain the same. But such transformations are due to a kind of metamorphosis, which does not necessarily improve or diminish the text.

As far as my own responsibility toward the text, I used to worry much more about its destiny in other languages, but now I tend to trust God and the ability or talent of the translator. I really enjoy knowing that the translator is committed, that he or she has a depth of experience and a reputation as a translator and, moreover, that he or she is very respectful and responsible. That puts me at ease. So you have to trust the other and be aware of the limitations of his or her task.

I believe that one human being's thinking can always reach or visit that of another, even if it occurs in another language. The question is to find a translator who is capable of abandoning his or her original "shell," and accepting the idiosyncrasies of the other's thinking and the other's language. That is why the translator cannot be someone unprepared, who hardly knows the language to be translated. One must know the culture from which the language to be translated originates as profoundly as one's own culture: that is, one has to recognize both the soul and the civilization of human experience. I have seen mistaken translations due to cultural limitations. If the translator is cultivated, if he or she masters the language in which he or she writes and the original language, I believe this is a great privilege. And I expect the translator to love the text and respect the writer, so that he or she won't mutilate the original.

The translator must make my text viable in the target language; he or she has to make me exist so that my ideas endure and the richness of my text is not lost. He or she has to look for equivalencies: not symmetrical correspondences, but rather fruitful analogies, so that the existence of my text is justified before the foreign reader. For the text will always remain mine; the translator is extremely generous, he or she lends talent and genius, but I am the one who will always sign the book. Thus, it is imperative for the reader to forget that the text is a translation.

I do not think that my texts are difficult, but they contain complexities. The work of art reproduces several ideas, and they are not always visible. The more you read great literature, the more you discover. The translator has to commit himself or herself to traveling and crossing all the layers of any single sentence of a text. One has to be able to take these layers, the archeology of the original text, to the other language. Every author—man or woman—works, explores his or her own language. Some authors more than others. I have always worked on my texts because I have always been sure that the text, the future text, is superior to my forces, and that my chance to reach the future text—the text which the work deserves—relies on my labor. I write many drafts, precisely because I believe in this progression of a text. At the same time, I know that I must not hurt the text and suffocate its emotion. I have to be careful, because a text may reach an extraordinary coldness and become pure artifact. The emotion is like a light dwelling above the text. The emotion is like the grease, not the saturated fat, but the fat that warms up and appeases the meat. This substance has to be maintained, and I need to imagine that the translator has access to it.

In my texts I recreate the views, experiences, and especially the memories, the archaic memories of women. For even when women did not write, they were witnesses to moments of life and death. I am convinced that the great male authors could only write their books because they had female sentimental advisors. These women transmitted to them the life experiences that they lacked. But the fact that I write about these memories does not mean that a man cannot be a translator of my books. Any translator can have a highly literary sensibility, and can be as multiple as I am. For I do not write as a woman, but rather as a woman and a man, as a multiple being. So I expect the translator to put on all these masks as he or she translates. Thus, my books have been translated by both men and women. Take *A República dos Sonhos* (The Republic of Dreams), for example: the Spanish translation was done by a man; the English translation by a woman; the French translation by a woman and a man, mother and son. Perhaps my short stories were mostly translated by women. I do not choose my translators—though I have always wanted to be translated, for example, by Gregory Rabassa and Helen Lane, who have both translated some of my texts. In any case, the translators give much more to a book than they receive credit for from their publishers, and I respect them greatly. In some cases you do feel a sort of estrangement, but then you realize that it is another language, and almost a new book with its own rules and impositions, its own aesthetic discipline. At first this bothered me, but then I came to understand it— I want to know that I am reading great English, French, or Italian, and that the writing is significant in each language into which it was translated. I also enjoy knowing that the text is no longer mine. I have read one of my texts in Galician for example, and it is very beautiful because it is as if that text had appeared before my own, because its language preceded my own language. It is a sort of hierarchical inversion that is very beautiful and touching. On the other hand, some languages have different demands, some are more rustic, more guttural, they have a more immediate breath, whereas others are more lyrical, they may soften your text, or make it sharper. Languages are living nature, they have flesh and blood, and they behave according to their own "biology."

I write my books regardless of the language of the reader, and this has not changed after my books began to be translated into other languages. I have always been very resistant, morally resistant to thinking about the readership and the publishing market. Thus, I do not think of any particular reader—or, if I were to think of the readers, I would idealize them. They would be good-looking, clean, well educated, and I would want them to like me. But if I did that, I would exclude all those who cannot even read yet. Of course I am joking, but there's some truth to it. I write for the isolated inhabitant of the Amazon basin, for instance, with the hope that some day he may read me; he or his son, and all the humblest people of my country. And I wouldn't mind if my texts were translated into other media too, I'm not biased about this. Like other languages, each medium has its own rules. Of course, I know that my text may eventually be translated, but when I write, I can't think about that. Just thinking about the text occupies me entirely.

NOTE

This essay is based on an interview with, and translated by, César Braga-Pinto at Rutgers University, New Brunswick, N.J., May 21, 1998.

Resisting Hybridity

Ariel Dorfman

History has taught me the need to be a hybrid, which I never wanted to be. I was born in Argentina and Spanish caught me, as I fell out of nothingness, into society, and therefore it was my first love. I used to be a territory in dispute, but now I understand myself as a bigamist of language. Now I share either two women, or two male languages share me as a woman, or through me they nourish each other, or I make love with one while the other watches and makes suggestions. At the moment the languages are like a reservoir, where you dip your hand in the one and you dip your hand in the other and they have mutually agreed on a truce. But most of my life has been a war between these languages.

I followed my father to the United States when I was two and a half. I caught pneumonia and I was isolated for three weeks in a pneumonia ward. When I came out, I refused to speak another word of Spanish for ten years. I wanted to belong, I wanted to blend in. I couldn't blend in, with parents who spoke Spanish (they also spoke Russian and Yiddish) and with a name like Vladimir, except in terms of language, to make believe I was a native English speaker. In 1954 I went to Chile, to encounter the language that I despised, that I really considered a barbarian tongue, the tongue of Chiquita banana. In Chile by a very slow process I became seduced by the Spanish language. It was a falling in love with Spanish as a language, with Chile as a country and as a community, with the revolutionary part of Chile in particular. Revolutions have a tendency to encourage this idea of starting anew, of providing a home for those who have no home. In Chile I gradually became bilingual, and much less of a gringo. When I went back to the United States, to Berkeley from 1968 to '69, I did so to test my Spanish/English identity and there made the ideological decision to never write another word of English again, a language I dubbed as imperial.

What I was rejecting constantly was the dual. I did not want to be a mongrel, I wanted to be pure. I invented myself and reinvented myself over and over again as a unique integral person, a person who had no cracks and no duality. I guess I was so divided and complex in my life inside, that I needed a unifying core of my personality that I could identify with. I had an identity that was under siege. I think that artists are one

55

step away from schizophrenics, and that this one step allows them to communicate in an articulate way, in a framework that people can understand.

Then came the Allende revolution, which I saw as a way out of exile. In the context of the revolution I could explore contradictions that I would not have been able to explore otherwise. A Spanish language exploration that gave me an anchor. But when the coup came, the positions of the languages changed in relation to their power. I went out into a world where English was going to be my major weapon against Pinochet, so how could I deny myself the use of English in that struggle? I began speaking and writing in English primarily as a pragmatic matter, using it in order to get rid of the need to speak it, so I could go back to Spanish. So English astutely found a way of safely smuggling itself back into my life. It has now become, however, the language that I survive in. I have reembraced that language I learned as a child as a bridge to my Spanish language experience. This memoir *Heading South* has allowed me to become a Latin American who writes in English, but still a Latin American.

In 1982, I was about to publish a book of essays called *The Empire's Old Clothes,* translated by somebody else. It was fine, but didn't express my newest thoughts, my own English-language experience. I felt I had to rewrite them, so, based on the translation, reworked them. As English reemerged I began to realize that there are things that I could say in English that I would never say in Spanish. There is a precision that English demands of me, where I learn to be lyrical in a spare way. Of course, first I needed somebody to translate and therefore betray the Spanish into English so that I could then rework it as if it were a text in English.

As soon as I finished *Death and the Maiden* in Chile in 1990 in Spanish, I translated it immediately into English, and worked with it in English from that moment on. I probably never would have gone through that experience if it hadn't been that what I wrote in Spanish was rejected by my own audience in Chile. In a way, they cast me into the world abroad that wanted the play. I took a fundamental step with *Death and the Maiden,* because English became the language of the play, even if I had written it first in Spanish.

I touched a raw nerve in the country. I wanted the play to become part of the healing process but in fact it showed me that the healing process did not include me. Because it wasn't accepted and embraced in Chile, it turned into the instrument of my expatriation. Historically, if I have to watch my country being globalized and integrated into the world market, I'd rather be where the real thing is happening, at the center of globalization rather than at the margins of globalization. *Death and the Maiden* became the final catalyst for my understanding that I would not ever be anything but dual in my life. The fracture that is shown in the play is my fracture; Paulina is going to be always, in some sense, an exile.

Speaking about fractures and multiplicity, I have worked in a great variety of genres, and in this way I am also a nomad. *My House Is on Fire,* the film I made with my son, was originally a poem, which I first turned into a story and finally into a film. The play *Widows* was first a poem and then a novel before I adapted it. *Reader* was a story first, then I made it into a play. I discovered that I can't adapt without someone else next to me, it's like translation. I need an intermediary. Braque said a work of art is not complete until it had destroyed the original concept. If the adaptation is going to be a work of art, it has to be really different. It's not only a problem of translating between languages (which is already a problem), it's translating and adapting the genre.

In translation, the work has to sound right in its new language, and yet it has to maintain enough strangeness in it, it has to have enough of a distancing process in it so that people will not feel entirely comfortable with what they are hearing or reading. I think this is the essence of my bridging, and I think it's the reason why I'm never going to be very popular. Maybe there is already that strangeness, a weirdness, in the way I write, because there's something irreducible, residual about my original experience, and any translator, including myself translating myself, has got to entice readers into that world so that they will be surprised by the difference. Using English for me allows the remainder to shine through, to resonate. Using English, as I did in *Heading South* or in op-eds for *The New York Times* or *The Los Angeles Times,* permits the Spanish to filter into the language. When you are bilingual in some ways you are constantly translating, or you are constantly taking into account the other language. I speak both English and Spanish like a native, though that is not entirely true. I speak each of them with a slight tilt or nod in the direction of the other. Each language is inhabited by the other. Very often they paralyze each other. You cannot talk about this use of languages without also talking about two simultaneous conditions: one is the evolution of one's own identity as a dual person, very much related to the political and geographic place you occupy, and the other is the intervention of history. You don't just switch languages, you don't just switch countries. Behind it is the rush of history and, unfortunately, a great deal of pain.

NOTE

These notes are based on an interview with Ariel Dorfman by Marcy Schwartz on April 1, 1998, in New York City.

A Translator in Search of an Author

Cristina Peri Rossi

I am not in the habit of choosing my translators; they choose me (they are generally women, women in love, seduced by a text). Professional translators don't interest me much. I believe that writing is a process of seduction, and translation a process of love. Even myself, when I have translated a book (*Family Ties* by Clarice Lispector or *The Traitor* by André Gorz), I've been in love with the text, seduced by it. (Other times, I've had to translate a book for purely economic motives, but that's another story.)

This translator in love with a text believes that the author's voice is his or her own voice, that the written words are those he or she would have liked to have written; in other words, he or she *identifies* with the author, and sometimes with the characters. Translation, this appropriation of another's text, inevitably leads to a symbiosis in which fidelity, betrayal, property, and appropriation are emotional and passionate mechanisms.

The translator pursues, as in love, an unobtainable object: one cannot *possess* another's text, just as one cannot rewrite it in another language without changing it. In passing into another language, the translated text always converts itself into something else, a transition that bothers the translator as much as the author. Both will feel, always, partially dissatisfied, partially frustrated. As in love, absolute fidelity is impossible, as is total identification (no one loves us as we wish to be loved, and we never manage to feel the same as the other person).

There are translators who obsessively pursue textual fidelity; they try to ignore that the *other* language is already in itself an infidelity with respect to the original. Others, however, stimulated by emotional symbiosis, attempt to rewrite the text in the other language, as if the author's voice were literally his or her own, as if the consubstantiation with the author transformed the two languages into one.

I have almost always had a very close, intimate relationship with my translators, a relationship that I would not hesitate to call erotic or amorous, since translation is a maneuver of language and language seeks to find form in something unnamable, desire.

No one knows the text to be translated better than the translator, since his or her task consists of plunging into the author's imaginary, his or her fantasies and desires. Because of this the relationship becomes a variety of psychoanalysis. It is, to a certain degree, vampiric, phagocytic, like love, and shameless, like pornography.

I remain fascinated by the relationships established between authors and translators, as difficult to write about, in fact, as true psychoanalytic sessions.

I don't choose my translators, I let them choose me.

After publishing the first edition of my novel *Solitario de amor*,[1] I received a curious letter. It came from France and was signed by a young man named Denis Tagu, forestry engineer assigned to a reforestation project in the Catalan countryside. The letter informed me that he knew a little bit of Spanish and that he liked to read in Spanish. A bookseller friend had recommended my book to him, and after reading it, he had wanted to read others. The one he had just read was *Solitario de amor* and he told me that he found reading it seductive and fascinating. He returned to France, to the town where the woman he loved was living, with a copy of the book for her. But there was a small problem: she didn't understand a word of Spanish. So, during the long and passionate nights ahead, while he made love to her he translated out loud the pages of my book. In this way, my written text intermingled with the oral text, still unwritten, of their love. He ended up translating the whole novel.

I read his letter fascinated by the interlocking series of mirrors: in my novel a man in love tries to seduce the woman he loves every night, as in real life a young Frenchman, the forestry engineer, reads fragments of the book to the woman he loves in order to seduce her. My spontaneous correspondent probably did not recognize the fragment of the *Divine Comedy* by Dante where Francesca, condemned to Hell for being lustful, relates how she was seduced by Paolo while both were reading about the amorous exploits of Lancelot the knight and the princess Guinevere. "That time, we read no further," says Francesca, alluding to the sinful seduction.

Of course I responded to the spontaneous translator's letter. I imagined that one night he would read my letter to his lover as before he had read my book to her, and that by now and forever after there were three of us in that bed: the two of them and the novel, *Solitario de amor*.

Denis Tagu sent me his spontaneous translation of my novel. From the moment I began to read it I realized that he had translated it into French exactly as I would have. In this way, the specular relationship multiplied even more: I had written the love script that he had wanted to pronounce to his lover, but he had accomplished the translation into French that I would have loved to have done. Some time later, the French publisher Phébus published Denis Tagu's translation, and I still consider it a beautiful and satisfactory version.

I met Diana Decker, the English translator of my poetry, casually, while I was delivering a lecture at a North American university. At that time, she was not a translator but a professor of Spanish in Washington. She was completely taken with my book of poems *Babel bárbara*[2] (Barbarous Babel), and I recognized in her ardor the libidinous component that converts a difficult translation into an act of love.

My lack of English was not an obstacle to our passionate encounters, when we would heatedly discuss whether the best way to translate "advenediza" into English was "outsider." When Diana Decker translates a poem of mine, and she has done many, I demand that she read it to me out loud in English. Her pronunciation in English is so impeccable that, even in a language in which I am basically deaf, I cannot help but admire it. And when a sound in her translation grates on me or a word seems too harsh or too weak, I interrupt her and I ask her to look for alternatives. Although it is impossible to imitate the sonority of Latin languages in English, between the two of us we manage to achieve an equivalent sonorous effect in the translation.

Often Diana Decker tapes our conversations (or versions, or disquisitions), and in this series of tapes one can hear us talk . . . about words, the topic of conversation that interests me more than any in the world.

I love to talk about words. And whom better to do it with than a translator who has savored, polished, weighed, explored, drunk, constricted, licked, and kneaded them like the lover's breast?

Translated by Daniel Balderston and Marcy E. Schwartz

NOTES

1. Barcelona: Grijalbo, 1988.
2. Barcelona: Lumen, 1991.

Trauma and Precision in Translation

Tomás Eloy Martínez

Translation is much more than an extremely attentive reading of a text. It also means writing it all over again, recreating it, making it reflect another culture. How does one produce in one's own culture something that is foreign, strange, and yet nevertheless ought to pertain to it in some way if it's going to be completely understood? Translation is always treasonous, but it is also a tradition of serving: the translator answers to two masters. Could this agent of exchange be the author, if the author speaks both languages? Not always. There are some successful examples, such as that of Carlos Fuentes and his U.S. collaborator in *The Old Gringo,* perhaps because Fuentes was trying to translate his Mexican culture of origin into the English culture of his upbringing. Other attempts have failed, such as that of Jorge Luis Borges and Norman Thomas di Giovanni, because Borges claimed his stories "seemed to have been written in English," and Di Giovanni followed his lead. In the end, the sound and the sense of certain words of Latin origin were demolished, like *unánime,* which in Spanish means both "one" as well as "everyone," and for which there is no satisfactory equivalent in English.

Some authors move without conflict from one language to another, from one culture to another. Vladimir Nabokov's Russian short stories are as elegant and intelligent as his American novels. At the same time, no one would deny that Conrad is an English author (even to the extent of his ideology). But *Finnegans Wake* in any other language than English, Dante outside of Italian, or *Martín Fierro* without its gauchesque musicality are unimaginable and, sometimes, even caricaturized.

There are authors whose texts resist being translated, such as Juan Rulfo or César Vallejo; others, of similar complexity, move into the other language almost without a trace of difference, such as Helen Lane's Roa Bastos or Aurora Bernárdez's Italo Calvino. It is nearly impossible for a text to emerge unharmed when it moves from one language into another.

The best translator can understand the most subtle respirations of the culture being translated and at the same time manage to reproduce in his or her own culture the tone of voice of the original. This ideal translator perhaps does not exist, because language doesn't only traverse cultures but also crosses from one time period into another. When Borges mentions El Bajo in his stories from the 1930s, the reader imagines a neighborhood with a particularly charged past: the arched walkways, the brothels, early movie projectors, daggers, the tango, Buenos Aires's amusement park at the time. In 1960, however, El Bajo became the refuge of the avant-garde artistic and theater crowd, and of progressive journalists. In 1990 it has become the extension of what in Buenos Aires we call "la City": the neighborhood of banks and stockbrokers. The arches are still there, along with some of the buildings from seventy years ago, but the name associated with the neighborhood means something different in each context.

How does one begin to explain all of this to an overwhelmed translator? As authors, we feel we are being translated carefully when the translator bombards us with questions, hundreds of questions for each book. Unfortunately, the only answer is to be literal, that is to say, one can only be guided by the text at hand. And thus is lost, whether in English, in French, or in German, the tone of an Argentine middle-class dialogue from 1970. Lost as well are Thomas Pynchon's continuous double entendres when his novels are translated into Spanish.

When I was growing up, I read Dostoevsky, Tolstoy, and Pushkin in Spanish translations that came from other translations. Few stories have left such an indelible impression on me as *Ivan Illich,* although there were elements of the plot that seemed confusing. Did he or didn't he go to the office when he was gravely ill? Much later, I read a direct translation from Russian, and another version in French, and this time the story was transparently clear. To this day I don't know if my difficulties in comprehension were rooted in my immaturity or in the flaws of a "double" translation.

A very interesting anecdote about translation concerns English and American detective novels in Argentina. The tendency was to translate into a neutral Spanish, in order to reach the greatest number of potential readers. (I especially admire the translations that Enrique Pezzoni did of Melville and of Nabokov, those that Cortázar did of Poe and of Marguerite Yourcenar, and those that Borges, or his mother, did of Faulkner and Virginia Woolf, in which one can recognize some of the rhythms of the original language.) The detective novels of El Séptimo Círculo, the series edited by Borges and Bioy Casares, were extremely conscientious in this sense, whether they were by authors such as Nicholas Blake or by Ellery Queen. In the late 1960s, the publisher Tiempo Contemporáneo tried to turn certain hard-boiled American crime novels, such as James Cain, Hammett, Chandler, into Buenos Aires slang, *lunfardo.* They came out unreadable, perhaps because their style went against the current.

I have worked very closely with the English, German, Portuguese, and, curiously, Bulgarian translators of my books. Sometimes I felt burdened with questions that were directed at a writer who was no longer me, but rather someone who had written a novel three, five, or ten years before with my name on it. Frequently, I had forgotten some of the references in certain passages—for example, references to the occult, or to the techniques of embalming—and I had to research them all over again to find the answers. The Italian translator of *Santa Evita,* for example, asked me why I mention "Corrientes Street" when according to a map he looked at, Corrientes is an avenue. It became an avenue in 1936, but from 1905 until 1936 it was a street. These are the details, trivial as they may seem, that make or break a book. In the final estimation, all writers ought to feel grateful for the disturbance of translators' inquiries, those flies that keep buzzing around our heads.

Translation is, after all, the final edition of a text, the test of its strength. It can also be its definitive defeat. I read fluently in French when I got to Caracas in 1976, but I had never read *Mort à credit,* the novel by Louis-Ferdinand Céline. Like every impoverished exile, I didn't have many books and happily accepted the opportunity to read the version that the local publisher Monte Avila had put out. I plunged into the novel, but ran screaming after reading the first two pages. It was awful! Two years later, I read it in the original and discovered, incredulous, that it was not at all the same book. The one I had read in Spanish was an invention, from beginning to end, written by an irresponsible man desperate for money who didn't know a single word of French.

NOTE

This essay is based on a conversation with, and translated by, Marcy Schwartz in New Brunswick, N.J. on February 25, 1999.

Writing and Translation

Ricardo Piglia

I think that the experience of the translator, in relation to the author of a book, is a strange relationship. I am of course very happy with the English translations, and I say it with utmost sincerity, that Sergio Waisman and Daniel Balderston have made of some of my texts, but I do not think the question has only to do with the topic of what there is in the style, or in the references, or in the errors of the text, and in what sort of changes can be made in the translation of a text, but that the interesting thing is the sort of work that is translation—because it would seem that it is a strange exercise in relation to reading, on the one hand, and property, on the other. I have always been interested in the relationship between translation and property, because the translator writes a new text that belongs to him or her, and at the same time does not. The translator is placed in a strange position, in the sense that what he or she does is move to a new language a kind of experience that does and does not belong there. The translator is a strange figure, moving between plagiarism and quotation; he or she makes a strange figure as a writer. A writer quotes a text, says someone said such and such a thing; or directly plagiarizes a text, as we all do on occasion—why? because we forget, or we like it too much—but the translator's exercise is a bridge between those two places. Translation is a strange exercise in appropriation. As Tulio Halperín Donghi has said, in the great founding texts of Argentine literature there are often translations incorporated in a direct way, as if Sarmiento or Echeverría, the founders of our national literature, thought of translation as something like the natural appropriation of one text by another.

I have the same relation with literary property that I have with social property: I am against it. I think that there is a game with property in the sense that what is put into question is the ordinary literary sense of intellectual property, by showing that literature's relations to property are very complex, just as they are very complex in society. Language is a common possession, in language there is no such thing as private property. We writers try to put marks or brands to see if we can stop its flow. Borges is an example of someone who tries to mark language as if he were taking possession of it; the words *mirror* and *labyrinth* seem ultimately to belong to writers such as Borges, but that is an illusion. In language there is no private property: language is public circulation—and flow. Literature interrupts that flow and perhaps that is what makes it literature.

For many centuries Latin functioned as the language of literature; that is to say, it was a language that was written but that nobody spoke. Today, the writer is in a similar situation. One has something like a repertory of texts, of reading and writing, that place a language in a written state. Besides, one owns the language that one speaks. Sartre said that we speak our mother tongue and write in a foreign language. That seems to me like something worth thinking about. One could speak about a different tradition, that of Nabokov or Beckett or Conrad, or of some Latin American writers such as Wilcock, who leave behind their mother tongue and write in a foreign language in a real sense; or of Borges, who works in a special, tense way with Spanish. In this case, we would have to discover the relationships among the languages that we read, write, and speak. It seems to me that this is relevant to a number of debates today.

It has often been said that the only exile that a writer experiences is the exile from the mother tongue, as it is in relation to that language that the problem of the localization of fiction should be considered. I would not say that it is a question of nationality, or even of one's home, the home the writer feels nostalgia for, and remembers, which would be that language. What does the writer's nationality mean, what sort of fidelity does he or she have to the language? The strangest case I know is Nietzsche's. Nietzsche said that a writer is forbidden from writing in any language other than the mother tongue. He said that anyone who wrote in any other language was an idiot, and that all he or she achieved by so doing was ruining his or her style. He himself was the greatest stylist that had ever existed in the German language because he was tied only to that language, because he had never tried to learn any others. But this always has much to do with Nietzsche's insistence on the idea that writing is the same as speaking. There is a very beautiful text of Nietzsche's on style, in a letter to Lou Andreas Salomé, where he offers recommendations on style and says something like this: style is in fact when one finds a way of writing that is the same as the way one speaks, not in terms of vocabulary but in terms of that faithfulness to a language of one's own that should not be contaminated. Another, and different, way of situating the discussion about translation is that writers work between languages, that they are situated among various languages, that they are unfaithful and cross from one to another. The most extraordinary case of this, the opposite of that of Nietzsche, would be Joyce. But even Joyce, although he changed everything, although he crossed and made everything flow into his language, even in his case the syntactic foundation of his work, even in *Finnegans Wake,* is the English language.

On the other hand, we writers have always debated whether we translate a preexisting reality, whether we work with a universe that we reflect. I have taken different positions about this over the course of time, but what I think now is that what we call reality, what we actually know reality to be—experience, history, politics, economic relations, structures of feeling, everything that one brings into a book—gives me the sense that what a writer truly does is to connect with that universe of the real that is meditated through language, in the sense that there really are social relations, existing forms of circulation, that function as the context that one takes as the point of departure. Translating from reality is just the writer's means of being in tune with a certain way the language works—social aspects of the language. For example, in politics: I don't know whether a writer translates or reflects political reality. Perhaps he or she reflects certain stories that circulate with regard to political situations, that circulate as social narratives, and then find their way into books. In that sense one could say that a writer is, to a certain extent, a translator of social language.

The other idea that I think is interesting is that translation is a good path, perhaps the best one, to follow if one is interested in knowing the history of literary style. Perhaps the history of successive translations of a text would mark better than anything else the mode in which literary style is fixed at a given point in time. For this reason one has to retranslate classic texts constantly, because it would seem that the translator is the one who is most closely connected with the models of style at any given moment. Comparing translations tells us about the history of a literary language more than literature itself. Or at least it is harder to see in the latter: the changes of style are less visible at times than when one reads different translations. For example, I have had the experience of reading various translations of Dante, from the first Spanish ones, including that of Bartolomé Mitre. One finds the translator in the translation, but one always finds the register of style that at that moment functions as a field from which one translates. That is, the translator does not translate freely, he or she translates with an implicit stylistic model. A writer does that also, but in the case of translations that difference may be more evident.

Now, with regard to the question of translatability, one could take one of two positions. I think, on the one hand, that there are obviously nuclei of language that are untranslatable. Poetry is in a sense untranslatable: in some sense poetry can only be read in the reader's mother tongue. We can read translated poetry, but the experience cannot be compared with that of reading poetry written in our mother tongue. It is possible that in poetry the relation between what remains beyond language and language itself is almost impossible to differentiate. On the other hand, the novel has the peculiar property of surviving the potential difficulties that stand in the way of the translator and of the reader.

I always use as an example something that Virginia Woolf says. She says that her friends—she is referring to friends who were setting the tone for English literature—felt that the best novel ever written was *War and Peace,* and that they all read it in English, because they did not read Russian; yet they agreed that it was the best novel that had ever been written, the proof of its greatness being that great novels can survive translation. Borges, surprisingly, said that great books are those that survive translation, they have something that goes beyond language.

NOTE

Based on a presentation at the University of California, Berkeley, by Ricardo Piglia and his English translators, Daniel Balderston and Sergio Waisman, in the spring of 1998. Transcription by Sergio Waisman, translation by Daniel Balderston.

II

Translating Latin America

A Conversation on Translation
with Margaret Sayers Peden

Margaret Sayers Peden

To have a conversation about something one loves talking about is a rare privilege. I am obviously better at speaking about my own experiences than I am about profundities of translation in general. So that's what I choose to do: talk about some problems I've encountered and some things that I think translation may be.

But I want to begin with a game—a game I call Translation Trivia. I sometimes wonder whether I should have packaged it. Perhaps there still is a market for it. I am going to pose twelve Trivia questions and give you the answers at the end of my remarks:

1. What is the gestation period of a whale?
2. According to late-Renaissance folklore, how could one keep sugar in a liquid state?
3. What North American movie idol once played Arsenio Lupin, the sophisticated French detective so popular in Latin American literature?
4. In a railroad yard, when is a sleeper not a sleeping car?
5. What was the hierarchy of Roman triumphal crowns?
6. Was the construction of a fifteenth-century ship such that an explorer could save himself from drowning during a shipwreck by clinging to the ship's wheel?
7. What is the specific genesis—no pun intended since the source is Exodus—of Michelangelo's statue of Moses with prominent horns? A most unfortunate occurrence in Latin culture!
8. What aromatic fruit was used during Medieval times to ward off the plague?
9. In a seventeenth-century setting is it a mistake to translate "hypnotized" as "mesmerized" or "outline" as "silhouette"?
10. Why would Antoine André Ravrio, clockmaker to French kings, have bequeathed to the workers who gilded his clocks a sizeable sum in the way of early workmen's compensation?

71

11. Who was the real-life prototype for Daniel Defoe's Robinson Crusoe?

12. What is the correct translation for the *Meleagris gallopavo*, the large game bird, a boon to pilgrims and also considered divine by certain Mexican tribes?

I hope someone will implore me to give the answers when I finish. Now this Trivia game is not, in my opinion, unrelated to our conversation today because I believe that a translator is one of culture's last generalists.

Who is a translator? What makes a translator? Well, you know the old saw about a camel being a horse put together by a committee. I think a translator is a person put together by a committee. To varying degrees a translator is composed of creative writer, scholar, archivist, innovator, and, often, a large portion of masochist. I'll suggest we consider some of these components, because I have fought battles defending some of them. I think no one would question that a translator is to a degree a creative writer. I mean I have reached the point where, if you will forgive such immodesty, I simply consider myself a writer, and am slightly insulted if that is questioned. That doesn't mean that I write original poetry and fiction, but I believe I'm a writer, and I think translators should be considered writers. Inarguably, I think translators are scholars, and this is a battle I have fought for years. Before the wonderful work done by the American Translators Association and the American Literary Translators Association, translation was considered to be what you did when you could do nothing else. You know, like teachers. If you can't do anything, you teach, and if you can't do anything else, you translate. I do both. You can see that I'm a little prickly about this attitude. But I would like to impress upon other people (not you who are already converted) how much time one spends in research if one does one's translation correctly. During the time I was translating—let me take as an example a monster work like *Terra nostra*—I spent an enormous number of hours in the library researching subjects I simply didn't know. Because I'm a very fussy person, I'm incapable of translating something I don't know anything about. So I would go to the library to read about fifteenth-century heretical sects which, believe me, I had very little information about prior to the *Terra nostra* translation. There is, similarly, a scene in the New World section that takes place before Columbus discovers the New World, in which the old man named Pedro is washed ashore upon a beach of pearls. Fuentes spends about three paragraphs on these pearls. I spent about three days in the library reading about luster, types, names, sizes, classifications. I could not be comfortable translating that section until I had read what I thought was necessary about pearls. So I do believe that research is a very specific ingredient in translations. That accounts for the creative writer and the scholar; the component of archivist derives from the fact that one is maintaining a culture, and that of the innovator from one's efforts toward inventing in a second language. And we all *understand* that portion which is masochist.

A translator is a person fascinated by puzzles. If you don't enjoy the puzzle of translating, find something else to do. A translator is a person who is challenged by problem solving. At the University of Texas-Dallas, *every* graduate student is required to take a course in translation, not because the school intends to turn out a population of translators but because the faculty at Dallas believes this course will do something to repair the instilled practice of gathering grinding masses of facts and never learning to apply them to problems. Translation is, in fact, simply a fast sequence of solving problems. A translator is also a person who will tolerate back-breaking work without public recognition. It takes a certain personality to do that. Along with the necessity to do research, I would name as an absolute necessity, willingness to work like an idiot day and night constantly, both in your home and when you're traveling. Asking questions when you go to a cocktail party. At my own university people now turn and run the opposite way when they see me coming, because I always have something I need to learn from somebody. How do you say so and so? what is that? and so on.

My next point is related. A translator is a person with the extroversion that allows pursuing perfect strangers for enlightenment on the customs of pre-Columbian Indian tribes or the hierarchies of Russian Czarist society. I am not shy about doing this. If I come to a passage in Neruda that has to do with birds, I have to know first of all what that bird looks like. I call over to the Biology department, and I say "Let me speak to your bird man." And when they put the bird man on the phone I say, "Can I call it this or am I on the wrong continent?" You can't have a bird living someplace it doesn't live. So you have to have that extroversion. And you have to have the introversion that sustains long hours before the typewriter or word processor, working in absolute solitude with only a set of dictionaries surrounding you. Might we agree, then, that the translator is a person who is put together by a committee? One with a different set of work requirements from those of most people I know.

Now there have been untold numbers of elegant definitions of translation. I should like to read one of my favorites given in 1611 by the authors of the King James version of the Bible and quoted by Donald Walsh:

Translation is it that openeth a window, to let in light; that breaketh the shell, that we may eat the kernel; that putteth aside the curtain, that we may look into the most holy place: that removeth the cover of the well, that we may come by the water.

One scarcely has the hubris? the presumption? to claim that his or her work allows the reader to look into the most holy place, but I do believe that any translation lets in light: the amount of light becomes only a matter of degree. I can't imagine even a bad translation that does not let in some light.

What do I believe about translation? What do I think translation is? I have come to believe a number of outrageous things about translation. I can argue to my satisfaction that it is possible and that it is impossible. I believe it is both. I can remember saying that I thought one actually had more freedom in translating poetry than in translating prose—that one was less confined. And now I add to that that I think the least room of all is allowed in the philosophical essay; I'll explain a little more about that. To say translation is impossible is to eat my own words, because when I was younger and much more naive and maybe had more energy, I believed that it was possible to translate *anything*. And in some recess of my mind I still have a tiny kernel of faith that on some ideal plane the ideal translation is possible. However, with more years and more translations and more problems I have become a bit more pessimistic about the *limitations* of translation. Maybe everything is a problem of semantics, because words solve our problems and words create our problems. I wrote in a note on translating concrete poetry that perhaps we need a new term for translation. You've read the many arguments comparing our terms and those in Romance languages—translate/traduce. I suggested we might use the term *transemantics*, which simply put is bringing meaning across. Practitioners would be called transemanticians.

Maybe we need a new triadic division. It is interesting how often divisions fall into triads. In politics, we have middle, center, and left; in society we have middle, lower, and upper classes. In translation, too, we have the middle road, the transliteration on one side, and on the other the version or the imitation. That division, though, I believe is based on the translator's philosophy—what he or she intends to do. The translator makes the decision: am I going to be ultraclose to the text? am I going to be ultradistant from the text? or am I going to try to settle for a happy medium? I think I have found that there is a different level of triadic division that has to do with the impositions that culture and language impose on us. Not our choice, but imposed upon us. Some of you know this as my Apple Philosophy.[1] Here I argue that a true translation—if a true translation is a possibility after Eden and Babel—is made available to us through closely related developments of linguistic and social patterns. In other words, we can most likely effect a close translation when we are working in a culture and language that have some shared background with our own. From translation I would move to a second division, that of substitution, a process that is involved in much of translation. Storm windows in English would be heavy shutters in

Spanish culture. "Shutter" nearly echoes the effect of the original language (storm windows), but it is a substitution, not a true translation. Then we move to a third division which I like to call explanation, that is using language to *describe* an object or phenomenon in the original that has no counterpart in the target language. A great deal what we call translation is indeed explanation, and this accounts for something that I think is an elementary principle of translation, that is, that your translation gets longer because you have to explain what you are "translating." Basically, then, I believe communication is possible. I mean that we can communicate between and among languages, but a true and perfect transmittal of every element of the original is impossible. Certainly we know that sound, meaning, metaphor can't come across perfectly.

Now I have a list of things that have to do with translation. I'm going to read them through and then expand on them a little. My first division is by genre, that is, translating poetry, translating prose, translating drama, translating essay. I began translating theater; then I switched to prose and with no little nervousness and a lot of desire, I switched to translating poetry and finally to non-fiction. The first non-fiction work I translated was a sequel to Neruda's *Memoirs*. It is called *Para nacer he nacido* in Spanish, which I suggested be published as *Passions and Impressions*. When I met Matilde Urrutia, she said, "Pablo never said *that*." "Well," I countered, "I am convinced Don Pablo would have approved it. Doesn't it sound Nerudian? *Pasiones e impresiones?*" "Oh, that sounds a little like Pablo," she admitted. My reason for resisting the literal "Born to be Born" is that it conveys all those thirties' resonances: "Born to dance, born to sing, born to. . . ." Then, there is also "Born Again," perfectly accurate as a translation but not for Neruda's little vignettes, so *Passions and Impressions* it was. Next came *Ariel,* a very tiny little book which greatly misled me. It was published in 1900 and is considered to be a philosophical aesthetic of enormous influence in the Latin American world, and totally out of print in English. The last translation was 1927. My difficulty in this translation was with the very, very self-conscious style. Very long sentences which I thought would modernize, making it more available to the contemporary reader. The book refused to do that, because Rodó is talking about beauty as a theme and is fitting his style to his subject. To separate the form from content simply does not work. Then my most recent non-fiction translation was *Sor Juana Inés de la Cruz o las trampas de la fe.* This book is enormous. And translating it I'm having the greatest difficulty with editors that I've ever encountered. Editors will accept my reading of a prose work. They will accept my reading of poems—and I do believe a translation is the closest reading you can find. But there's not an editor alive who'll accept my reading of expository essays. Now, I don't think my essay style is that bad. For a while I *did*. I was beginning to feel really battered. I think that if my most recent translation had been my first, I would never have translated another book.

How do I begin a translation? To me the overall most important key to the translation is to find its voice. Who is telling? Who is narrating? Who is singing? In the case of *Terra nostra,* you know the narrative voice in that book is like a set of Russian dolls. You open one, and there's another inside. With this novel we began translating in the middle, because Fuentes was still revising the beginning. A couple of times I said to him, "Carlos, I really want to know who the narrator is." And he would rub his hands with glee and say, "I'll send you some more." And he would send more pages, and he never would tell me. Of course, very profound scholarly articles have been written on that question. I can tell you that Fuentes *never* told me. But in ordinary circumstances, once I can find the voice, other things begin to fall into place.

The next general topic on my list is that of the translator as literary critic. A translator enters a text very deeply, more deeply, perhaps, than the literary critic. For example, Dennis Kratz, the incoming president of the American Literary Translators Association, is a medievalist; he—rather obviously—wrote his dissertation on a medieval subject. It was published and received favorable critical attention. Then he decided to translate the work he had analyzed in his dissertation. He found that he had disproved much of what he had written. He had to revise the ideas expounded in his doctoral thesis.

It had been observed that you must be a dictionary addict if you are a translator. At the same time, I caution you not to be a dictionary *slave,* because that is as much a trap as not using dictionaries. I love dictionaries, I collect dictionaries. I collect human dictionaries—yes, I think dictionaries on the hoof are very often very much better than those on the shelf. But again, you must not always trust your native informants because they can occasionally be absolutely convinced of something that is totally wrong, just as I am sometimes very often totally wrong in English because of the way I read a work. Take all the things you can into consideration, but become aggressive about pursuing informants and about pursuing and collecting dictionaries.

To the degree it is possible, immerse yourself totally in the author you're translating. That's a very big dose of discipline to give yourself. But each author has his own secret and specific use of language that will be revealed to you only as you know him or her better. A quick illustration comes from translating Neruda's three collections of *Elemental Odes*—which will be published by California. When first I came across the word *corola,* I thought I would not translate it with the cognate "corolla" when it was used, for example, for sun or sunfish. But as I came across this word more and more frequently, I thought, "what am I doing to Neruda's language?" "Corolla!" obviously refers to anything round that has lines radiating from it. So I went back and put "corolla" in all the places he had used "corola." You may not agree that that's the correct solution, but at least I had a broader base upon which to make a judgment. I truly recommend that you become an expert in your writer and learn everything that's possible about that writer. That's a very large order, and it's an idealistic suggestion, but it's one that I make.

Often I am asked about "improving" a text. I put that in quotation marks because one of my workshop students in Columbia, Missouri, was saying the other day, "But this is awkward, and I'm going to have to improve it." Do you remember Miller Williams's phrase on this? He calls it the sin of improvement. One does not have the freedom to "improve" a text, a concept that also has a certain inherent arrogance. Beyond that, if a book is bad in the original language, it will probably be bad in the second language and really should not be translated to begin with. Here I think the context makes all the difference in the world. If I were translating for a State Department official and he stated something in a very foolish way, I would not only want to improve that for him, I would be obligated to do so. Obviously one can change a text under different situations.

Under translating prose I have questions of rhetorical level, augmentation, narration versus dialogue, texture, specific problems in translating for the theater—which I shall now move down under poetry because I think it's closer to translating poetry than it is to translating prose. The "rhetorical" level is that business of finding the voice. Who is the person speaking? Is the style elevated? Does it have a certain anti-quated sound? Is it colloquial? I find poetic "speech" very easy to trans-late. Not poetry, but poetic speech. The best example I can give you is in my translation of Sor Juana de la Cruz. How many of you know her? I think she is, to begin with, the most remarkable woman ever to be born in our hemisphere. I think her "Respuesta a Sor Filotea" (1691) is one of our most incredible documents. It is our first statement of a woman's right to study and teach. It's a beautiful work, and when I began to translate it, I went to Vern Williamsen, the Golden Age specialist at my university (because I have been trained as a modernist), and I said, "Vern, if you were translating Lope de Vega, how would you translate it? Would you try to make it a little archaic or would you like to make it contemporary?" He said, "It was contemporary when he wrote it; I'd put it in today's language." I went to our Quijote specialist, Howard Mancing, and asked him the same question and got the same answer. So I started out with a very clear view, especially since so much of what Sor Juana says speaks to us today. I thought, "I'm going to make her sound as though she were speaking today." I tried to do that, consciously, but the rhetorical level would not "stay down." The content dictated the tone. Sor Juana was saying things that would sound strange to a North American woman today; if they were said in our parlance, they would sound out of joint. I have the feeling that rhetorical levels will find themselves if we let them do it.

To move from narration to dialogue, I find narrative much easier to translate. Since so much translation really is substitution or explanation, you have more elbow room to do that in narrative than in dialogue. Dialogue is inescapably direct, which is why theater is so difficult to translate. In theater also we find all-important matters of cadence and pace. You've seen plays that seemed to drag on forever? Well, you can do that to a play by allowing your translation to become too wordy.

Moving to poetry. Under this grouping I list form, structure, choosing between meaning and sound, ambiguity, multiple meaning, interpretation. All problems of translation are concentrated in poetry. I become a little impatient when I go to translation meetings, and people who translate poets act as if they are from Mt. Olympus. And imply to people who translate prose, "Gosh, if I just had the time, I'd do that in a couple of weeks." I do recognize that problems are more concentrated in poetry, and I've come to have a lot of quirks in translating poetry. For example, I've become an absolute fanatic about form. Let me start with some extreme examples.

When I started translating the Neruda *Odes,* I was immediately struck by the form. These are long, skinny poems that seem to snake down the page. This is very interesting, since they were first published by a newspaper, and Neruda must have been very sure about the form of these poems that are so inappropriate (formally) for newspaper publication. I had to fight against letting the lines get longer and the white space smaller. White space is important in *any* poem because it's silence, and in poetry silence is as important as speech, but in these poems space is particularly important. I had an epiphany when I was very close to the end of the translation. I happened to reread Neruda's Nobel acceptance speech, in which he praised Ercilla, the poet, he said, who invented Chile by naming. Then he says, Latin America is a continent of vast spaces waiting to be filled with names, and it is the poet's obligation to fill those spaces. Suddenly I thought, the *Odes* are Neruda's Chile, *his* invention. Basically these odes are about the rocks, the sea, the birds, the flowers, the food of Chile. And these odes that go down the page *look* like Chile. I don't think Neruda sat down and said, "I'm going to write a poem in the shape of Chile." I don't think he meant to do that, but something, I am convinced, was happening in his consciousness as he sat in his house in Isla Negra and looked out at his sea and thought of his country and thought of those words—that poets invent their country. This experience confirmed my conviction that form is all-important. A second illustration. After I translated some of Sor Juana's poems and they were already in print, I went to a conference at Arizona State University on Translators as Creative Writers. We were invited to come read our translations with comments on how we solved some of the problems. During the day

Robert Bly, William Arrowsmith, and W. S. Merwin got up to read their poetry, and each made specific mention (it seemed like a plot) of the tackiness of translating poetry today in meter and rhyme. And there I sat with my little book in meter and rhyme. Then I began to get annoyed, and decided when it was my turn to tell them why. But when my turn came, none of them was there. I still think I was right. Sor Juana de la Cruz lived in an enclosed world. She was a cloistered nun. I've walked through her convent and seen the architectural shape of the place she lived, the black and white spaces where light exists only in contrast to shadow. Beyond that, she lived in a strongly ordered hierarchy of female-subservient-to-the-male, male-subservient-to-the-Church, in such a strictly ordered world that to remove her from those formal bound-aries seemed to me an absolute betrayal of her entire life. And those were my reasons for translating her poems the way I did; following her meter and rhyme.

The extreme, of course, is a concrete poem, those fun games where a poem about a vase has to look like a vase. I'm not suggesting with the Chile analogy that all forms telegraph the content, but that the translation should *look* like the original poem. Not all poems, of course, *can* be translated. Take the example of the Spanish poem which is nothing but a list of towns. Now that seems to be really untranslatable. Would you agree? Translation is a constant tightrope act, and your decisions happen so fast that *you* are like a tightrope walker: you make a decision and go a little farther; make a decision and go a little farther. You must decide in each poem what is the most important thing or groups of things to try to convey because you can't convey them all.

And finally we come to the question of interpretation, because if I said that every translation is reading, I think the opposite is true as well: every reading is a translation. It comes down to the way you hear the work in the language into which you're translating.

I am going to illustrate this with a funny thing about Neruda. (I never met Neruda, and that's always been a sorrow of my life—that I came too late in my career to meet Neruda.) But when I began the *Odes,* I did everything I could to make up for not having met him. I read most of Neruda's poetry and all the criticism I could find. I lis-tened to recordings of Neruda's reading—because he had a very spe-cific, sonorous, almost monotone, way of reading. While I was trans-lating, I had the opportunity to go to Chile to meet Matilde Urrutia. We were invited to Isla Neruda to spend the day and have lunch with her. I suddenly felt I knew the poems in a way I had never known them before and, of course, came back and scribbled over a lot of them. After I had seen his sea, his rocks, his sky, I had much better insight into what these poems were about. I had already done "Ode to Wood." Well, I was so moved by that ode I thought he must be an unusually skilled craftsman. But just as I was working on it, I came across a picture of Neruda sitting outside his home at Isla Negra.[2] He was sitting at a wobbly table that looked as if it had been put together by a kindergarten class. Neruda was an inveterate collecter, collecting everything, and when his collection would get too big, he'd add another room on the house. You get these chambers of rooms you go through filled, filled, filled with collections. I had imagined this great worker with wood, and when I went through the house with Matilde and reached his study, it was marvelous, all lined with rough-hewn wood. Everything smelled of wood. It smelled like a fireplace, it smelled like split logs. (On his desk, by the way, were pictures of the adolescent Baudelaire and Edgar Allan Poe.) On his desk was a cup with the pencils all sharpened. You got a shiver down your back because those pencils were ready to write. Opposite was a beautiful window overlooking the stormy Chilean sea. I thought I'd never get another chance; I had to ask, "Was Pablo a great worker of wood?" I thought Matilde would fall down laughing, "He was a disaster with a hammer, absolutely terrible; you ran when he picked up a hammer because no telling who could be killed." She did say that he oversaw absolutely every nail and panel that went into the house. My interpretation of the *Odes,* however, was greatly affected by that visit.

One more anecdote and then back to Translation Trivia. I have had marvelous working partnerships with most of the people I've translated. I've done more with Fuentes than anyone else: six of his novels and a collection of short stories and a novella yet to come out. Fuentes is the ideal person to work with in that he has impeccable English. Of course, he does not want to spin his wheels rewriting his books in English; he wants to go on to something else. I repeat, he is wonderful to work with, and he is very cooperative. There are a million Fuentes stories, but the funniest thing may have happened when we went to pick him up one night at the train station in St. Louis. (This was the period when he would not fly.) As we begin to drive to Columbia, Missouri, a fat rain began to fall, immediately turning into an absolutely paralyzing snowstorm. Carlos is a nervous traveler; I noticed his knuckles were getting white holding onto the dashboard. So we pulled into a little motel in Wentzville. Not many travelers that night, nor was there food at the motel, and we were starved. We had to pile into the car again and find a restaurant. When we returned, we heard the most bloodcurdling sound I've ever heard in my life. The snow had stopped, the temperature had dropped twenty degrees, everything was a sheet of ice, and the air was still, the way it is when the world is frozen. Again the bloodcurdling screams. We looked across the way and there sat this big eighteen-wheeler with a load of pigs, all screaming. I don't mean squealing, I mean screaming. (Now here's some inside information: you can find their cousins in "The Old Gringo" because Carlos used those pigs in that novel.) But when we went out to breakfast the next morning, Carlos was fidgeting to tell us this story. His wife Sylvia had been expecting him in Columbia, so before he had left for the restaurant, he called to say he wasn't in Columbia but would get in touch after dinner. She returned his call while we were out, and the man at the desk told her, "Sorry, no Mr. Fuentes here." So she hung up and called the number again, and once again he said, "There's no Mr. Fuentes here." She insisted, "But of course he's there, how else would I have this number, why am I calling this number?" He said, "Lady, we're in the middle of a snowstorm here. There ain't but three people checked in and that was a couple and their Mexican chauffeur." That's one of Carlos' favorite stories, so I'm not telling tales out of school.

1. Now. What is the gestation period for a whale? It depends on the species, well, yes, but in general terms, about fourteen months. The calves are liveborn. The mother often has a midwife helping her. They nudge the newborn calf up to the surface for air until it's strong enough to swim on its own.

2. What was the late-Renaissance folk lore for keeping sugar in a liquid state? This is from Sor Juana. She says in the "Respuesta" that all you have to do is put a few drops from a quince or some other bitter fruit. She adds that if you put the yolk of an egg in syrup, it will hold together; if you put the *white* of an egg, it will shatter.

3. All right, what North American movie idol once played Arsenio Lupin? John Barrymore played the part. The supporting cast was Charles Corbin, Ella Raines, and Maurice LeBlanc—who, incidentally was Lupin's creator.

4. In a railroad yard, when is a sleeper not a sleeping car? When it's what we call a railroad tie. That's a sleeper. A "durmiente" is an absolute correspondence between British English and the Spanish. I almost translated it wrong in a play *Los invasores*. There were bums in the trainyard, and I thought they were bums *sleeping*.

5. What is the hierarchy of Roman triumphal crowns? These were the civil, for one who fought his way into a hostile camp; the mural, for one who scaled the wall; the obsidianal for one who liberated a beseiged city. The obsidianal was not made from gold or silver, but from leaves and grasses flourishing on the field where the feat was achieved. What? the civic crown was for saving a fellow citizen from death? That's wonderful! I'll go back to my source and have him beg forgiveness.

6. Was the construction of a fifteenth-century ship such that an explorer could save himself from drowning by clinging to the ship's

wheel? No, even though Pedro in *Terra Nostra* does so. According to Lionel Cassens in *Illustrated History of Ships and Boats,* fifteenth-century explorers such as Columbus used a horizontal tiller. The ship's wheel was still in the future. No, I didn't correct it. I queried Carlos about this, but he wanted Pedro saved by a wheel. And it makes very little difference since *Terra Nostra* synthesizes times and spaces.

7. Why does Michelangelo's Moses wear horns? This comes from the Vulgate. I was using the King James Version in translating Sor Juana who takes up Moses' ascent of Mount Sinai. Fortunately I realized she would not have been using the King James Version but the Douay based on the Vulgate. Here it says "that Moses knew not that his face was horned from the conversation of the Lord."

8. What aromatic fruit was used to ward off the plague? Bergamot. The orange pear-shaped fruit was worn inside a cloth mask with glass coverings for eyeholes, and a beak. Today Bergamot rind is still much prized in perfumery.

9. In a seventeenth-century setting is there an objection to translating "hypnotized" as "mesmerized" or "outline" as "silhouette"? Yes, Mesmer and Silhouette had not been born.

10. Why would Ravrio have bequeathed to the workers who gilded his clocks a sizeable sum as workmen's compensation? Ravrio's workers suffered from lead poisoning acquired during the gilding process. Had the usage developed differently, we might say instead of "Mad as a March hare," "Mad as a Ravrio gilder."

11. Who was the real-life prototype for Daniel Defoe's Robinson Crusoe? He was Alexander Selkirk, a sailor shipwrecked off the coast of Chile, as recorded in *The Journals of Captain Woodes Rogers.*

12. What is the correct translation for *Melaegris gallopavo?* The popular name for the large game bird native to this hemisphere is "turkey." The *guajalote* (as it is called today in Mexico, and reported by an English traveler in 1860 as *huexolotl* "from the gobbling noise it makes," OED), was mistakenly called "turkey" because of an original confusion with the Guinea-fowl. So our native American bird was thought to be a fowl from Guinea, which lies on the western coast of Africa, known to the ancients and imported from Guinea via Turkey, hence its name—but a bird that more properly should have been called an "Americus" or even a "Vespucci."

And with that bit of speckled etymology, typical of a translator's trivia, I think it's time to close.

NOTES

This essay was transcribed by Serafina Clarke, Tad Palmer, and Rebecca Soglin; edited by the author with Marilyn Gaddis Rose.

1. In *Latin-American Literary Review*.

2. See twenty-minute film "Yo Pablo Neruda."

Words Cannot Express . . .
The Translation of Cultures

Gregory Rabassa

TO A FOREIGN GIRL
This valedictory effusion
Pleads in a tongue you do not speak
And yet for it by fond illusion
Your understanding I would seek.

—Alexander Pushkin
(Translated by Walter Arndt)

A most important word in almost any sphere of life is the word *misunderstanding*. We have international misunderstandings that can lead to war, although sometimes said misunderstanding is cultivated and intentional. There are emotional misunderstandings that bring on lovers' quarrels, showing that words convey feeling as well as meaning. Then, closer to home, there are critical misunderstandings, as an author who has received a bad review will attest. If we take a close look at cases within these categories we will find that every so often the misunderstanding does not come from a wrong interpretation of the words involved, but, rather, from a misconception of what they stand for, an unawareness of the cultural barnacles that cling to them and change their shape as they drift along cultural tides and eddies. These verbal accretions occur at all levels of linguistic expression: as individuals, we all have our own little private quirks, assigning new, unheard-of, and even absurd shades of meaning to ordinary words, the stuff of poetry, as it were; groups are quick to organize words into an exclusive jargon or an intimate argot; the public media are all too willing, it seems, to let solecisms take the place of accepted expression, even encouraging grammatical banality in the name of populism. I can only say that *vox populi vox dei* runs the risk of leading one into atheism. As nouns so frequently become verbs—*to impact,* for example, giving a possible new and inaccurate picture of what an impacted wisdom tooth is—one is inclined to ponder whether or not our culture is tending more and more toward passivity and away from action, keeping in mind that in Greek the Creator was the *logos,* while in Latin he was the more properly Roman *verbum.*

These changes within a language that we see in operation at all times in line with the examples I have just mentioned are the causes of its changing course as it develops, along with the fact that it has so often been put into an alien mouth, as is evinced by the various offshoots of Latin, official and otherwise. To go further, in modern times we see divergences, acceptable or not, taking place within modern languages as they leave the metropolis and take root in the colonies. Not only do they begin to differ in sometimes minor, sometimes major, ways from the old mother tongue, but also among themselves as the different lands begin to take their own peculiar effect. In the meantime, of course, back home the language is also changing to a degree where often the colonial version is closer to the ancient ways than the one that stayed behind. These changes are usually due to changes in attitude rather than simple linguistic misuse. (Let me pause here to add another item to my list of horrors: the case with which we make adjectives out of nouns in order to avoid a nice, round phrase. *Attitudinal* is one of these freakish sports.)

In some cases, emotion can be expressed in ways that have no need for accompanying words, as we know from silent movies, which call for little verbal explanation. If Pushkin's words to the foreign beauty are put forth in a proper way, he should have no fear that they will not be understood. Julio Cortázar, in *Rayuela* (Hopscotch), illustrates this most eloquently with his invention of *glíglico,* the language of love:

> —Sí, y después nos entreturnamos los porcios hasta que él dice basta basta, y yo tampoco puedo más, hay que apurarse, comprendés. Pero eso vos no lo podés comprender, siempre te quedás en la gunfia más chica.[1]

> Yes, and then we trewst our porcies until he says he's had enough, and I can't make it anymore either, and we have to hurry up, you understand. But you wouldn't understand that, you always stay in the smallest gumphy.[2]

As can be seen, the best way to translate *glíglico* is to put it into Gliglish. In both cases the author's intent overcomes our lack of knowledge of the language and we know all we have to know concerning what's going on. This is a manufactured case of linguistic difference, but it does illustrate that sometimes language is unnecessary to convey meaning and mere utterance will do the job. A whole concept can lurk hidden in a simple "Hmmm" or *"Pues."* In Portugal, *pois,* all, by itself, will often stand as an affirmative reply. We might think of these as oral punctuation, and that will help us respect the importance of the latter when meaning is put onto paper.

Things have a built-in ambiguity about them, often brought on by the traditional way in which we consider them. A more accurate way of looking at things and defining them would be the way that Ortega y Gasset recommends, that we define a thing by its use, so that if I take off my shoe and use it to drive a nail into the wall, for that moment it ceases to be a shoe and becomes a hammer, thus avoiding the absurd notion of driving a nail with footwear. It also brings us back to the *Quijote,* where Sancho wisely solves the problem of whether the item under discussion is a barber's basin or Mambrino's helmet by describing it with the portmanteau word *baciyelmo.* Would that the innate ambiguities of objects could be so cogently expressed by those of us who are neither Sancho Panza nor James Joyce. If things are ambiguous, words are even worse. If beauty is in the eye of the beholder, meaning is in the mind of the observer. A word, like an object, will take on new meanings with new uses. Most often this is due to some cultural influence upon the language, some attempt to convey a new idea or action or description when there is no traditional term extant. In this way a language diverges in its different geographical and cultural areas. The Puerto Rican in Buenos Aires innocently announces that he is going to catch the bus and is forthwith arrested as a child molester *(Voy a coger la guagua).*

This last example shows us how the translator must be doubly aware of possible ambiguities on both sides. He must be wary of adding any as he puts a word into his own tongue, and, ideally, he should try to preserve any possible ambiguity or double-meaning that lies in the original. As an aside, but one having to do with our cross-cultural theme, let us consider that last phrase, double-meaning. As it stands, it is quite clear: one word, two meanings. If we put it into French, however, and then use that French version, *double entendre,* in English, it almost always carries a connotation of something naughty. This may be due to the fact that ever since the nineteenth century strait-laced outsiders have looked upon France as the hub of erotic delinquency and freedom. This is illustrated by the bilingual misinterpretation of a Brazilian family whose daughter is learning French. Her brother teases her at the dinner table by asking her how one describes the various parts of the body in French and she dutifully goes through the list of *main, jambe, tête,* and so forth, until finally he asks her how they say neck and she replies *cou,* which brings out an *"Ai, minha filha"* from her mother and a comment by her father to the effect that only the French would have the audacity to call a neck *cou,* the confusion being with the Portuguese word *cu* which describes the nether end of the digestive tract.

Very often we guess at the meaning of a word by its context and get it wrong. Sometimes, however, a near miss by the right person, someone of importance, can add yet another meaning to the word as it makes its way down through the centuries. In such a way we now have the widely accepted solecism *normalcy* in English, coined by Warren Gamaliel

Harding when he meant to say normality, and, yet, old Gamaliel may have been right, because what he meant was only a certain facet of normality and his neologism, ugly as it is, fills the bill in that sense. This notion was put forth by Borges when he told his translator, *"No escribas lo que digo, sino lo que quiero decir,"* thus making full use of the ambiguous Spanish term *querer decir,* meaning both "to mean" and "to want or to try to say." The turbulent and often absurd political whirl of Latin America is many times the basis for malicious humor, usually directed at the individual in charge as a reflection on his feeble intelligence. Much of this humor is at the same time based on words and terms that are easily misunderstood by such a person. One of these *piadas* deals with General Costa e Silva when he was military dictator of Brazil and was on a state visit to Paris. His wife, Dona Iolanda, complained to him, *"O, Artur, faz uma semana que estamos em Paris e ainda não fui para o Louvre."* ("Say, Artur, we've been in Paris a week and I still haven't gone to the Louvre.") His reply was, *"Eu também. Deve ser coisa da água."* ("Me too. It must have to do with the water.") This illustrates the fact that the general's mind was not on art but on other more earthly matters and he took it for granted that everyone else felt the same way, showing the danger in voting one's own feelings and sense without regard for other possibilities. The translator must be above this; he must be careful, but he also must have some inner instinct for what is just right, for the proper choice among possibilities, and this instinct is one that he has been unconsciously cultivating all along by astute observation of the culture or cultures within his experience and learning. The craft of translation calls for someone along the lines of Clausewitz's ideal military commander (who was certainly no Costa e Silva): "What this task requires in the way of higher intellectual gifts is a sense of unity and a power of judgement raised to a marvelous pitch of vision, which easily grasps and dismisses a thousand remote possibilities which an ordinary mind would labor to identify and wear itself out in so doing."[3] We go back to the Louvre for another presidential visit by a military man to show how misunderstanding fits the circumstances of a person's limited capacity. President Fulgencio Batista of Cuba was making the rounds of the museum on a state visit of his and, as he knew very little about art, he had a well-educated aide follow along behind and whisper in his ear what he should comment concerning certain paintings. "This is a fine example of Impressionism. . . . This is a fine example of Impressionism. Ah, yes, Picasso's gray period. . . . Ah, yes, Picasso's gray period." They finally came to the Mona Lisa and the aide whispered, *"¡Qué cara! ¡Qué gesto!"* ("What a face! What an expression!"), and Batista, *"¿Qué carajo es esto?"* ("What the hell is this?").

There are ever so many examples of pitfalls with individual words, as the example of the Puerto Rican in Argentina shows. These can be avoided if the translator remembers that he must be a doubter at all times, prepared to smell a rat at every turn, to be absolutely devoid of self-confidence, except that he be confident that he will be on the lookout for such hazards. The Portuguese language has split even farther apart than the Spanish, so that if a Brazilian in Lisbon is told to queue up, *fazer bicha,* he will be outraged because he has understood that he's been told to become a drag queen. In Portugal *moça* more often than not means prostitute, while *rapariga* is simply girl; in Brazil it is exactly the reverse. Now with television there is a new acculturation in the world. What had been regional expressions, usages limited to a certain country or locality, have become international as they spread out over the air waves. Brazil has many more facilities for the production of *telenovelas* than does Portugal, so that members of the younger generation in Lisbon and elsewhere now often ape the customs and language of Rio and São Paulo, much to the despair of their elders. This effect should be obvious, however, as we have seen how rock music, as a kind of lowest common denominator, has practically obliterated local musical expression the world over. In music, as in language, a variation of Gresham's Law seems to obtain.

When cultures cross and mingle, there is a good deal of exchange, especially in language. A word will first come over as a sort of exotic addition that makes something commonplace seem foreign and exclusive. The word, if it survives the first encounter, will settle into local usage and eventually, over a long period of time, will become part of the language, as was the case with so many French words brought into English by the Normans. Of course, pronunciation soon goes native too, making the word in question all the more natural. This can be seen in English proper nouns as Beaulieu becomes Bewley, Beauchamp Beecham, and so on. As the word settles in, however, it often takes on a meaning that is a shade different from what it once was. If we walk down Third Avenue and see the sign *bar,* we know that it stands for a neighborhood watering place, a saloon, unpretentious and working-class. If we see the same sign in Latin America, though, it will signify something different. As a foreign term it has much more cachet and refers to what at home we would call a cocktail lounge or something along those lines. In reverse, that area behind an American house paved with bricks and furnished with benches and a grill is called a *patio,* something quite different from the Spanish *patio,* whence its name, which is a descendant of the Roman atrium, and if we wish to keep on with word development, the Spanish *atrio* no longer designates an inner courtyard, but, rather, the front of a church. There are times when we even try to improve upon the adopted term. The word *lingerie* somehow doesn't sound French enough when pronounced correctly, so a plusquam Gallic version has been developed by those who have no French but damn well know how it ought to sound, that abomination *lahnzheray.*

The translator must be modest, then, must be careful, cannot impose himself, and, yet, he must be adventurous and original, bound all the while to someone else's thought and words. In this sense translation is a baroque art, one where the structure is foreordained but where the second artist must decorate it according to the lights of his own culture. His genius is secondhand in a sense, but he still has a chance to strut his stuff within the limits before him. Machiavelli lays out a path that well might be that of the translator in relation to the author he is translating: "Men almost always prefer to walk in paths marked out by others and pattern their actions through imitation. Even if he cannot follow other people's paths in every respect, or attain to the merit [virtù] of his originals, a prudent man should always follow the footsteps of the great and imitate those who have been supreme. His own talent [virtù] may not come up to theirs, but at least it will have a sniff of it."[4] As can be seen even from this example, we have trouble with the translation of that Machiavellian bugbear virtù, which is not virtue and yet in some ways is. Here, indeed, we can quote the French autres temps, autres moeurs. Time and custom have both been at work so that the word virtù has lost many of its Florentine facets even in modern Italian, and Anglo-Saxon attitudes down through the years have made Machiavellian a nasty word.

These same cultural differences, however, may lie unnoticed until someone sets out to translate a book. Those who have gone into the trade after years spent mastering the other language are usually startled to find that a novel that had been a swift and easy reading gives them all sorts of problems when it comes down to translation. Most often this is not due to a difference in words, but in the way that they are strung together: syntax. There has never been a study that attempts to look at grammar and syntax from a cultural point of view except for a few notions concerning personal pronouns and forms of address. Perhaps it is too broad and vague and therefore forbidding. If such is to be done, I should think that translation is the place to find the contrasts. By the same token, I lament the trend that has been dominant over the past half century or so of exiling translation as a tool for the learning of language from the classroom. It is precisely by attempting to put something into another tongue that we see the important differences between the two and often in this way gain a touch of insight into how the people who think that way think. Otherwise we will go about prating like parrots in a kind of Pavlovian infancy and although our pronunciation is divine, we have little sense of what we are really saying.

Unfortunately, there is no way we can preserve the grammatical structure of the original in a translation to show that this book was really written in Spanish or Portuguese or whatever. To do so would be to produce some kind of gibberish that would be unintelligible to both sides. At the same time, however, there ought to be some kind of undercurrent, some background hum that lets the English-speaking reader feel that cultures do not translate easily. To make Martín Fierro a cowboy is to ruin the poem. The gaucho and the cowboy lived on the plains, rode horseback, herded cattle, and fought Indians, yet it is ludicrous to think of John Wayne as a gaucho. It is the culture that matters, and culture is most often made up of the lesser details: squatting and sipping *mate* or drinking black coffee, wearing *bombachas* or chaps, relying on the pistol or the long knife. These small things add up to make the similarities disappear. The talk of the gaucho is peculiar to his caste, as is that of the cowboy, but they are not interchangeable, and to translate gaucho speech into cowboy dialect would be to ruin the effect. Here is where the translator cannot follow the writer from the other side of the fence, but must be most creative himself. Keeping custom in mind, he must conceive of an English that the gaucho would speak if he spoke English. This will, of course, be pure invention, but if successful it will not only bring a language across the divide, it will bring a culture. The translator, then, who is most often adjured to be faithful, must also be inventive. Let us remember that the same language that gave us the canard *traduttore, traditore* also gave us *Se non é vero, é bentrovato*.

Our culture has the closest grip on us in those areas that are most intimate. A person will continue to curse instinctively in his native language if he hurts himself years after he has left his homeland and become part of another culture. And there must be something deeply personal about arithmetic, because the last thing a person gets to do naturally in a new language is to figure and count. These close things also make matters difficult for the translator. When it comes to translating curses, a literal version is usually worthy of a curse itself. Different peoples have different concepts of how to insult or demean each other. The Anglo-Saxon is quick to denounce someone's illegitimate background, while in Spanish it would be relatively mild to call someone *bastardo*. Call an American "cuckold" as an insult and more likely than not he won't know what you're talking about, but call a Spanish-speaker *cabrón* and you'd better be ready to fight. I recently came across a translation of Carlos Fuentes where the expletive *coño* was translated literally, making for a rather puzzling sentence and showing that curses are ill-served by close translation. The translation of curses really illustrates the essence of the act: we are really translating the spirit and not the word. In many cases there is a coincidence, but here and there spirit and word part in the new language and in those cases we must hew close to the spirit. *Hijo de puta* is not the literal translation of "son of a bitch," but it is of the spirit behind the expression and hence most accurate.

Even so, some languages are richer than others in foul language. It may be that those societies that still must deal with horses and other living creatures have richer vocabularies than those of us who deal with dull machines. You can't berate a non-hearing Oldsmobile or Volkswagen with the same fervor that you can a team of mules. Beyond that, we may have lost individual creation with the homogenized speech fed us on radio and television and the repetitive utterances that pass for song lyrics (babe-uh babe-uh ad infinitum). I was distressed for my culture when I was translating Jorge Amado's *Tocaia Grande* (which came out as *Showdown* in English as the meaningful place-name of the Portuguese was impossible to render into a cogent translation) and had to start repeating myself with words denoting the male member after the seventh or eighth time while Jorge went merrily on through fifteen or sixteen versions, all in good, common usage in the state of Bahia. I will stick to translation in this case and leave interpretation to the anthropologists.

The fact that language is culture and culture is language is brought out most sharply when one tries to replace his language with another. A person can change his country, his citizenship, his religion, his politics, his philosophy, and now even his sex more easily and smoothly than his language. It is the very sound of the language that sings the culture it represents, and this is the oral aspect that is lost in translation and this may be what Robert Frost was thinking or feeling when he defined poetry as what's lost in translation. The language of the "jabberwocky" is not English and yet it can only be felt through English, just as one of Alfonso Reyes's *jitanjáforas* can only exist when surrounded by Spanish. We translators, then, by our very act of translating are divesting the work of its most essential cultural aspect, which is the sound of the original language. After this it is ever so essential that we preserve whatever slim shards of the culture may be left lying about, and the way to do this is to acculturate our English as if it were his mother tongue, as if England had not lost the "purple land," perhaps, and not to produce a cowboy stumbling clumsily about in *bombachas* and *chiripá*, uncertain about defending himself with a *facón*.

NOTES

1. Julio Cortázar, *Rayuela* (Buenos Aires: Editorial Sudamericana, 1963), 104.

2. Julio Cortázar, *Hopscotch*, trans. Gregory Rabassa (New York: Avon Books, 1975), 95.

3. Carl von Clausewitz, *On War*, ed. and trans. Michael Howard and Peter Paret (Princeton: Princeton UP, 1976), 112.

4. Niccolò Machiavelli, *The Prince*, ed. and trans. Robert M. Adams (New York: Norton, 1977), 16.

Infante's Inferno

Suzanne Jill Levine

There are many puns, some in English, others in French.

—G. Cabrera Infante

Cabrera Infante refused to call *La habana* a novel even though all writing is fiction to him. *La habana* is a memoir, on the edge of autobiography, signaled already in the title by *"Infante."* Alliteration, the autobiographical *"Infante,"* and the subterranean inferno metaphor for Havana and the female sex in both *Tres tristes tigres* and *La habana* make *Infante's Inferno* a logical title. But there are other reasons that do not immediately meet the ear. What strikes the reader of the original title is not only its playful alliterative form, the explicit reference to "Havana" and in comic self-deprecation to a "Dead Infante," but also the visible parody of Ravel's *Pavane pour une infante défunte.*

I have discussed the dialogue between Spanish and English in TTT, and how this dialogue is both represented and sabotaged in translation. *La habana* introduces yet another interlingual conversation, between French and Spanish, evident already in the title beneath the title. As Cabrera Infante said in his introductory letter about *La habana,* "There are many puns, some in English, others in French" (February 1, 1979). How does the close relationship between the Romance languages Spanish and French translate into English? And if the *pavane* motif is essential to the book, as suggested, how does one justify its loss?

La habana is a Dantesque voyage, in search of not one but many Beatrices, in search of not divine but profane love: The erring narrator discovers that true love is ultimately sexual obsession, that communion is an illusion. In this parodical inversion the dead Infante remains caught in the circles of the hell and heaven of Havana, a memory, a book, an infinite Proustian discourse.[1]

The English title is fateful and faithful: *Dante ante Infante.* Dante *and* Virgil (*io,* or "I"). As Virgil is Dante's guide to the underworld of the dead in search of Homer, so does the narrator, guided by Dantes and Virgils (and Sapphos) seek memory but also the I, " his writerly identity." If *La habana* satirizes Dante's search for true, divine inspiration by suggesting that the lover, like the writer, is alone, imprisoned in his own discourse, it also exalts in biblical dimensions the illusion of creation, Literature. Between Infante and Dante, another essential and Cuban Virgil intercedes: José Lezama Lima. His *Paradiso* (1967), a direct homage to Dante, re-creates a young poet's birth as writer and as sexual being in the urban paradise of Havana, providing a discursive Joycean and Proustian as well as Dantesque space for *La habana* to come.

The following translated correspondence traces, from another perspective, the multistaged evolution of the title.

When the original was still in manuscript, and before I translated *"La Plus Que Lente,"* Cabrera Infante wrote (December 2, 1978), "What do you think, seriously, of the title *Dry Dreams* for our next book?" As early as September 6, 1979, he was naming titles, some of which prefigured his next book, *Holy Smoke*: "I'm thinking of *To Havana and Not Havana*.[2] Or *Havana is not a Cigar* or perhaps *Havana Si, Havana No*.[3] But all are too glib, slick, and though parodic not grave enough for my *Difunto Infante*." The title had to be parodic but not merely burlesque: *Gravity* was needed.

SJL to GCI, September 22, 1979: *"Dry Dreams* is good. Another: *Pavana for a Havana Lost* (playing with Paradise Lost). (Here are a few for your amusement but not for the title: Dry Dreams of a Wet Back Afternoon of an Infinite, Nocturnal Omissions)."

SJL to GCI, August 8 1980: "A possible title: *In Old Havana*.[4] In the interview [with Julián Ríos, *Espiral* 51] you suggest that DIVINE BODIES would be a good title for HAVANA, do you take it back?"

Sometime later, Carlos Fuentes commented to me that he had come up with the title *Infante's Inferno*: I passed this comment on to Cabrera Infante (SJL, August 15, 1981):

> This title, Fuentes' sinister idea, is certainly funny but could lead to the book being taken Holly too lightly (you know what I mean, I can just hear a critic saying "I had a hard if not hot time getting through Infante's Inferno . . ."). Infante's Inferno could turn the book into Havana for a Dead Duck, but what the hell . . . let's dive right in, if nothing better emerges from the Calldron.

Cabrera Infante quickly corrected me, reluctant to assume anxiety over a false influence, Fuentes (September 28, 1981):

> Dearest Daughter, *Infante's Inferno* is not an invention of Fuentes or by Morel but my own onus. Don't you remember? Please check up on my scarlet letters. The whole concoction was mine. I simply told Fuentes about this possible title in Old San Juan, P.R. and he gave me this bit of information that there was a book by some war correspondent called Durante's Inferno.

Sure enough (GCI, June 22, 1981):

> I fear that we haven't found our title (viscount? marchioness?) yet. But remember tardy TTT. HAVANE I don't like. HAVANA FOR A DEAD INFANT is a compromise with the original. And infant, as you know, is too tender, a baby, a suckling babe. It's almost HAVANA FOR A DEAD FOETUS! . . . I modestly think that one of the alternatives is INFANTE'S INFERNO because it's alliterative, Dantesque and slightly comical. There is besides, a book by a war correspondent in WWII, famous then, called Durante's Inferno.

In the same letter, Cabrera Infante continues,

> The title, finally, will be determined by the publisher, as it happened last time. But I've thought of another which maintains Havana (which as you've seen, is essential to the book) and at the same time something of the original infante (though no Ravel) besides being a wordplay, holding its pun high in salute. This title would be Havana for a Knight and to make it more obvious (there are always slow, lip-readers) we'd add another epigraph to the King Kong one saying:
>
> > "But you were in Havana for a night,
> > Just gettin' the feel of the land."
> >
> > (Mae West in "Havana for a Night")
>
> These lines come from her best record of the same title, a parody of the bolero "Vereda tropical" with English lyrics by Oscar Hammerstein. . . . Mae West fits in with the theme of blondes and false blondes in the other epigraph . . . and with the mythic women of cinema and of the century, Fay Wray clutched by K.K., Mae West squeezing men in her hands. The fact that the reference is a popular song and not a symphonic piece doesn't matter. Nor that the title seems cheaper than the original (which always happens in the translation): The American reader doesn't know the original, nor Ravel's Pavane for that matter. . . . What's important is that there be a humoristic, slightly anachronical, pop element. There are also anachronisms in Infante's Inferno—and if Infante gets lost, it's always there in the author's name above.

The essential "effects" of the title (though "cheaper") should be "humoristic, anachronical, pop," that is, parodical.

Finally (October 1, 1982) he pronounced: "Our title is: *Infante's Inferno*," and in longhand, "This will make Dante Difunto."[5] This last joke has serious connotations. Within Cabrera Infante's poetics of translation, the Old becomes the New; the past (Dante) is transformed, displaced, translated into the present (Infante). The Old is paradoxically defunct and reborn.[6]

If Ravel and Havana disappeared explicitly from the title, they were emphatically regained in the book, Havana a protagonist to whom many pages and puns serve homage, as in an alliterative pun, *"La habana . . . La Vana"* (237), which became a rhyming alliteration, "Havana, the Vain, Then" (135). Then, again, there's the *habanera* motif that we maintained by leaving the word for Havana woman in Spanish, since the English reader could associate it with the musical form *habanera*. And Ravel became a musical leitmotif as we reveling Ravelrousers of the unraveling word elaborated on Ravelian Jokes—for example, in *"La Plus Que Lente,"* where Ravel, Debussy, and even Satie now play a more principal role than in the original, especially Cabrera Infante's favorite, Satie, who didn't even appear in the original passage.

The following is yet another instance of "unraveled Ravel" (to quote John O'Hara's *From the Terrace*) regained—cited from the chapter titled *"Todo vence al amor,"* turning Virgil's *Amor vincit onmia* upside down, in a kind of verbal 69:

The original:
"Bueno, yo cultivo mis flores" dijo y abrió el libro y volvió a leer, como con furia ahora: verso versus verso. (270)

Literal Translation:
"Well, I cultivate my flowers" she said and opened the book and started reading again, as if with fury now: verse versus verse.

The "transelaboration"—"Love Conquered by All":
"Je vais m'occuper de mon jardin," she said and was kind enough to translate for me: "Time to go back to my flowerbed." Merde! Je vais cracher sur la tombe de Couperin, I should have said, but she had opened her book and was reading with a kind of fury now, verse versus verse. (160)

Virginia, the girl pursued on this occasion by our incessant Don Juan, is in a library. À la *Satyricon,* GCI satirizes throughout the book the Frenchified cultural pretensions of the Cuban bourgeoisie.[7] The contrast between people's pretensions and their more authentic vulgarity recurs as a constant dialectic throughout *La habana,* as it does in Puig's *Boquitas pintadas.* Virginia is reading Baudelaire's *Flowers of Evil* under false pretenses, or rather trying to outpun the narrator by turning Baudelaire cutely into Voltaire's gardener. The only jokes the narrator tolerates are his own, and they are his own, and so he replies with a "ready repartee," alliterating, *como con furia ahora,* to mock the (to his mind) mock-intensity of her reading: verse versus verse.

We not only substituted but elaborated on jokes, out of necessity, but equally compelling was the perverse "pleasure of the text." The Spanish parody of Voltaire's *"Je vais cultiver mon jardin,"* that is, "Yo cultivo mis flores," is based on the proximity of French and Spanish, a similarity that, as with the original's title "Havana for a Dead Infant," dissipates when English supplants Spanish. The "transelaborated" English version appropriately introduces French and exposes the disturbing, comical presence of (mis)translation implied in the original, now explicit in the translation. My *trouvaille* was inspired by a recording of Ravel's *Le tombeau de Couperin: "Je vais cracher sur la tombe de Couperin,"* in which Boris Vian's *J'irai cracher sur vos tombes* overflows into Ravel's homage.[8] This translated passage becomes more allusive, more musico-literary than the original, and perhaps more sexual, *cracher* suggesting French slang for "orgasm," *cracher dehors.* Alliteration lurks too, invisibly, in the conjunction of "should . . . she."

The humor, born of the close union between languages, works here because of a Gallic cultural perspective shared by Anglo and Latin America. Postcolonial Latin America has looked to Europe and North America, compensating for a lack of critical dialogue by *translating* into its own terms the so-called mainstream culture.[9] The hypocrisy in Cuban society mocked by the narrator originates in the alienation between model—be it popular North American or highbrow French culture— and Cuban reality. This distance between model and copy is a universal experience, certainly a very American experience: The North and South American aspiration to appear European is part of what is both alienated and authentic about America. The French phrase in the English translation accents thus the correspondence existing po(e)tentially between *La habana* and *Infante's Inferno.*

BETWEEN TEXTS AND SEX

With its myriad sexual episodes, *La habana* is a picaresque bible, or better, one thousand and one lustful Cuban Nights (and days). How to reproduce the clichés and folklore that constitute *choteo,* a local language of sex and jokes?

"Amorpropio," title of the chapter that describes briefly, ecstatically, the adolescent's discovery of masturbation, produced in my associations a biblical heading: "Love Thyself." Amor propio, properly speaking, means "self-love," "self-esteem," but here it is used more literally than figuratively to signify sexual self-love-making. "Self-Love," or even the Gallicism "Amour-Propre" could have been perfectly proper titles but just didn't seem as ironical as the original "Amor propio," playing literal love against a metaphoric sense of pride or vanity. *Amor propio* is such a common expression in Spanish; the word *propio* seems so concretely attached to ownership, loudly stressing the narrator's inevitable attachment to his own instrument of love. "Love thyself," taken from the rhetoric of the Bible (which, as Cecil B. De Mille was not the first to discover, is a very erotic book) reproduces a playful tension, between literal and figurative, between "good" and "bad" self-love, or perhaps between love and sex.[10]

Cabrera Infante responded ingeniously (February 24, 1980): "About Love Thyself's title, what do you think of Love Thy Neighbour? One's own penis lives practically next door, as a crow flies—or is it as the fly crows? . . . Now jokingly, I found the title a trouvaille. (Please note the correspondence between found and trouvaille , , ,) Velly goo." His humorously pornographic suggestion "Love Thy Neighbor" gave me the solution for the title of the next chapter, "Amor trompero."

The narrator begins this episode with a popular Spanish refrain: "Amor trompero, cuantas veo, tantas quiero" ("False love: The more women I see, the more I want"), which corresponds semantically more or less to the English saying "The grass is always greener. . . ." "Love Thy Neighbor" struck me as the appropriate introduction to this episode, which recounts the narrator's repeatedly unsuccessful attempts to seduce girls and women in movie theaters. "Neighbor" is comically accurate since the narrator would sit strategically next to unknown females, who literally became his temporary neighbors. "False Love" would not bring to the English reader's mind a popular saying like the profanity of "Love thy neighbor." The biblical "Love thy neighbor" lives up to the book's many double intertextual entendres, if not literally to "Amor trompero." "The grass is always greener" was incorporated into the text, substituting the original refrain, and Cabrera Infante parodically elaborated on it with "Your neighbor's grass is where it's green."[11]

One final folkloric sampler: the metamorphosis of episode VI, titled "Mi último fracaso" (my last failure, 315) into "You Always Can Tell." This episode explores the perennial penial theme of an adolescent's sexual initiation, the narrator's (miss)adventures in brothels, and his final quasi-successful encounter with a streetwalker. As he takes leave of her, at the chapter's end, she remarks that she didn't think she'd have any customers that night, to which he responds, "You see?" so that she can complete the phrase with the punch line from a song in Spanish. "You never know." Immediately he thinks of an answer to her answer but doesn't utter it aloud, another line from another bolero: "You will be my last failure." "My last failure" does not evoke a song or a singer, the campy Olga Guillot, and therefore cannot epitomize the chapter's popular theme, which the Cuban reader would immediately recognize.

My first thought was "Better Late Than Never," a popular saying that could celebrate the character's first participation in sexual intercourse after discoursing upon it for three hundred pages. Then "You Never Can Tell" came to mind, working well as the girl's parting words (changing "You never know" to "You never can tell"). But, as the final phrase has to be the narrator's mental repartee, Cabrera Infante suggested "you always can tell," an ironic echo, the narrator a constant echo of his narcissistic obsessions. Perhaps Freud was our (unconscious) guide, particularly in his essay on "The Antithetical Sense of Primary Words," in which he shows that yes often means no and vice versa: Could not the same apply to always and never?

"You Always Can Tell" covers a multitude of "sins": 1) The narrator automatically approaches the cruising *fletera* not knowing but somehow knowing that she is one, thus, "you always can tell"; 2) "Mi último fracaso" is an affirmation that suggests the negative yet affirmative "You Never Can Tell," and the uncertainties of sexual initiation; 3) "Mi último fracaso" recalls another text, a song, just as *La habana para un infante difunto* recalls Ravel, asserting the verbal, the literary over a reality described. You always can *tell*, a misquotation from the lexicon of clichés, very much emphasizes the *telling* of this tale of tails in which even when the narrator can't always do he can always tell.

NOTES

1. "Memory ruled by the city does not show encounters and visits, but, rather, the scenes in which we encounter ourselves." Peter Demetz, intro. to Walter Benjamin's *Reflections* (New York: Harcourt Brace Jovanovich, 1978) 1, xvii. Benjamin's (and Breton's) view of the city streets as the "only place of authentic experience" coincides with GCI's—all of them preceded by that *flâneur* par excellence, Baudelaire.

2. Inspired in Hemingway's Caribbean drama (glorified in film by a young Lauren Bacall and her man Bogart) *To Have and Have Not*, in turn inspired in a phrase from *Don Quixote*—the Haves and the Have Nots. The title of the final chapter, or epiphanic "epilog," came out of these Havana jokes: "Movies Must Have an End" (my italics).

3. Poking fun at Fidel's anti-yanqui slogans.

4. Cinematic allusion to *In Old Chicago*.

5. The process/reasoning behind choosing the allusion-saturated "Inferno" for the title can be illuminated by the following statement by Umberto Eco:

> The idea of calling my book The Name of the Rose came to me virtually by chance, and I like it because the rose is a symbolic figure so rich in meanings that by now it hardly has any meaning left: Dante's mystic rose, and go lovely rose, the War of the Roses, rose thou art sick, too many rings around Rosie, a rose by any other name, a rose is a rose is a rose, the Rosicrucians. The title rightly disoriented the reader who was unable to choose just one interpretation. . . . A title must muddle the reader's ideas, not regiment them. (Postscript to The Name of the Rose 3)

6. Enrico Mario Santí speaks of writing as "spatial difference," exposing "the sign's inherent lack and its need to be supplemented by an endless chain of other signs." *Pablo Neruda: The Poetics of Prophecy* (Ithaca: Cornell UP, 1982), 162. He cites Neruda's Cantos in *The Heights of Machu Picchu*, which salute

Dante but which displace his wor(l)d in the New World, (re)interpreting Mesoamerica in Western terms. The historical process of interpretation and creation is described here as a "process of translation by which the past is transformed, with all its attendant revisions, into the present. It is the act of translation . . . that provides the culmination to the earlier revision of literary history by becoming the figure that adopts Western signs as part of a new beginning" (161).

7. The French are the first to satirize their own classics. In Renoir's film *Boudu Sauvé des Eaux* (1932), a gentleman approaches the bookstore where Boudu the bum has found a home, asking, "Do you have *Fleurs du Mal?*" To which Boudu responds, "This is a bookstore, Monsieur, not a flowershop. " The avid reader goes off in a huff.

8. Vian was a (quitessentially French) jazz enthusiast who "doubled as a Dixieland trumpeter in Paris clubs." See E. J. Hobsbawm, "The Jazz Comeback," *New York Review of Books,* Feb. 12, 1987, II.

9. Jameson, F. "Postmodernism and the Consumer Society," *The Anti-Aesthetic: Essays on Postmodern Culture,* ed. Hal Foster (Port Townsend, WA.: Bay Press, 1983), 112. Jameson claims that cultural movements define themselves by displacing a previous cultural period (postmodernism seeks to displace modernism). Here Jameson quotes Octavio Paz's essay on translation and metaphor (from *Los hijos del limo*), which describes Hispanic culture as enriching itself by "translating" other cultures into its own terms. This process is compared to translation in which the text doesn't completely become another but rather the emphases are switched: The marginal becomes central and vice versa (123).

10. Jean Jacques Rousseau distinguished good narcissism *(amour de soi)* from bad narcissism *(amour-propre),* healthy self-esteem from unhealthy vanity. The ironic "Love Thyself," like GCI's, plays with the tension between these two poles (no pun intended), adding a hidden, third connotation, onanism.

11. See p. 94. Also SJL to GCI (August 8, 1980): "About to start work on "Love Thy Neighbor"—seeking equivalents for the refrain 'Amor trompero . . .' I now have two possibilities (aside from the literal); 'Love thy neighbor as thyself. What is thy neighbor's covet not' or, more earthy, 'the grass is always greener.' How's that for horse sense?"

The Draw of the Other

James Hoggard

I've been asked a number of times: *Why do you spend so much time trans-lating?* But before I can answer, a rapid series of questions follows: *How can you spend so much time translating other people's work and still have time or energy for your own? Don't your poems, stories, essays end up taking a back seat? Why let something like translation get in the way?*

The reasons are many, and they're all fundamental to my sensibility. They're also fundamental to the sensibility of many other people. Even before I could read, and certainly before I started writing and translating, stories caught my attention; and it wasn't too much longer before I began to discover that I thought in stories, that a lot of people exchanged information through stories, that the *sense of the other* exerts a powerful draw on a lot of us. Stories, in effect, are our paths to the world; and by stories I'm certainly including poems, that idiom so often considered the most intense of the arts.

Whether in verse or prose, stories work best when they evoke situations, when they convey, whether suggestively or directly, a person thinking or acting in an identifiable context; and that's true of lyrical as well as narrative poetry. But what does an idea like that have to do with translation? Plenty, because translation demands an immediate and intense recognition of *the other,* those figures outside (and sometimes wickedly inside) self that stir one's curiosity. When I was a child and youth, figures such as Aeneas and Beowulf, Odysseus and Hamlet, and the Little Engine That Could seemed like good friends of mine, and so did the dolphins leading ancient ships. Language, I was learning, made the world available; and a turn toward translation, it now seems, was inevitable.

Years ago, an extended metaphor in "The Function of the Artist," an essay by the novelist Borden Deal (*Southwest Review,* Summer 1966) seized my attention so vividly it became an important point of reference. Talking about storytelling in terms of prehistoric people gathered around a fire at night, Deal referred to the mountain range close by. Its size and rock face were formidable. Worse, the creatures that lived on its far side were viciously threatening. One didn't dare go there. Each community, though, Deal told us, usually included someone who was more daring or imaginative than the rest. Through fact or invention he'd maneuver his way into that distant, terrible realm, and he'd come back home with stories. At night he'd tell them to the people huddled in the shimmering small light. As he told them what the world was like on the other side of the mountain, the range of the puny light the people were clustered near began growing. The size of their world began expanding as they realized that they, too, might go beyond where they had been and now were. Curiosity was making them increasingly courageous, and so it should; after all, they were already, however cautiously, imagining themselves in what, just a short time before, had been an alien realm.

Several years after reading the Deal essay I began reading Octavio Paz. I started thinking, though, that I'd rather read him in the original, so I started learning Spanish. The effort seemed more natural than dramatic. Years earlier, when I was a child, my uncle had given me a Latin text. Diving into it, I was having a fine time learning how my new friends had spoken and written more than two thousand years ago. Later I studied other languages.

Then a request came: Would I be interested in writing a poem for a conference on and with Jorge Luis Borges? Of course. Besides, I had never been to Maine, and it was time to go some place new. One afternoon there, I met Oscar Hahn, a poet from Chile who was living in the States. Wanting to sharpen my Spanish, I told him I'd like to translate him, and a couple months later the typescript of his first major collection came in the mail, with a note that the book was getting ready to be published in Buenos Aires. What I saw intrigued me. But what about "my own work"? Had I gotten distracted from that? No. In fact, I had begun to understand more acutely than before that studying someone else's work in a different language sharpened my understanding of my own language.

Specifics, however, are more immediate than generalities, and obliqueness often more fruitful than directness. I'm thinking particularly now of "Por qué escribe usted?" ("Why Do You Write?"), a sonnet by Hahn, now an important contemporary poet of the fantastic. Two elements of it are striking: its edginess of tone and the fact that it's written in the form of a list that's relentless in its impatient rush to conclusion:

> Porque el fantasma porque ayer porque hoy
> porque mañana porque sí porque no
> Porque el principio porque la bestia porque el fin
> porque la bomba porque el medio porque el jardín
>
> Porque góngora porque la tierra porque el sol
> porque san juan porque la luna porque rimbaud
> Porque el claro porque la sangre porque el papel
> porque la carne porque la tinta porque la piel
>
> Porque la noche porque me odio porque la luz
> porque el infierno porque el cielo porque tú

Porque casi porque nada porque la sed
porque el amor porque el grito porque no sé

Porque la muerte porque apenas porque más
porque algún día porque todos porque quizás

All items in the list begin with *porque* ("because"), not *a causa de*
("because of"). The rhythm of the work is abrupt; there's nothing
friendly about it. Still, a translator wants to make sure he's not naively
misreading the work; maybe there's a smoother option that one's not
aware of; phrases, after all, can evoke numerous possibilities.

When I came to this poem, I had been working with Hahn's poetry
for years, so I decided to check directly with him. I asked him if he really
had meant for the poem's rhetoric to sound so impatient, even initially
odd. I told him I wanted to make sure I hadn't misread the attitude that
the speaker of the work was conveying. No, he told me, it's as edgy in
Spanish as my version was in English, even a bit odd in construction.
Then he told me how the poem had developed.

Along with others, Hahn had been asked by an editor in France to
write a piece explaining why he wrote. Hahn said that he tried to compose an answer, but what kept coming out sounded stupid; he even
hated the question. There were too many factors drawing one to song
and story to convey them fairly in a brief statement. The more frustrated
he became with the assignment, the angrier he got. He even started feeling, he said, like a child having a temper tantrum. After throwing up his
hands and spewing, he said, he started spraying a list down on paper.
Surprised, he noticed his tension diminishing. A new poem was forming.
He started revising it, shaping it into a sonnet. The form itself was an
act of rebellion: the editor had asked for prose.

It was time now to polish my translation. Curbing an impulse
toward gracefulness, I kept the "because" construction rather than the
friendlier "because of" option. The matter of accuracy, of course, was
important; but one was also reminded of something that translators,
critics, and general readers need to keep in mind: fine artists know what
they're doing. Original impulses may be nebulous, but the final terms of
execution rarely are; and Hahn's mastery had been noted by important
voices for years.

There was still the question of form: how to convey in English what
he had done in Spanish. I kept studying the poem. Two matters became
increasingly vivid. In rhythm and syllable count the lines varied. Hahn
had not been controlled by a metronome, and some of his rhymes were
approximate rather than exact. In form and tone he was combining gestures of spontaneity with a context of order. My translation would do the
same. In other sonnets of his that I had worked with, four-beat lines in
English seemed to be more crystalline than the five-beat form. Hahn did
not pad his lines in Spanish, and neither should his translator. Spanish

was often notably more polysyllabic than English, and one wanted the work in its new language to be as natural in effect as it was in its own. Equivalences, then, were more important than quantitative mirroring.

In "Por qué escribe usted?," however, Hahn's lines were longer than those in other sonnets he had published. I had to respect the variation, and I needed to keep his sense of form. So I decided to follow a six-beat rather than the standard five-beat line in English. Rhyme was also a factor. In the closing couplet and several other places, for example, I rearranged some of the words to achieve in English rhymes that were comparable to those in the version in Spanish. In the next to last line and the poem's final phrase, for example, *Porque la muerte porque apenas porque más / . . . porque quizás* became "Because death because more because scarcely / . . . because maybe." Drawn intensely into the world of the other, I reexamined the demands and tendencies of my own language and sensibility. I was also, though obliquely at first, meeting in this poem concepts of forces that drive and modify many, including me. So "Why Do You Write?" one is asked then hears an answer:

> Because yesterday because today because the ghost
> because tomorrow because yes because no
> Because the beginning because the beast because the end
> because the bomb because the center because the garden
>
> Because góngora because the earth because the sun
> because rimbaud because the moon because saint john
> Because the bright because blood because paper
> because flesh because skin because color
>
> Because hell because heaven because night
> because I hate myself because you because light
> Because nothing because thirst because almost
> because love because clamor because I don't know
>
> Because death because more because scarcely
> because someday because all because maybe

Again and again we're reminded that work in translation becomes as personal as any work that one does. Through it one learns and relearns the powerful draw of the other, and through that other we begin to see more clearly the textures of the places and languages we live in. Understanding the importance of the lesson Deal taught, we realize that new songs and stories are already forming, on both sides of the mountain, and there's a wealth of news to bring to the fire.

Anonymous Sources:
A Talk on Translators and Translation

Eliot Weinberger

Some years ago, Bill Moyers did a PBS series on poetry that was filmed at the Dodge Festival in New Jersey. Octavio Paz and I had given a bilingual reading there, and I knew that we would be included in the first program. The morning of the broadcast, I noticed in the index of that day's *New York Times* that there was a review of the show. This being my national television debut, naturally I wondered if their TV critic had discovered any latent star qualities in my performance, possibly leading to a career change, and I quickly turned to the page. This is what he wrote: "Octavio Paz was accompanied by his translator,"—no name given, of course—"always a problematic necessity." "Problematic necessity," while not yet a cliché about translation, rather neatly embodies the prevailing view of translation. I'd like to look at both terms, beginning with the one that strikes me as accurate: necessity.

Needless to say, no single one of us can know all the languages of the world, not even all the major languages, and if we believe—though not all cultures have believed it—that the people who speak other languages have things to say or ways of saying them that we don't know, then translation is an evident necessity. Many of the golden ages of a national literature have been, not at all coincidentally, periods of active and prolific translation. Sanskrit literature goes into Persian which goes into Arabic which turns into the Medieval European courtly love tradition. Indian folk tales are embedded in *The Canterbury Tales*. Shakespeare writes in an Italian form, the sonnet, or in the blank verse invented by the Earl of Surrey for his version of the *Aeneid;* in *The Tempest,* he lifts a whole passage verbatim from Arthur Golding's translation of Ovid. German fiction begins with imitations of the Spanish picaresque and *Robinson Crusoe*. Japanese poetry is first written in Chinese; Latin poetry is first an imitation of the Greek; U.S. poetry in the first half of this century is inextricable from all it translated and learned from classical Chinese, Greek, and Latin; medieval Provençal and modern French; in the second half of the century, it is inextricable from the poetries of Latin America and Eastern Europe, classical Chinese again, and the oral poetries of Native Americans and other indigenous groups. These examples could, of course, be multiplied endlessly. Conversely, cultures that do not translate stagnate, and end up repeating the same things to themselves: classical Chinese poetry, in its last eight hundred or so years, being perhaps the best literary example. Or, in a wider cultural sense of translation: the Aztec and Inkan empires, which could not translate the sight of some ragged Europeans on horseback into anything human.

But translation is much more than an offering of new trinkets in the literary bazaar. Translation liberates the translation-language. Because a translation will always be read as a translation, as something foreign, it is freed from many of the constraints of the currently accepted norms and conventions in the national literature.

This was most strikingly apparent in China after the revolution in 1949. An important group of modernist poets who had emerged in the 1930s and early 1940s were forbidden to publish and were effectively kept from writing; all the new Chinese poetry had to be in the promoted forms of socialist realism: folkloric ballads and paeans to farm production and boiler-plate factories and heroes of the revolution. (The only exceptions, ironically, or tragically, were the classical poems written by Mao himself.) Yet they could translate foreign poets with the proper political credentials (such as Eluard, Alberti, Lorca, Neruda, Aragon) even though their work was radically different and not social realist at all. When a new generation of poets in the 1970s came to reject socialist realism, their inspiration and models were not the erased and forgotten Chinese modernists—whose poems they didn't know, and had no way of knowing—but rather the foreign poets whom these same modernists had been permitted to translate.

Translation liberates the translation-language, and it is often the case that translation flourishes when the writers feel that their language or society needs liberating. One of the great spurs to translation is a cultural inferiority complex or a national self-loathing. The translation boom in Germany at the turn of the nineteenth century was a response to the self-perceived paucity of German literature; translation became a project of national culture building: in the words of Herder, "to walk through foreign gardens to pick flowers for my language." Furthermore, and rather strangely, it was felt that the relative lack of literary associations in the language—particularly in contrast to French—made German the ideal language for translation, and even more, the place where the rest of the world could discover the literature it couldn't otherwise read. Germany, they thought, would become the Central Station of world literature precisely because it had no literature. This proved both true and untrue. German did become the conduit, particularly for Sanskrit and Persian, but it is also became much more. Its simultaneous, and not coincidental, production of a great national literature ended up being the most influential poetry and criticism in the West for the rest of the century. (And perhaps it should be mentioned that, contrary to the reigning cliché of Orientalism—namely that scholarship follows imperialism—Germany had no economic interests in either India or Persia. England, which did, had no important scholars in those fields after the pioneering Sir William Jones. Throughout the nineteenth century, for example, Sanskrit was taught at Oxford exclusively by Germans.)

In the case of the Chinese poets, their coming-of-age during the Cultural Revolution meant that they had been unable to study foreign languages (or much of anything else) and thus were themselves unable to translate. But to escape from their sense of cultural deficiency, they turned to the translations of the previous generation, and began to discover new ways of writing in Chinese, with the result that Chinese poetry experienced its first truly radical and permanent change in some 1,300 years.

Among U.S. poets, there have been two great flowerings of translation. The first, before and after the First World War, was largely the work of expatriates eager to overcome their provinciality and to educate their national literature through the discoveries made in their own self-educations: to make the United States as "cultured" as Europe. The second, beginning in the 1950s and exploding in the 1960s, was the result of a deep—and already half-forgotten—anti-Americanism among American intellectuals: first in the more contained bohemian rebellion against the conformist Eisenhower years and the Cold War, and then as part of the wider expression of disgust and despair during the civil rights movement and the Vietnam War. Translation—the journey to the other—was more than a way out of America: the embrace of the other was, in the 1960s, in its small way, an act of defiance against the government that was murdering Asian others abroad and the social realities that were oppressing minority others at home. Foreign poetry became as much a part of the counterculture as American Indians, Eastern religions, hallucinatory states: a new way of seeing, a new "us" forming out of everything that had not been "us."

By the early 1970s, of course, this cultural moment was over, and the poets, for different reasons, became detached from the intellectual and cultural life of the country, as they vanished into the creative writing schools. There are now more U.S. poets and poetry readers than in all the previous eras combined, but almost none of them translate. The few who do, with two or three notable exceptions, are all veterans of the 1960s translation boom. The end of a general anti-Americanism among American writers and readers may have led to a happy populace of literati, yet it is one that is singularly nationalist (but without overt flag waving), isolationist (but without overt xenophobia), and uninformed. Unbelievably, or all too believably, the total number of literary translations—fiction, poetry, plays, literary essays, and so on—from all languages, published by all the presses in the United States—large, small, and university—comes to about two hundred a year. The number of poetry translations—including the Greek and Roman classics and inevitable new Neruda and Rilke volumes—is usually around twenty-five or less. The entirety of world literature in English translation may be the only field where it is still possible to keep up with all the new publications in the field.

Paradoxically, the rise of multiculturalism may have been the worst thing to happen to translation. The original multiculturalist critique of the Eurocentrism of the canon and so forth did not lead—as I, for one, hoped it would—to a new internationalism, where Wordsworth would be read alongside Wang Wei, the Greek anthology next to Vidyakara's *Treasury*, Ono no Komachi with H. D. Instead it led to a new form of nationalism, one that was salutary in its inclusion of the previously excluded, but one that limited itself strictly to Americans, albeit hyphenated ones. Today nearly every freshman literature course teaches Chinese-American writers, but no Chinese, Latinos but no Latin Americans. In terms of publishing, if you are a Mexican from the northern side of the Rio Grande, it is not very difficult to get published; if you're from the southern side, it is almost impossible. There are probably fewer than a dozen living Mexican writers who have been translated and published in the United States, and only two or three with some regularity. In contrast there are many millions of dollars pouring into Chicano Studies departments, Chicano literary presses, special collections at libraries, literary organizations, prizes, and so on. In terms of Mexican Americans, this is necessary and healthy, but it has also meant that, in terms of translation, readers in the United States now have less contemporary Mexican literature available to them than they did in the 1960s.

Translation is a necessity, for the obvious reason that one's own language has only created, and is creating, a small fraction of the world's most vital books. It is also perhaps the best source for the genuine news from abroad. Mexico, hardly an obscure corner of the globe from a U.S. perspective, is a case in point: The American perception of Mexico has radically changed in the last forty years, and the beginning of that change has a precise date. For much of the twentieth century, what we knew in English about Mexico came from the foreign writers who had been inspired, moved, and sometimes repelled by their visits there: Malcolm Lowry, D. H. Lawrence, Aldous Huxley, Katherine Anne Porter, Hart Crane, Graham Greene, and Langston Hughes, among them. Then, in 1959, the *Evergreen Review* published a special issue called "The Eye of Mexico," edited by Ramón Xirau with the assistance of Octavio Paz. This was the first highly visible introduction of Mexican literature in the United States and one that was much discussed at the time: the first news of writers such as Paz, Rulfo, Fuentes, Sabines, Poniatowska, Arreola, and others, as well as León-Portilla on the Náhuatl concept of art. We were, at last, hearing from the Mexicans themselves.

That magazine issue led to numerous books in English by these writers and, from that moment on, it was not only Mexico that was inspiring U.S. writers, it was Mexican literature. For the general reading population, Mexico could now be seen through Mexican eyes. What was once a set of stereotypes began—though of course this work is far from complete—to take on a human face.

The same principle is at work south of the border. With the exception of Paz—who was a true internationalist—and a very few others, Mexican writers have tended largely to ignore U.S. literature beyond certain classics, to see it as part and parcel of the monstrous culture that has brought the world McDonald's and the Marines. This, in the last ten or fifteen years, has begun to change, and many Mexican writers are becoming increasingly interested in that world of U.S. culture that, from the outside, remains hidden in the back streets behind the neon signs of the mass market. It may begin with the translation of a few poems but— as has been historically the case many times—a few cultural artifacts often grow into a more general national understanding. Mexico has gone from a clichéd anti-Americanism to the point where its new President is calling for a kind of binational citizenship—a massive cultural change that is not attributable solely to migration and cable TV.

This importing of American literature into Latin America is not part of the Coca-Colaization of the planet: poetry particularly always moves through underground channels that have little to do with the dominant and corporate cultures, and U.S. poetry has always been written in spite of, and not because of, the State and the culture at large. Moreover, unlike Coca-Cola—which you either drink or you don't—poetry is a dialogue. To take two examples: The poetry of Octavio Paz was radically altered by his readings of U.S. poetry, particularly Pound and Williams. The translations of Paz's poetry, in turn, were tremendously influential for certain U.S. poets of the 1960s and 1970s. These same poets are now being translated in Mexico and have attracted wide interest. In short, there are now younger Mexican poets who are influenced by the American poets who were influenced by Paz who was influenced by American poetry. Translation is not appropriation, as is sometimes claimed; it is a form of listening that then changes how you speak.

The second example: In 1913, Ezra Pound, inspired by his discovery of Chinese poetry, writes the manifesto "A Few Don'ts by an Imagiste." Published in *Poetry* magazine that year, it is enthusiastically read by a young Chinese poet named Hu Shih, who is studying in Chicago. Hu returns to China and, in 1917, publishes his own, quite similar, manifesto, "Tentative Proposals for the Improvement of Literature," which becomes known as the "Eight Don'ts," and sets off a literary revolution, the May Fourth Movement of 1919. The story is more complicated, but it may be summarized as this: Hu Shih found in American poetry what Ezra Pound thought he had found in the Chinese. Like the protagonist of a Sufi parable, the poet went to the other side of the world to discover what was at home. Perhaps it is a parable for all translation.

The necessity of translation is evident; so why is it a problem—or, as they now say, problematic? Milan Kundera famously considered the poor translations of himself as—and only a man would write this—a form of rape, and he characterized the bad translations of Kafka as betrayals in a book called *Testaments Betrayed*. All discussions of translation, like nineteenth-century potboilers, are obsessed with questions of fidelity and betrayal. But in the case of a writer such as Kundera, who came of age in a society dominated by the secret police, "betrayal" carries an especially heavy weight. We know what a translation is supposedly a betrayal of, but is it unfair to ask to whom the text is being betrayed?

And one can never mention the word *translation* without some wit bringing up—as though for the first time—that tedious Italian pun *traduttore traditore*. Luckily, the Italian-American philosopher Arthur Danto has recently and I hope definitively laid it forever to rest:

> Perhaps the Italian sentence betrays something in the cultural unconscious of Italy, which resonates through the political and ecclesiastical life of that country, where betrayal, like a shadow, is the obverse side of trust. It is an Unconscious into which the lessons of Machiavelli are deeply etched. Nobody for whom English is a first language would be tempted to equate translation and treason.

The characterizations of translation as betrayal or treason is based on the impossibility of exact equivalence, which is seen as a failing. It's true: a slice of German pumpernickel is not a Chinese steam bun which is not a French baguette which is not Wonder Bread. But consider a hypothetical line of German poetry—one I hope will never be written, but probably has been: "Her body (or his body) was like a fresh loaf of pumpernickel." Pumpernickel in the poem is pumpernickel, but it is also more than pumpernickel: it is the image of warmth, nourishment, homeyness. When the cultures are close, it is possible to translate more exactly: say, the German word *pumpernickel* into the American word *pumpernickel*—which, despite appearances, are not the same: each carries its own world of referents. But to translate the line into, say, Chinese, how much would really be lost if it were a steam bun? (I leave aside sound for the moment.) "His body (her body) was like a fresh steam bun" also has its charm—especially if you like your lover doughy.

It's true that no translation is identical to the original. But no reading of a poem is identical to any other, even when read by the same person. The first encounter with our poetic pumpernickel might be delightful; at a second reading, even five minutes later, it could easily seem ridiculous. Or imagine a fourteen-year-old German boy reading the line in the springtime of young Alpine love; then at fifty, while serving as the chargé d'affaires in the German consulate in Kuala Lumpur, far from the bakeries of his youth; then at eighty, in a retirement village in the Black Forest, in the nostalgia for dirndelled maidens. Every reading of every poem is a translation into one's own experience and knowledge— whether it is a confirmation, a contradiction, or an expansion. The poem does not exist without this act of translation. The poem must move from reader to reader, reading to reading, in perpetual transformation. The poem dies when it has no place to go.

Translation, above all, means change. In Elizabethan England, one of its meanings was "death": to be translated from this world to the next. In the Middle Ages *translatio* meant the theft or removal of holy relics from one monastery or church to another. In the year 1087, for example, St. Nicolas appeared in visions to the monks at Myra, near Antioch, where his remains were kept, and told them he wished to be translated. When merchants arrived from the Italian city of Bari and broke open the tomb to steal the remains, Myra and its surroundings were filled with a wonderful fragrance, a sign of the saint's pleasure. In contrast, when the archdeacon of the Bishop of Turin tried to steal the finger of John the Baptist from the obscure church of Maurienne, the finger struck him dead. (Unlike dead authors, dead saints could maintain control over their translations.) Translation is movement, the twin of metaphor, which means "to move from one place to another." Metaphor makes the familiar strange; translation makes the strange familiar. Translation is change. Even the most concrete and limited form of translation—currency exchange—is in a state of hourly flux.

The only recorded example of translation as replication, not as change, was, not surprisingly, a miracle: Around 250 B.C., seventy-two translators were summoned to Alexandria to prepare, in seventy-two days, seventy-two versions of the Hebrew Bible in Greek. Each one was guided by the Original of all Original Authors and wrote identical translations. Seventy-two translators producing seventy-two identical texts is an author's—or a book reviewer's—dream and a translator's nightmare.

A work of art is a singularity that remains itself while being subjected to restless change—from translation to translation, from reader to reader. To proclaim the intrinsic worthlessness of translations is to mistake that singularity with its unendingly varying manifestations. A translation is a translation and not a work of art—unless, over the centuries, it takes on its own singularity and becomes a work of art. A work of art is its own subject; the subject of a translation is the original work of art. There is a cliché in the United States that the purpose of a poetry translation is to create an excellent new poem in English. This is empirically false: nearly all the great translations in English would be ludicrous as poems written in English, even poems written in the voice of a *persona*. I have always maintained—and for some reason this is considered controversial—that the purpose of a poetry translation into English is to create an excellent translation in English. That is, a text that will be read and judged *like* a poem, but not *as* a poem.

And yet translations continue to be measured according to a Utopian dream of exact equivalences, and are often dismissed on the basis of a single word, usually by members of foreign language departments, known in the trade as the "translation police." They are the ones who write—to take an actual example—that a certain immensely prolific translator from the German "simply does not know German" because somewhere in the vastness of *Buddenbrooks,* he had translated a "chesterfield" as a "greatcoat." Such examples, as any translator can tell you, are more the rule than the exception. One can only imagine if writers were reviewed in the same way: "the use of the word 'incarnadine' on page 349 proves the utter mediocrity of this book."

This is the old bugbear of "fidelity," which turns reviewers into television evangelists. Now obviously a translation that is replete with semantical errors is probably a bad translation, but fidelity may be the most overrated of a translation's qualities. I once witnessed an interesting experiment: average nine-year-old students at a public school in Rochester, New York, were given a text by Rimbaud and a bilingual dictionary, and asked to translate the poem. Neither they nor their teacher knew a word of French. What they produced were not masterpieces, but they were generally as accurate as, and occasionally wittier than, any of the existing scholarly versions. In short, up to a point, anyone can translate anything faithfully.

But the point at which they cannot translate is the point where real translations begin to be made. The purpose of, say, a poetry translation is not, as it is usually said, to give the foreign poet a voice in the translation-language. It is to allow the poem to be *heard* in the translation-language, ideally in many of the same ways it is heard in the original language. This means that a translation is a whole work; it is not a series of matching *en face* lines and shouldn't be read as such. It means that the primary task of a translator is not merely to get the dictionary meanings right—which is the easiest part—but rather to invent a new music for the text in the translation-language, one that is mandated by the original. A music that is not a technical replication of the original. (There is nothing worse than translations, for example, that attempt to recreate a foreign meter or rhyme scheme. They're sort of like the way hamburgers look and taste in Bolivia.) A music that is perfectly viable in English, but which—because it is a translation, because it will be read as a translation—is able to evoke another music, and perhaps reproduce some of its effects.

But to do so requires a thorough knowledge of the literature *into which* one is translating. Before modernism, poems, no matter from where, were translated into the prevailing styles and forms: the assumed perfection of the heroic couplet could equally serve Homer,

Kalidasa, or the Chinese folk songs of the *Book of Odes*. The great lesson of modernism—first taught by Ezra Pound, but learned, even now, only by a few—was that the unique form and style of the original must in some manner determine the form and the style of the translation; the poem was not merely to be poured into the familiar molds. Thus, in Pound's famous example, a fragment of Sappho was turned into an English fragment, ellipses and all, and not "restored" or transformed into rhyming pentameters.

This was based on a twofold, and somewhat contradictory, belief: First, that the dead author and his literature were exotic, and therefore the translation should preserve this exoticism and not domesticate it. Second, that the dead author was our contemporary, and his poems—if they were worth reading—were as alive and fresh as anything written yesterday. An unrestored Sappho was "one of us" precisely because she was not one of us: a foreign (in the largest sense) poet pointing to a way that our poems could be written today.

Modernism—at least in English—created extraordinary works in translation because they were written *for* modernism: written to be read in the context of modernist poetry. The cliché that the only good poetry translators are themselves poets is not necessarily true: the only good translators are avid readers of contemporary poetry in the translation-language. All the worst translations are done by experts in the foreign language who know little or nothing about the poetry alongside which their translations will be read. Foreign-language academics are largely concerned with semantical accuracy, rendering supposedly exact meanings into a frequently colorless or awkward version of the translation-language. They often write as though the entire twentieth century had not occurred. (This is especially true in the Asian and Middle Eastern languages.) They champion the best-loved poet of Ruthenia, but never realize that he sounds in English like bad Tennyson. Poets (or poetry readers) may be sometimes sloppy in their dictionary-use, but they are preoccupied with what is *different* in the foreign author, that which is not already available among writers in the translation-language, how that difference may be demonstrated, and how the borders of the possible may be expanded. Bad translations provide examples for historical surveys; good translations are always a form of advocacy criticism: here is a writer one ought to be reading and here is the proof.

Translation is an utterly unique genre, but for some reason there is a perennial tendency to explain it by analogy. A translator is like an actor playing a role, a musician performing a score, a messenger who sometimes garbles the message. But translation is such a familiar and intrinsic part of almost any culture that one wonders why there is this need to resort to analogies: we do not say that baking is like playing the violin. One analogy, however, is exact: translators are the geeks of literature.

Translators are invisible people. They are often confused with simultaneous interpreters—even at bilingual poetry readings. According to a survey of my own clippings—which I happen to have, but any translator could tell you the same story—90 percent of book reviews never mention the translator's name, even when they are talking about the author's so-called style. When they do, the work is usually summed up in a single word: *excellent, mediocre, energetic, lackluster.* Discussions of the translation longer than one word are nearly always complaints about the translation of a word or two. When my edition of Jorge Luis Borges's *Selected Non-Fictions* rather weirdly won a major award earlier this year—a prize that is normally never given to a translation or to a dead author—the press releases and news articles did not mention my name, and even my own publisher took out an ad congratulating Borges, wherever he is, but not me.

Translators sometimes feel they share in the glory of their famous authors, rather like the hairdressers of Hollywood stars, but authors tend to find them creepy. As Isaac Bashevis Singer said:

> The translator must be a great editor, a psychologist, a judge of human taste; if not, his translation will be a nightmare. But why should a man with such rare qualities become a translator? Why shouldn't he be a writer himself, or be engaged in a business where diligent work and high intelligence are well paid? A good translator must be both a sage and a fool. And where do you get such strange combinations?

"Why shouldn't he be a writer himself?" is the great and terrible question that hangs over the head of every translator, and of every author thinking about his translator. One might say that the avoidance of the question—not the response to it—has been the recent flood of publications in which translators explain themselves.

Some translators now claim that they are authors (or something like authors), which strikes me as a Pirandellesque confusion of actor and role (or, closer to our times, a Reaganesque confusion). It began some twenty-five years ago in the United States as a tiny microcosm of the larger social currents. Translators began to come out of their isolation and anonymity to form groups, such as the Translation Committee of the PEN American Center, where they could share the tales of misfortune of their underpaid, entirely unrecognized, and often exploited occupation. This led to demands, as a group, for thoroughly justified material concessions: the translator's name prominently featured on the book and in all notices of the book, a share in the author's royalties and subsidiary rights (rather than a flat fee—degradingly known as "work for hire"—with no subsequent rights or income), and some sort of "industry standard" for translation fees. Simultaneous to the slow acceptance of these demands was a proliferation of conferences and lectures on translation as an art. This in turn coincided with the rise of so-called theory in the universities, and there is, perhaps, no subject in literature more suited for theoretical rumination in its current modes than translation: the authority of the author, the transformation of the sign, the tenuousness of signifier and signified, the politics of what is/isn't translated and how it is translated, the separation of text and author, the crossing of (or impossibility of crossing) cultural barriers, the relativism of the translation as discourse, the translator as agent of political/cultural hegemony, and so on. All of which are sometimes interesting in themselves, but generally unhelpful when one actually translates. (As Borges said, "When I translate Faulkner, I don't think about the problem of translating Faulkner.")

With this preoccupation with the translator—and the self-evident and now excessively elaborated corollary that everything is a form of translation—the translator has suddenly become an important person, and explaining translation a minor but comfortable academic career and a source of invitations to conferences in exotic climes. Small wonder, then, that the advance guard of translators and their explainers are now declaring that the translator is an author, that a translated and original text are essentially indistinguishable (because an original text is a translation and/or a translation is an original text) and, most radically, that the sole author of a translation is the translator (who should therefore have one hundred percent of the rights and royalties to the books).

This strikes me as presumptuous, if not hubristic; and it may well be time to raise the banner of the translator's essential and endearing anonymity. In the United States, we can no longer use the word *craft*, which has been taken over by the so-called creative writing schools, where the "craft" is taught in "workshops." So let us say that translation is a trade, like cabinet making or baking or masonry. It is a trade that any amateur can do, but professionals do better. It is a trade that can be learned, and should be (though not necessarily institutionally) in order to practice. It is a trade whose practitioners remain largely unknown to the general public, with the exception of a few workers of genius. It is a trade that is essential to a literate society, and—let's raise a banner—whose workers should be better paid.

For me, the translator's anonymity—his role as the Man Without Qualities standing before the scene, a product of the *zeitgeist* but not a direct maker of it—is the joy of translation. One is operating strictly on the level of language, attempting to invent similar effects, to capture the essential, without the interference of the otherwise all-consuming ego. It is the greatest education in how to write, as many poets have learned. It is a prison in the sense that everything is said and must now be re-said, including all the author's bad moments—the vagaries, the repetitions, the clichés, the clinkers—while strictly avoiding the temptation to explain or improve. It is a prison, or a kind of nightmare, because one is in a dialogue with another person whom you must concede is always right. But it is also a liberation. It is the only time when one can put words on a page entirely without embarrassment (and embarrassment, it seems to me, is a greatly underrated force in the creation of literature). The introspective bookworm happily becomes the voice of Jack London or Jean Genet; translation is a kind of fantasy life.

In my own case, the other I have bizarrely inhabited—or more exactly, has inhabited me—since I was a teenager is Octavio Paz. But the curious thing is that, in terms of a history of a relationship between an author and a translator, it was not very interesting at all. It was full of discussion, but uniquely entirely without unpleasantness, for Octavio himself was a prolific translator and understood the process, as many writers do not. I would send him drafts of the translations; he would comment on them, often illuminating what had been, for me, obscure. We would sometimes debate back and forth, but in the end, he always gave me the last word, for although he knew English extremely well, he also knew that I knew it better. A few times, when I was translating poems that had not yet been published in book form, he would change a word or two or a line of the original after seeing the translation—for translation, as another reading, often points out or magnifies flaws in the original. (Or it erases them: At a reading, Octavio once said, "I have many doubts about myself in Spanish, but I love myself in English." This is a fairly common sentiment: Valéry preferred himself in Spanish, Goethe in Nerval's French, García Márquez in English. It is less a tribute to the translator than a recognition that translation gives a writer a critical distance in which to read himself.) A few times, we jointly came up with an English word that did not correspond to the Spanish original, but rather to his original intent—sometimes because he felt it was inadequately expressed in Spanish or because he wanted to take advantage of the vast and often more precise English vocabulary. And I have invented a few titles that were quite different from the originals, and which I would not have done without the author's participation.

One result of this (for me) lifelong collaboration is that I probably know Paz's work better than anyone. But it is a very specific kind of knowing: I could not necessarily write a critical study of Paz that would be better than any other, for my expertise is entirely microscopic. Rather the way a certain kind of art historian knows a painter—brush strokes, palette, technique—I know all his favorite words, syntactical constructions, punctuation, stylistic tics and gestures; I could spot a forgery a mile away. Yet when asked to talk about Paz's work in general, I may be less articulate than other readers, as I am a tree surgeon rather than an ecologist.

My personal relationship with Octavio is another story, a subject for the memoirs I hope I forget to write in extreme old age. The author-translator relationship, however, mine or any other, has no story. It is one that has never been told (as far as I know) by any author, beyond a few passing complaints, and only rarely by translators, usually in the form of amusing intertextual anecdotes. This is because the story has only one real character: the author. The translator, as translator, is not a fully-formed human being; the translator, in the familiar analogy, is an actor playing the role of the author. Sometimes we, the audience, are aware of the actor "doing" the role brilliantly or poorly, sometimes we forget he is an actor at all (the "invisibility" that is often still considered the translation ideal, particularly for prose). But in either case, reflections on that role remain one-sided: Olivier may write a memoir of his Hamlet, but Hamlet will never write of his Olivier.

I also happen to be, however inconsequentially, both translator and translated. Though it is hard to imagine that I occupy anyone's fantasy life, everything I write is regularly translated into various languages. For the ones I don't know, I merely let them go, and hope that I am not mistaken for a dinosaur in Krakow or Petersburg. Every translation is merely another reading, and no writer—though some try mightily—can control how he is read. For the languages I somewhat know, I glance here and there, sometimes with the realization that the translator has written the exact opposite of what I said. (It is a discovery that induces a kind of vertigo, for one begins to believe that the exact opposite is no less worthy a statement, and perhaps not all that different.) In the case of the Spanish translations, I go over every line for the least theoretical of reasons: I personally know some of my readers and must see them after they've read the text. There I've had three kinds of translators: At one extreme, a brilliant poet whose language is so elegant he makes the original look like a bad translation. At the other, a well-meaning naif with whom I felt like an aged dissolute as I explained in a blizzard of faxes that, to cite only a few, a "hit man" is not a man who hits, and that one does not "inject" LSD. In the middle is my regular and ideal translator: an excellent writer who knows (usually more than I) whatever subject I'm talking about, has successfully invented a "style" or "voice" for me in Spanish, and whose only shortcoming is a question of probably insurmountable cultural difference: coming from the tradition of the Spanish Baroque, he needs to be continually reminded that the funny part of a New York joke occurs at the end of the sentence.

Because of the nature of what I write, and the technicalities of publishing—abroad I publish in mass-circulation intellectual magazines and cultural supplements of newspapers, which appear frequently, and in the United States I appear in literary journals, which are infrequent— it is usually the case that my writing is published first in translation. I pertain, in a small way, to a new kind of writer in this new era of global culture: one who is more visible abroad or in translation than at home or in his original language. To write knowing that one will be translated poses a set of problems that are new for writers (or more exactly, were previously only known to Goethe and Heine) and are shared not only by these authors-for-translation but also by, among others, the recent generation of African Francophone and Indian Anglophone writers: How much should one sacrifice the domestic in order to reach the foreign? How much can one "explain" to the outside world without alienating the readers of one's own world? How far can one represent one's culture—which is, after all, why many translated writers are read—without the often untranslatable local expressions, allusions, terminology, native species? How to remain idiosyncratic in one's own language—to keep one's writing from turning into a room at the Holiday Inn, the same in Samarkand or Cleveland? In short, how translatable should one allow oneself to be? These questions are only beginning to be posed, not answered.

The old German Romantic dream of a World Literature beyond nationalisms, of a literature produced by the translated—who have now become the transplanted, diasporic, international—has already had unintended consequences. Among them is the great translation tragedy of our time: the Salman Rushdie case.

It is rarely said that the *fatwa* and its subsequent global mayhem, riots, and deaths were the result of a mistranslation. Rushdie's book was named after a strange legend in Islamic tradition about the composition of the Qu'ran, which was dictated to Muhammad by Allah Himself through the angel Gabriel. According to the story, Muhammad, having met considerable resistance to his attempt to eliminate all the local gods of Mecca in favor of the One God, recited some verses that admitted three popular goddesses as symbolic Daughters of Allah. Later he claimed that the verses had been dictated to him by Satan in the voice of Gabriel, and the lines were suppressed. The nineteenth-century British Orientalists called these lines the "Satanic verses," but in Arabic (and its cognate languages) the verses were known as *gharaniq*, "the birds," after two excised lines about the Meccan goddesses: "These are the exalted birds/ And their intercession is desired indeed." In Arabic (and similarly in the cognate languages) Rushdie's title was literally translated as *Al-Ayat ash-Shataniya*, with *shaytan* meaning Satan, and *ayat* meaning specifically the "verses of the Qu'ran." As the phrase "Satanic verses" is completely unknown in the Muslim world—which Rushdie apparently didn't know—the title in Arabic implied the ultimate blasphemy: that the entire Qu'ran was composed by Satan. The actual contents of the book were irrelevant.

Translators were among those who paid for this mistake: In July of 1991, the Italian translator of *The Satanic Verses*, Ettore Capriolo, was stabbed in his apartment in Milan, but survived. Days later, the Japanese translator, Hitoshi Igarashi, an Islamic scholar, was stabbed to death in his office at Tsukuba University in Tokyo.

As far as I know, Rushdie has never made any extended comment on Hitoshi Igarashi. It would take another kind of novelist—Dostoyevsky perhaps—to untangle the psychological, moral, and spiritual meanings and effects of the story of these two: the man who became the most famous writer in the world at the price of what seemed until recently to be life imprisonment, and the anonymous man who died for a faithful translation of an old mistranslation, paying for the writer's mistake.

Translation is the most anonymous of professions, yet people die for it. It is an obvious necessity that is considered a problem. (There are never conferences on the "pleasures of translation.") Yet it is a problem that only arises in the interstices when one is not casually referring to some translated bit of literature: the Bible, Homer, Kafka, Proust. . . . Could it possibly be that translation essentially has no problems at all? That it only has successes and failures? There is no text that cannot be translated; there are only texts that have not yet found their translators. A translation is not inferior to the original; it is only inferior to other translations, written or not yet written. There is no definitive translation because a translation always appears in the context of its contemporary literature, and the realm of the possible in any contemporary literature is in constant flux—often, it should be emphasized, altered by the translations that have entered into it. Everything worth translating should be translated as many times as possible, even by the same translator, for you can never step into the same original twice. Poetry is that which is worth translating, and translation is what keeps literature alive. Translation is change and motion; literature dies when it stays the same, when it has no place to go.

Can Verse Come Across into Verse?

John Felstiner

Since verse translation forms both the means and the end of this book, the cherished axiom that translating poetry is a betrayal must come into account as well. Let us assume that we find the language of any fine poem in a unique, inalienable state. Does a "version" or "rendering" inevitably do just what those terms imply—turn the poem into something other than it is? Or, assuming that the translator aims to compose a new poem that speaks for itself, and yet aims to speak for the original in all its integrity: does one purpose preclude the other? These questions have a rich lineage that traces back two thousand years—a sign of vitality if also of vexatiousness. From Cicero and Horace through Saint Jerome to Ezra Pound and Walter Benjamin, the problem of verse translation has remained essentially the same. Octavio Paz phrased it in the title of a 1970 essay: "Translation: Literature and Literalism."[1]

Are there alternatives to verse translation? A trot can clarify diction, imagery, structure;[2] thorough explication can provide an intellectual grasp. Both procedures have their place. But since verse, unlike most prose, is involved bodily and specifically in its own tongue, no amount of paraphrase or interpretation can substitute for hearing a poem in one's native language. Only a verse translation, I have come to believe, can yield a vital, immediate sense of what the poet meant.

Although practitioners of the art have made major statements on its theory, and have also detailed their awareness of what gets lost in translation, the poets themselves have seldom taken the chance, except vaguely and unofficially, to convey their own sense of loss. Only the man who voiced them can really know what it feels like to have these subtly cadenced lines, *Ya no sois, manos de araña, débiles / hebras, tela enmarañada,* transmuted hypertrophically into "All that spidery fingerplay, the gimcrack / device of the fibers, the meshes' entanglements—you have put them behind." But Neruda did not expect much anyway from English versions of his work.[3] He was once asked into what language his poems translated best:

Italian, because there's a similarity of values between the two languages. English and French . . . do not correspond to Spanish—neither in vocalization, nor in the placement, color, or weight of the words. This means that the equilibrium of a Spanish poem . . . can find no equivalent in French or English. It's not a question of interpretive equivalents, no; the sense may be correct, indeed the accuracy of the translation itself, of the meaning, may be what destroys the poem. That's why I think that Italian comes closest.[4]

Clearly Neruda laments the loss in translation of the very thing that makes him love to write: a poem's blend of sounds and rhythms, of tones and overtones, which he calls "equilibrium" because they have a physical presence for him. But this lament resembles a view of verse translation that never gets beyond the weary dualism of style and content. Bring over a poem's ideas and images, and you will lose its manner; imitate prosodic effects, and you sacrifice its matter. Get the letter and you miss the spirit, which is everything in poetry; or get the spirit and you miss the letter, which is everything in poetry. But these are false dilemmas, and the distinction they imply plays no part in Neruda's poetry. I doubt he would stand by the notion that his poems can yield a "sense," a "meaning" distinct from their form, an "interpretive equivalent." He must have known, or at least guessed from his own experience translating Shakespeare and others, that the translator of a poem whose music and meaning work indivisibly is not performing some stereoscopic feat, any more than the poet was in writing the poem. Let us admit that to really translate a poem is impossible—impossible yet fascinating—and start from there. Verse translation at its best generates a wholly new utterance in the second language—new, yet equivalent, of equal value. Perhaps the passage from Spanish into Italian generates nothing new. In preferring that minimal displacement, Neruda was expressing a residual uneasiness at being translated at all. Apart from the fact that translation would promote his currency abroad, the idea of new utterance, new incarnation, may not after all have appealed to him when it applied to his own poetry.

His work as a translator over the years also shows that Neruda was less interested in re-creating other writers' work through verse translation than in drawing emotional sustenance from them, or simply making them available. During his twenties he translated Baudelaire's "L'Ennemi," a fragment of Rilke's *Malte Laurids Brigge* (from Gide's translation), two pieces from Joyce's *Chamber Music,* Blake's *Visions of the Daughters of Albion* and "The Mental Traveller," and part of Whitman's *Song of Myself.*[5] All these are literal renditions that read well, and show Neruda not so much making these poets come alive in Spanish as affiliating himself with various romantic sources. Later in life, as he traveled and found himself translated everywhere, he often did versions from his friends' or his translators' work—a heartening form of literary exchange.

For Shakespeare's quadricentennial in 1964, Neruda wrote a playable and often moving version of *Romeo and Juliet*, though he made little attempt to echo Shakespeare's absolute felicities.[6] He was well aware that compared with English verse, Spanish tends toward spreading, and he found himself needing "two or more lines for each one of the original."[7] When Juliet parts with Romeo, for instance, in Act Two, scene two, she says, "This bud of love, by summer's ripening breath, / May prove a beauteous flower when next we meet." Clearly Neruda is not at home, rhythmically or verbally, in the four lines that splay out from Shakespeare's two: *Este botón de amor con el aliento / de las respiraciones del verano / tal vez dará una flor maravillosa / cuando otra vez tú y yo nos encontremos.* I do not know whether it could be done better in Spanish. Certainly Neruda knew that a loss could occur in going either way between two languages. This state of affairs did not stimulate him to be inventive as a translator, and it also left him doubtful that his own poetry might survive translation intact.

"It seems to me," he said, "that the English language, so different from Spanish and so much more direct, often expresses the meaning of my poetry but does not convey its atmosphere."[8] Again I would question this abstraction of meaning from atmosphere, seeing how palpably Neruda's verse can shape its perceptions out of sounds and rhythms. *Hambre, coral del hombre*, he says at Macchu Picchu (X), and what that means can scarcely be separated from how it sounds. Here indeed one has to wrestle with words to shape an English verse fully equal to the Spanish. "Hunger, the human coral," gets exactly the rhythmic pattern that Neruda has, but means something different. To say "Hunger, coral of man," likens hunger to coral more accurately, but less compellingly. "Hunger, coral of humankind," avoiding a specific gender, ties both "hunger" and "coral" into the sounds of "humankind"—but not nearly so closely as Neruda does, with *hambre* kept from *hombre* by only a single vowel, and with *coral* between them, its vowels modulating from one word to the other. The upshot is not so much that we get the letter in English and miss the spirit, as that translators must try for better and better verse.

Neruda's doubts about translation were shared by the Peruvian César Vallejo, often linked with Neruda though they wrote quite differently. "Everyone knows that poetry is untranslatable. Poetry is tone," Vallejo said. Poems reach out to us with the "cardiac rhythm of life," and despite translation "their tone remains, immovable, in the words of the original language."[9] Certainly Vallejo's own idiosyncratic and complex poems resist translation. But in a way, the difficulty of translating Neruda well stems from his not being difficult to translate adequately. He exhibits no struggle with language or with silence as Vallejo does. Even in the anguished mood of *Residencia en la tierra* he hardly ever doubts his element, any more than a swimmer does. However surprising or disconnected his images, words for what he has to say do not fail him, and their face value is seldom unclear, which means for the translator that a semblance of Neruda's poetry comes fairly easily.

One does not feel the poet's words struggling against their referents, because for him their source and validity came from nature. "The word was born in the blood,"[10] Neruda believed, and he said he "began to write from a vegetal impulse."[11] This prelexical source of poetic language means that a translator can often rely on the common nouns in English—"tree" for *árbol*, "dew" for *rocío*—to express what Neruda had in mind. He might be called an Orphic poet, animating the things of the world by summoning and naming them. When he says *amapola*, in translation it remains a poppy, and of course a *cóndor* stays a condor. Thus, it is not usually a semantic originality in Neruda that confronts the translator. What makes his verse difficult to translate is first its sensuousness, which either may or may not find an equivalent in English, a sound and rhythm of equal value. Second, and at a deeper level, he is difficult to translate for the same reason that an average Chilean has trouble grasping some of his poetry. When Neruda has lit on an image intuitively, the translator must sometimes make an unguided choice. What does *mares poblándose* (literally, "seas peopling themselves") refer to? The face value of the phrase may not be in doubt, but is the literal translation convincing and compelling? The choice between "peopling" and some other word such as "thronging" or "swarming" has still to be made.

The question of verse translation continues to exercise translators, critics, and sometimes poets, because it goes deeper than judgments of loss or gain. Sooner or later the translator asks, Where does the nature of poetry subsist? In ideas, imagery, diction, pattern, sound, or rhythm? In all those together, of course, but perhaps most in sound and rhythm, which are specific to their own language. At one point during his last days, Neruda talked with a guest about Lithuanian translations of his poetry. They were only fair, she said, but he assured her: "Don't worry. The rhythm is all right. . . . For a poet, that's what counts."[12] To show what a difference rhythm makes, here are two of Whitman's lines that Neruda translated. In *Song of Myself,* section two, we hear:

> Urge and urge and urge,
> Always the procreant urge of the world.

We hear the dense monosyllabic "urge" copulating throughout line one; the way the word can (only in English) act as verb and noun at once; the line's taut trochaic beat released into a flow of dactyls in line two; Whitman's astonishing (and Shakespearean) "procreant" instead of "procreative"—and all of these things leave Neruda's version sounding rhythmically bulky:

Impulso, impulso, impulso,
siempre el procreador impulso del mundo.[13]

A friend of Neruda's remembers him working assiduously on his Whitman translation in Madrid in 1935, searching for the right words.[14] Maybe that word-for-word adherence was the trouble, since his own verse at the time, his "material songs" to wood, wine, and celery,[15] were astir with the procreant urge and the rhythm he did not confer on Whitman. Like Shakespeare, Whitman often eludes everything but mere wonder. This test points up an inalienable quality in the finest poetry, something at once meaning and music, that remains organic to the tongue it is created in. To respond to this quality, a translator moves between two extremes, neither settling for literalism nor leaping into improvisation, but somehow shaping a poem that is likewise inalienable and organic. It follows from this that the language of translation should ordinarily be the translator's native tongue and that the translator must in some sense be a poet.

What Neruda felt was getting lost in English translations of his verse might more precisely be called its physical body rather than its atmosphere. A good example occurs in "Agua sexual," the epitome of *Residencia en la tierra*. Even the English title, "Sexual Water," dissipates the surprise of the adjective by making it subordinate to the noun, whereas Spanish syntax places the adjective *sexual* in an emphatic position without losing the force of the noun *agua*. The poem's first line beautifully manifests what Neruda called the vocalization, placement, color, and weight of Spanish words: *Rodando a goterones solos / . . . cae el agua*—literally, "Rolling in large single drops / . . . the water falls." These are some options in English:

> Running in single drops (Hays, 1943)
> Rolling drop by drop (Eshleman, 1962)
> Running down in big and distinct drops (Wright, 1967)
> Rolling in big solitary raindrops (Walsh, 1973)

Hays's version makes clear why Neruda called English "so much more direct": down to six syllables, with the adjective "single" *(solos)* preemptively limiting the noun instead of climactically following it, and *solos* kept to one meaning instead of connoting "alone" as well as "single." Even with the more likely "rolling" instead of "running," Hays would lack the fullness of Neruda's sonorous back vowels, the *oh*'s and *ah*'s pulsing through *Rodando a goterones solos*. Wright transcribes Neruda faithfully at the expense of his own rhythm, and Walsh specifies raindrops, thus failing to suggest the sweat and sperm that come later in the poem. Taking off from Eshleman and Wright, another option might be "Rolling down drop upon drop." Yet that could still be improved. At least it satisfies the criterion of being exact yet idiomatic, and shows that, other things being equal, rhythm is what counts. The French version—

"Roulant à grosses gouttes seules"—says just what the Spanish does but too tersely.[16] Only Italian, as Neruda said, can make a rhythmic, aural, and semantic equation with *Rodando a goterones solos:* "Rotando a gocciolones solos." It's beautiful, but is it translation? Yes, and no. In an obvious sense, the Italian does come as close to Neruda's poem as it's possible to come—but not through any particular virtue in the translation. Only the inherited virtue of a cognate diction, grammar, and syntax stands the Italian in such good stead, so that it would actually be more accurate to speak here of transliterating from Spanish. It must in fact be a little dull to readjust Neruda into Italian; translators working in other languages need have no envy. Since English, as Neruda said, is "so different from Spanish," forging a new version in it takes the translator through a process kindred to that of the poet.

Translating a poem often feels essentially like the primary act of writing, of carrying some preverbal sensation or emotion or thought over into words. Anyone who has slowly shaped an original sentence knows what it feels like to edge toward a word or phrase and then toward a more apt one—one that suddenly touches off a new thought. The same experience holds for poets, generating a line of verse, who find that the right rhyme or image when it comes can trigger an unlooked-for and now indispensable meaning.

So it is in the to-and-fro of verse translation, where finding how and finding why to choose a particular rendering are interdependent. In its own way the translator's activity reenacts the poet's and can form the cutting edge of comprehension. At times it even seems (to the enthusiast, at least) that only those insights feeding into or deriving from the task of translation are exactly legitimate, germane to the poem. This is not to limit or belittle the act of comprehending a poem, but to enlarge the responsibility of translating one.

The vital question about Macchu Picchu—is the place still alive to move us now?—turns quite literally into a question of translation. In Canto IX, Neruda composes seventy-two highly figurative epithets to Macchu Picchu, telling off as many attributes of the abandoned city:

> Triangled tunic, pollen of stone. . . .
> Buried ship, wellspring of stone. . . .
> Coral of sunken time.

At one point in the sequence occurs a key image, "Gale sustained on the slope," followed by another that translators have seen in various ways:

> *Inmóvil catarata de turquesa.*

Leaving alone the variations on "cataract of turquoise" or "turquoise waterfall," *inmóvil* raises the most interesting possibilities, since it concerns the potential of Macchu Picchu. The first English translation made it "Motionless cataract of turquoise," and semantically that will do.[17] It embodies well enough the paradox of a downflow that has no movement. Yet "motionless" renders this precious source of energy more inert than I think Neruda's poem would have it. Tarn's version also takes away energy by saying "Still turquoise cataract"—a fine image in itself, as of something shining seen from afar and arrested aesthetically.[18] The word *still*, at least for me, carries echoes of those crucial moments in *Four Quartets* when perishable life is transformed by spirit, "at the still point of the turning world."[19] Such echoes heighten Neruda's image, but may do so misleadingly. Given the preceding epithet, "Gale sustained on the slope," and given Neruda's desire to reanimate the dead at Macchu Picchu, the turquoise cataract needs to be more dynamic than "still" would allow. It needs to be seen as much under the aspect of history as of art. At one stage in my own translating I tried "moveless," but that seemed precious; then "unmoving," if only to keep a potential energy in the word, but its negative prefix felt too strong; then "stilled," but this reads some outside force into the original.

Perhaps for once a better translation was waiting there all along in the exact cognate of *inmóvil:* "immobile." The English prefix *im-,* counterpoised against the root word *mobile,* builds up a palpable tension that expresses something we need to know about Macchu Picchu. Like an "immobile turquoise cataract," the ruined yet revisited city is being sustained, poised against whatever has stalled but not finally stopped its energy. The poet finds a word to say as much; sometimes the translator also does. Small points of tuning, like this one, can make the difference between a locked, tragic sense of Latin American history and the dynamic, prophetic sense motivating Neruda.

NOTES

1. Octavio Paz, *Traducción: literatura y literalidad* (Barcelona: Tusquets, 1971); rpt. as "Teoría y práctica de la traducción," in Paz, *El signo y el garabato* (Mexico City: Joaquín Mortiz, 1973).

2. Willard Ropes Trask, in *Translation* 6 (Winter 1978–79): 263–65, says he translates verse only into prose. But his prose versions have the qualities of verse. A good literal prose version of *Alturas de Macchu Picchu* by Tom Raworth appears in E. Caracciolo-Trejo, ed., *The Penguin Book of Latin American Verse* (Baltimore: Penguin, 1971), 128–50.

3. Neruda read widely in English, and his translations from Blake and others show a solid grasp of the language. I am not sure whether he had an exact sense of idiomatic English.

4. Rita Guibert, *Seven Voices,* trans. Frances Partridge (1972; rpt. New York: Random House, Vintage Books, 1973), 35–36. This is the most extensive

interview with Neruda available. I have altered it very slightly in one spot, but have not seen the original Spanish.

5. These translations were published in small magazines: Baudelaire, 1967; Rilke, 1926; Joyce, 1933; Blake, 1935; Whitman, 1935—see *Obras completas,* bibliography. The first four are reprinted in OC, III, 763–81.

6. William Shakespeare, *Romeo y Julieta,* trans. Pablo Neruda (Buenos Aires: Losada, 1964).

7. Quoted in Hernán Loyola, "Neruda traduce a Shakespeare," *Aurora* (Santiago) 2.5 (Jan.–March 1965): 150.

8. Guibert, 36.

9. César Vallejo, "La nueva poesía norteamericana" (1929), in *Aula Vallejo, 5–7,* ed. Juan Larrea (Córdoba, Arg.: Univ. Nacional, 1967), 67–70.

10. Neruda, "La palabra," in *Plenos poderes* (Buenos Aires: Losada, 1962); OC, II, 974.

11. Neruda, "Viaje por las costas del mundo" (1943), OC, II, 563.

12. Ugné Karvelis, "Une Journée à Isla Negra," *Europe* (Paris), nos. 537–38 (Jan.-Feb. 1974): 49.

13. Walt Whitman, "Pasto de llamas," trans. Pablo Neruda, in *El aviso de escarmentados del año que acaba y escarmiento de avisados para el que empieza de 1935* (Madrid: Cruz y Raya, 1935), 61–64; rpt. *Repertorio Americano* 922 (Sept. 20, 1941): 265.

14. Luis Rosales, "Prólogo," in Pablo Neruda, *Poesía,* 2 vols. (Madrid: Noguer, 1974), I, 40.

15. "Entrada a la madera" (Entrance into Wood), "Apogeo del apio" (Apogee of Celery), "Estatuto del vino" (Ordinance of Wine), OC, I, 229, 230, 232.

16. Neruda, *Résidence sur la terre,* trans. Guy Suarès, 105.

17. G. R. Coulthard, in *Adam.*

18. *The Heights of Macchu Picchu,* trans. Nathaniel Tarn.

19. T. S. Eliot, *Four Quartets:* "Burnt Norton," II.

III

Critical Approaches

Reading Latin American Literature Abroad:
Agency and Canon Formation
in the Sixties and Seventies

María Eugenia Mudrovcic

On 24 July 1981, the *New York Times* announced the imminent publication in English of Ernesto Sabato's *Sobre héroes y tumbas*. In the note, entitled "Publishing: A Novel's Long Trek Into English," Edwin McDowell didn't comment on the "highly acclaimed novel" as much as he denounced the long and troublesome process the book went through before it could be published in the United States "20 years after its publication in Spanish and long after its translation into French, German, Italian and other languages" (24). A few days later, on the front page of the *New York Times Book Review* (where a decade or two earlier it would have been unthinkable to talk about a Latin American novel), Robert Coover reviewed what he called "a masterpiece," and did not fail to question the inexplicable delay of the translation: "We in the English-speaking world are the last to get the news" (1). From the time it was first published in 1962, *Sobre héroes y tumbas* had received outstanding reviews and had sold well in Latin America and Europe; it was that success that soon sparked the interest of Holt, Rinehart & Winston, with whom Sabato finally signed a contract in 1969. The book, however, did not in fact appear in the late sixties because of Sabato's dissatisfaction with the translations undertaken by Patricia Emigh; and Holt unilaterally cancelled the contract in 1974. Resubmitted to "at least four major trade publishers" (i.e., Knopf, Grove, Viking, and Penguin), Sabato's second novel didn't find a willing U.S. publisher until 1978, when the Center for Inter-American Relations—"a New York-based organization dedicated to promoting hemispheric understanding" (McDowell 24)—finally reached an agreement with David Godine, and also assumed the full cost of the translation.

Even though the *New York Times* gave the novel some coverage, the 1981 piece did not mention the terms of the final contract, which were made public later by Ronald Christ, at the time the director of *Review,* the literary journal of the CIAR. "When no publisher was able to offer an advance for this translation and no subvention was available from the Center for Inter-American Relations' limited translation program, Helen Lane and I,"—Christ stated—"with the cooperation of the book's author and publisher-to-be worked out a novel agreement. Helen Lane agreed to translate small sections of the book when she could steal time from better paying projects; Ernesto Sabato agreed to offer consultation when needed, and to go on waiting; Mr. Godine agreed to publish the book no matter how long it might take to complete the translation; and the Center agreed to pay Helen Lane for those translated snippets with proportionally small sums filched from other sources, such as the budget for office supplies. The paperclip fund we called it" (Christ 17).

The *New York Times'* note did not give any information about the earliest phase of the negotiation process, when, following Emir Rodríguez Monegal's recommendation, Scribner's rejected the English rights to the book in 1966. Writing from Paris, the first director of *Mundo Nuevo* was quite categorical in his report: "*Sobre héroes y tumbas* is a distinguished failure" (1966a). More years would still need to pass before Monegal would become the arbiter of literary value for the establishment in the late sixties and seventies—a period when José Donoso's literary agent could write: "Granted, Emir has clout. . . . If Emir says yes, he is good and he does have the respect of his contemporaries in his home ground, it often happens that the book is done. This is real power, of course, but given the realities of the world, somebody has to exercise it" (Brandt 1973). Nevertheless, it seems that Monegal's early judgment of the novel ended up playing some role in the otherwise inexplicable delay of its translation into English. In publishing terms, Sabato was what is called a no-risk author: a best-selling author in Argentina, and widely translated (and sold) in Europe (the French edition was immediately reprinted after selling out 7,000 copies). Furthermore, his first novel, *The Outsider,* was published by Knopf in 1951, and made him known in the United States. Yet none of these credentials—crucial in any decision-making process on a translation—seemed to matter when publishers were considering buying the English rights to his second and most successful novel.

But, far from being exceptional, *On Heroes and Tombs'* "long trek into English" is, in the broader context, a more common event than it initially appears to be. When Latin American literature finally found its place in the U.S. book market, it had gone through a no less arduous and difficult process. Only after a long struggle for recognition did it "succeed" in the sixties and throughout the seventies. This success was not only due to its aesthetic value, as both Latin American and U.S. critics frequently maintain, but, more importantly, it was the result of the active promotion by formerly friendly critics, translators, and publishers. The lobbying efforts of the Center for Inter-American Relations eventually gained Latin American literature entry into the New York establishment. Likewise, the critics and translators gathered around

Review also played a key role in determining the authors and works that have since become what U.S. readers take to be the Latin American canon. In this essay, I intend to reconstruct this institutional space within the literary translation industry in the United States (what Bourdieu would call "the kitchen" of a cultural field), and, from there, look at the Center's role as a mediator for Latin American literature; especially, at the power it exercised over which books and authors were imported, translated, and read.

Historically, U.S. publishers have been reluctant to translate the literature of their southern neighbors into English. Such publication projects were often perceived as high risk and non-profitable ventures. It seems as if many publishers found a kernel of truth in the statement Russell Baker made in his *New York Times* column: "Americans will do almost anything for Latin America except read about it."[1] There have been exceptions, however, mostly framed by occasional peaks of enthusiasm for the region, which then sparked exchange programs for scholars, distribution of grants and fellowships, book publishing, and conferences. One of the moments of apogee came with President Franklin Roosevelt's Good Neighbor Policy. During World War II, U.S. political interest in Latin America grew, as did their economic interests, given the area's potential as a future market. In fact, "the State Department showered largess; [and] where official money was unavailable or insufficient, it was generously supplemented by private grants, notably by the Rockefeller Foundation" (Cline 59).

In this context, Alfred Knopf, considered at the time to be one of the great purveyors of literature in translation,[2] decided to feed the official appetite for all things Latin American while, at the same time, exploring new markets and adding "exotic" names to a list of authors that already included some Latin Americans (Alberto Blest Gana's *Martín Rivas* [published in 1918], Isaac Goldberg's *Brazilian Literature* [1922], *The Destiny of a Continent* by Manuel Ugarte [1925], and *The Eagle and the Serpent* by Martín Luis Guzmán [1930]). By the late fifties, and long after public interest in the region had come to an end during the postwar era, Knopf had become the biggest publisher of Latin American literature in the United States. Its catalog was extensive and displayed such heterogeneity that it is difficult (at least today) to "read" the policy or vision that governed the selection of titles. Besides the special attachment to Brazilian literature that Blanche Knopf showed since her first trip to Latin America in 1942 (Jorge Amado, Graciano Ramos, Guimarães Rosa, and Gilberto Freyre were among the authors in whom Knopf heavily invested) the press's list didn't seem to be governed by any specific criteria other than author popularity, publisher instincts, and circumstantial awareness of specific works. Unintelligible as it might be, Knopf's list—which brought together authors as disparate as Ricardo Palma, Alfonso Reyes, María Luisa Bombal, Eduardo Mallea, Ciro Alegría, Germán

Arciniegas, Alejo Carpentier, Ernesto Sabato, Adolfo Costa du Rels, and José Suárez Carreño—certainly suggests that up to the 1950s what was understood as "Latin American literature" in the United States was varied, if not arbitrary.

During the years of its commitment to Latin America, Knopf had to overcome many obstacles. That the reading public and critics had little, if any, knowledge of the history and literary tradition of Latin America made it almost impossible to get New York reviewers to show interest in Spanish or Portuguese books in translation—in those rare reviews the commentaries were usually not favorable. It was not until 1962, with the appearance of *Gabriela, Clove and Cinnamon* by Jorge Amado, that a novel issued by Knopf became a bestseller both in New York and throughout the United States: "These earnings of yours"—Alfred Knopf wrote to Amado—"are probably greater than any Latin American novelist has ever received from a North American publisher." High costs and low sales figures were another problem Alfred Knopf had to face when it came to publishing translation of Latin American literature: "Brazil has meant to me a great deal during the past quarter of a century. . . . I have involved my firm in substantial financial losses in trying to promote its literature" (qtd. in Rostagno 33). Another problem for publishers was finding competent translators. Alfred Knopf was fortunate though: a pioneer in the profession, Harriet de Onís, "naturally" became his main translator, and subsequently played a central role in the decision-making process for the Latin American project. Some critics believe that she was the one who "decided which novels would be translated into English" (Rostagno 34). Whatever the extent of Harriet de Onís's power may have been, her monopoly over the translation market visibly declined by the mid-sixties, when a new generation of translators, professionally more sophisticated, emerged, mainly grouped around the Center for Inter-American Relations.

But, within this general context, Knopf's loyalty to Latin America was exceptional. Other U.S. publishers' interest in Latin America disappeared altogether as soon as the "good neighbor" enthusiasm declined, and when official and private funds essentially dried up. By the end of the fifties, the Cold War had shifted priorities, attention, and funds to Asian and Soviet studies, and no major university was undertaking any significant program with a Latin America focus. It was the bitter reception given to then Vice-President Richard Nixon on his 1958 trip to the region, and the successes of the Cuban insurgency commanded by Fidel Castro in 1959, that suddenly revived U.S. interest in Latin America. As in the pre–World War II days, the U.S. government generously supplemented various programs: funds were made available through the Alliance for Progress, Title VI of the National Defense Education Act, Fulbright grants, or the Peace Corps. As a direct result of federal and private support, many major U.S. universities experienced a boom in Latin American Studies.[3] The same enthusiasm was also directed at Latin American literature. Robert Mead wrote enthusiastically in 1978:

> Since about 1960, when the so-called boom in the "new Latin American literature" began to be visible, U.S. publishers, readers, and critics have all shown an unprecedented degree of interest in Latin American authors, . . . dozens of novels and poems were speedily translated, often by excellent hands; and English language critics began to evaluate these books in a variety of media: *Time, The New York Times, The New Yorker, The New York Review of Books, Atlantic, Harper's,* and so on. Courses in Latin American literature in translation were offered on many university campuses, and professors of literature who five or ten years before might have asked (and sometimes did) "Is there a Latin American literature" quickly became specialists in Borges or Cortázar in English. (2–3)

Judging from publishing statistics, it is easy to understand Mead's euphoria: before 1960 there were 146 Latin American titles published in translation in the United States, fifteen years later the number had almost tripled, reaching a total of 414.[4] In large part, the responsibility for this burgeoning interest in Latin America—unpredictable in the pioneering years of Knopf's "good neighbor" venture—was in the hands of the Inter-American Foundation for the Arts and the programs on translation undertaken by its successor, the Center for Inter-American Relations.

Founded in 1962 by Rodman Rockefeller, the Inter-American Foundation for the Arts (IAFA) was born to promote intellectual exchange between the Americas. The context within which IAFA was inscribed (still raw was the burning impact of Bay of Pigs invasion) smacked of Cold War ideology. The Rockefeller family it was associated with (Rodman was Nelson's oldest son, and like his father, he had a passion for Latin America)[5] and the emphasis placed on inter-American dialogue (a recycled idea from the Good Neighbor Policy) led many Latin Americans to the conclusion that the Foundation was the artistic wing of the Alliance for Progress. "Though never overtly stated, the intention behind IAFA was to counteract the impact of Cuba's cultural revolution on Latin intellectuals. IAFA's goal was to show U.S. interest in the art of its alienated neighbors, hoping thus to allay suspicion and rancor" (Rostagno 103).

To get the New York establishment involved with Latin American intellectuals, that is, to open a "dialogue" between the United States and Latin America, the Foundation organized symposia in four different locations over a period of five years—Bahamas (1962), Puerto Rico (1963), Chichén Itzá (1964), and Puerto Azul (1967). Following the format of a retreat rather than the formality of an academic congress (the stress was placed on "informality" but at the same time also on "seriousness") each symposium gathered about fifty participants in a remote and paradisiacal resort to discuss openly about topics that were no less open. Emir Rodríguez Monegal, a frequent delegate to the meetings, described the working sessions as "completamente abiertas" despite the fact that "en este tipo de simposio ninguno de los participantes puede atribuir luego públicamente a nadie una opinión determinada. Si uno quiere comunicar al mundo su opinión, es libre de hacerlo; pero no debe repetir lo que sus colegas dijeron con entera libertad" (1968a, 93). Paradoxically, the symposia were not meant to be forums for the production of ideas, nor spaces for voicing or proselytizing IAFA's politics. By far, socialization was their major (though not always openly stated) goal. The list of attendees—which, other than Latin Americans anxious to gain access to the U.S. cultural scene, included prominent American writers, accredited publishers, and key figures in the New York establishment—was also a map of the network soon to become the launching pad for the Latin American boom.[6]

But what the IAFA expected to emerge "naturally" from the meetings did not in fact emerge as hoped. The symposia's accomplishments were rather meager. They helped to create "a spirit of community" and "camaraderie" among the participants.[7] However, this sense of community proved to be only temporary—it evaporated soon after the literary gatherings came to an end. Less effective was the IAFA's impact on the New York publishing structure. During this period, only a few contracts were signed: Scribner's published Beatriz Guido's *End of a Day* (1966); Farrar, Straus and Giroux hired Alberto Girri as a Spanish consultant; New Directions issued Nicanor Parra's *Poems and Antipoems* (1967); and Harper and Row published Luis Harss's *Into the Mainstream* (1966). It was clear by the third gathering in 1965 that the symposia had lost their original significance and were instead becoming more "a jet set affair than an intellectual convention" (Rostagno 104). Under heavy attack by the Organization of American States, and aware that its cultural agency was having only a limited impact but unprepared to take over programs more extensive than the famed symposia, the IAFA was obliged to redefine its role, merging in 1967 to become known as the Center for Inter-American Relations.

Toward the end of 1966, Rodríguez Monegal received a formal request from the IAFA. José Guillermo Castillo asked him to recommend those contemporary novels the Uruguayan critic considered worthy of translation into English. This inquiry, or survey, was the first stage of a program, entitled "Publishing Latin American novels in the U.S.," whose final goal was "interesar a las casas editoriales norteamericanas en publicar tanto autores jóvenes como algunos de los más conocidos que no hayan sido publicados en este país anteriormente." After gathering the opinions of sixty Latin American critics and publishers, and deciding which of those recommended novels were "más interesantes," the Foundation planned to pay for the translation of the most representative passages and introduce them, along with synopses and critical opinions on each of the novels, to different U.S. publishers. If the "packet" were to be accepted, the IAFA would be able to cover "los costos restantes de la traducción o aumentaría la suma destinada a estos fines por la editorial, con el objeto de atraer los mejores traductores." The project, to be carried out in 1967, never was completed under the auspicies of the IAFA. Instead, it became the starting point for one of the most successful programs with which the Center for Inter-American Relations was identified for a long time.

José Guillermo Castillo, acting as director of the Center's Literature Program, redesigned his initial plan on translation: to make it more workable and effective he implemented some structural changes. The survey, for instance, was replaced by a selection committee comprising Rodríguez Monegal, Alexander Coleman, Alastair Reid, Gregory Rabassa, John Simon, and Mark Strand. To facilitate and guarantee the translation cycle, the Center recruited skilled translators and also helped to train new ones. On subsidy policies, subventions amounting to half or all of the translation fee—a figure ranging between $2,000 and $5,000—were made available to publishers to reduce editorial costs. In addition, the Center relied heavily on public relations: it seems that Castillo's charm won over not only reluctant editors but also famous reviewers, and "many of the boom novels [were contracted] over lunch and at cocktail parties" (Rostagno 108).

Ten years after being founded, the Center's literature program had already sponsored the translation of more than forty-five books, most of them written by "almost every major Latin American author to become known in this country," starting promisingly with Gabriel García Márquez's *One Hundred Years of Solitude* (1970). For its large-scale assault on the publishing market, the Center was acclaimed by many translators as a "model organization": "Despite the unquestioned quality of contemporary Latin American writing, it owes a significant measure of its positive response from American readers to the vision and innovative leadership of the Center for Inter-American Relations" (de Rosa 40). Well known and highly regarded by U.S. editors, by the mid-seventies the Center no longer needed to search New York for willing publishers since the editors themselves were by then calling on the Center for its advice and assistance. The euphoric reaction to this response is evident in the Center's annual report for 1975–76, where Gregory Rabassa stated: "the modest inscription" indicating the Center's assistance for translations is "a sort of hallmark for good literature" and also "an important ingredient in the [book's] success" (qtd. in de Rosa 39). In this role of clearing-house or "symbolic banker" for Latin American literature, in less than a decade the Center had become precisely the type of promotional, sponsored institution that David Rockefeller had in mind when he first established the Center's headquarters at 680 Park Avenue in 1967.

"With exasperating sluggishness, the effects of the boom in new Latin American literature are beginning to be felt even here in the United States"—this is how Rodríguez Monegal opened his introductory essay to *Review* '68, the Center's literary journal, which was a key component of its promotional machine.[8] As the journal's first director, Monegal bitterly complains about the delay ("the best critics had systematically refused to take any Latin American book seriously"), attributing it to "blind literary prejudice" (1968b, 3). For the Uruguayan critic, it was thus necessary to stimulate—as he states programmatically in his closing paragraphs—first, "knowledge of the new Latin American literature in the U. S.," "more and better English translations" and, finally, "the kind of criticism capable of orienting the American reader toward these translations" (1968b, 12–13). Read as a manifesto, the text self-imposes a mission that, in a broader sense and somewhat predictably, appropriates or duplicates the mission made public by the Center. What goes without saying, on the other hand, is what Rodríguez Monegal understands "Latin American literature to be and, more importantly, how it must be read." In other words, *Review*'s self-imposed mission was not only to help to improve the perception and appreciation of Latin American literature in the United States, but also to "produce" it: to produce its meaning and its value.[9]

To place Latin American literature into the U.S. mainstream—the English title of Luis Harss's *Los nuestros* as *Into the Mainstream* seemed quite an appropriate choice—*Review* needed to de-emphasize the social realism correlation that U.S. critics commonly associated with Latin American literature and to replace that image with one closer to what the New York cultural elite believed to be "contemporary" or "modern." Needless to say, Modernism as such—what in the Latin American context was consecrated as "the Boom"[10]—represented the tendency that historically better suited the aesthetic dictates of the Cold War, "not so much for what [modernist works] said or represented, but for what they did not say or represent, for their scrupulously maintained neutrality as purely self-referential languages of form, or what Guilbaut calls their 'political apoliticism'" (Larsen 773).[11] Controlling the production of value and reputation in the United States at the time, the modernist ideology created the standard of authority against which Latin American works and authors were judged and authorized. Its traces can easily be found as commonplaces in reviews, critical analyses, reading reports, or other spaces that formed part of the structure of value making. It appeared within the allusions to the unprecedented "universality" of Latin American authors—especially common in reviews of Borges's work: "Argentina has no national literature, but has produced a literary mind that is as mysterious and elusive as the fretted shadows on the moonlit grass" (37), as a *Time* reviewer commented on his *A Personal Anthology*. It also appeared within the repeated mention of a "revolutionary" language that had succeeded in breaking with traditional regionalism—a commonplace usually hidden behind the no less uncommon biological metaphor: "When one compares the experimental narratives of Fuentes in México or Cortázar in Argentina with the nationalistic or indigenista works of the recent past"—Robert Clements wrote for the *Saturday Review*—"it becomes clear that the Latin American novel has reached maturity" (quoted in Rodríguez Monegal 1968b, 11). Or it appeared within the abuse of what Bourdieu calls "privileged references" that bring legitimacy to Latin American authors by measuring them against such writers as Joyce, Faulkner, Dos Passos, Sterne (for instance, *Time*'s article announcing García Márquez's Nobel Prize was headlined, "Literature: A Latin Faulkner" ["Magic" 88]).

The Center can be considered a good proponent of the monopoly of art inherent in the system of literary patronage. As an institution, it selected the titles to be translated, paid the translation fees, provided the translators, guided its protégés through the New York publicity and editorial structure, worked to guarantee a successful reception and a good selling rate, and even paid airfare, if writers couldn't afford to travel to a promotional event. This way of doing things established a solid web of professional and nonprofessional loyalties that linked the Center to "its" writers, critics, and translators ("The art business, a trade in things that have no price," Bourdieu stated, "belongs to the class of practices in which the logic of the pre-capitalist economy lives on" [741]). In addition, the interdisciplinary nature of the services performed made the Center a versatile enterprise, able to intervene in different fields of cultural production. The publishing and promotion of Latin American books alternated with monthly offerings of poetry readings, panel discussions and guest lectures, and conferences co-sponsored with the P.E.N. American Center were followed by editorial advice offered to literary journals interested in launching special issues on Latin American literature (e.g., *Tri-Quarterly, Mundus Artium, Nimrod,* and the *Hudson Review*). The Center was able to maintain its multimedia activities due in large part to what Ronald Christ called "promotional alliances" with publishers such as Roger Straus of Farrar, Straus and Giroux, Cass Canfield of Harper and Row, and John MacRae of E.P. Dutton, or with New York reviewers and editors who became regular readers of the Center's protégés—figures such as novelist William Kennedy (*Quest* and *The New Republic*), editor Nona Balakian *(New York Times),* editor Robert Silver *(New York Review of Books),* and reviewers John Simon and Mark Strand.

Through this large-scale assault on different cultural fields (art, journalism, university presses, and similar institutions), and its political and economic connections,[12] the Center made a considerable impact in bringing Latin American literature into the cycle of consecration—especially during the first decade of its activities, which was a key period for Latin American canon formation in the United States. Perhaps the tidy control maintained over key areas of production and circulation was enough to suppress any criticism of the Center's monopolistic power or the enormous influence its decisions had on the translation market. Only minor expressions of discomfort are recorded in this respect, such as that of Donoso who, after plotting how to corner friendly reviewers for his books published in the United States, wrote in a letter to Ronald Christ: "Is it all repulsive conniving and intriguing and using people? I feel a bit guilty. But it's sink or swim this time and I'm scared. I have to play all my cards and play them right. I'm hoping for paperbacks of *Coronación, Hell Has No Limits* and *This Sunday* to come out of all this" (1976).

In sociology, a form of art that establishes its aesthetic meaning (and value) assisted by the intervention of agents or middlemen usually is called "art of dissemination" (García Canclini 91). The Center had, however, a broader impact as a cultural agent, not only because it consistently intervened in the circulation of Latin American literature in the United States, but also because it modified the existing relations between writers, brokers, and readers. The pyramidal structure imposed by its monopolistic patronage consequently diminished the relative autonomy of the cultural field, altering the horizontal bonds that traditionally have linked authors, critics, and public. That is why Latin American modernism in the United States mainly struggled in a "field of belief" (Bourdieu 74–111), battling for legitimation and value, rather than competing for a specific audience capable of materially appropriating its works. At this point, the continent's literature was in the stage of creating its reputation rather than selling books. With the exception of two titles— *Gabriela, Clove and Cinnamon* and *One Hundred Years of Solitude*— no Latin American book made the U.S. best-seller lists until the late seventies (Castro-Klarén and Campos). The boom then can be blamed— as in fact Angel Rama did blame it (1972)—for its *vedetismo* ("charisma" was conveniently exploited to make the boom author's names), its *exclusivismo* ("entering the field of literature," wrote Bourdieu, "is not so much like going into religion as getting into a select club" [77]), but certainly it cannot be accused of *best-sellerismo*, not at least in the United States.

Sensing the specific laws of the publishing market, its system of classification and the structured space of its discourses, the Center took advantage of "success" as a guarantee of Latin American literature's value ("in the ['bourgeois'] market, the successful get more successful" [Bourdieu 101]). It also restricted access to the U.S. cultural field, carefully selecting which authors to endorse or which works to translate (inflation of such endorsements would have lessened their value). In this context, Modernism worked as a politics of exclusion more than as a category of inclusion, and this explains why a number of recognized Latin American authors have not achieved full boom status in the United States—Miguel Angel Asturias, for instance, dismissed by *The New York Times* as "a Guatemalan windbag" who "inexplicably won the Nobel Prize" (Leonard 14), or Alejo Carpentier, whom Monegal considered "in no position to accept to be translated and published by an American house" (1966b), or Ernesto Sabato (to return to this essay's first example). Referring at length to what he viewed as Monegal's political criteria for reading and evaluating Latin American literature, and especially for determining the Latin American canon, Carlos Fuentes wrote in 1977:

> He leído con irritación su antología publicada chez Knopf [*The Borzoi Anthology of Latin American Literature*] . . . Por mucho que los estime, no creo que la novela latinoamericana sea un proceso destinado a culminar en Cabrera Infante y Sarduy. One must not confuse the kings with the jesters! . . . RM adopta la actitud de los "críticos" realistas-socialistas: la calidad literaria es definida por la posición política. Y en este caso, mientras más a la derecha, mejor escritor!! (1977)

Envisioning *Review* as a natural site for the determination and dissemination of value, Monegal was perhaps the most active "mover and shaker"—as Carl Brandt once called him (1969)—of the Center's Literature Program.[13] But he also was one of its least visible agents, following closely the law of the cultural field that dictates that any promotional exercise that, in the business world, takes the overt form of publicity must be euphemized in order to become symbolically more effective (Bourdieu 77). This same law of the market was wisely applied and respected by the Center, while, in the background, it was deciding what should be imported from Latin America and how it should be read.

It is difficult to imagine what Latin American literature in the United States might have looked like today without the Center's intervention and patronage throughout the sixties and early seventies. What would have happened, for instance, if the United States had followed the horizontal pattern of diffusion and consecration, such as the one followed in the French cultural field (Molloy; Bareiro Saguier)? As impossible as it is to know for sure, one can still speculate: arguably, the Latin American canon would likely be a more heterogeneous, diverse, and more open body of texts (and authors). It would also be a more unstable, and perhaps even more flexible canon than it actually has turned out to be for the U.S. readership. But, whatever its forms are, or might have been, it is clear that those forces intervening at the time were not just literary, but also political and economic, re-invoking the central role of the Cold

War and the Center for Inter-American Relations in producing what is now—rightly or wrongly, accurately or not—called "Latin American literature" in the United States.

NOTES

1. In a *Time* review of Faustino González-Aller's *Niña Huanca*, R. Z. Sheppard repeated almost the same statement: "we would do anything for Latin America except read about it" (105).

2. For more details on Alfred Knopf's commitment to literature in translation, see Knopf, Rostagno, and Sayers Peden.

3. Luso-Brazilian Programs were initiated in 1959–1960 at New York University and the University of Wisconsin, followed in 1961 by Latin American graduate programs at UCLA, Columbia, Florida, Texas, Tulane, Wisconsin, Yale, Cornell, Illinois, NYU, and Stanford.

4. For details on titles and bibliography, see Shaw's *Latin American Literature in English Translation*.

5. See Kutz and Berman.

6. Among the Latin American participants in the IAFA's symposia were Carlos Fuentes, José Donoso, Nicanor Parra, Juan Rulfo, Emir Rodríguez Monegal, Marta Traba, Beatriz Guido, Leopoldo Torre Nilsson, and Gustavo Sáinz. The U.S. delegation was no less diverse: it included Edward Albee, William Styron, Oscar Lewis, Robert Lowell, and Arthur Miller, among the writers; while Alfred Knopf, James Laughlin (New Directions), Roger Klein (Harper and Row), Tad Szulc *(New York Times)*, Richard Rovere *(New Yorker)*, Jack Newfield *(Village Voice)*, Jason Epstein *(New York Times Review of Books)* represented the "New York establishment," as Coser once called the group of the most influential literary brokers based in New York.

7. In his memoirs, Donoso recalled some moments where the illusion of belonging to the same inter-American *patria* was probably shared by many Latin Americans during the symposia: "un grupo armaba un alboroto tremendo en el corredor del hotel jugando trivia . . . : quién hizo el papel de Prissy en *Lo que el viento se llevó*, quién fue el iluminador de *Philadelphia Story*, . . . poder contestar a algunas de estas cosas totalmente absurdas asentó de cierta manera mi sensación de pertenecer a una generación internacional y contemporánea— uruguayos y yanquis, peruanos y mexicanos—, ya que participábamos todos de los mismos mitos cosmopolitas a cuyos personajes aludíamos, y que para nuestra generación estos mitos triviales . . . tenían una vigencia por lo menos tan grande como los heroicos mitos nacionales" (1983, 77–78).

8. A key component of the Center's promotional machine, *Review* was first launched as a yearly collection of reprinted reviews of Latin American books—"a re-view of reviews"—to become, under Ronald Christ's direction (1970–1979), "a full-fledged literary journal." During this second period, which was the Center's most effective one in establishing a Latin American literary canon in the United States, the journal's editors discontinued the practice of

reprinting material and initiated new sections: "Focus" (with in-depth material on a single work or author), "Texts" (a section featuring works by lesser-known Latin American writers), and "Topics" (a section on translation, film, theater, and photography).

9. *Mundo Nuevo* was, in more than one sense, *Review*'s closest model. Paraphrasing Monegal, it can be said that the New York journal on Latin America literature was a reborn version of *Mundo Nuevo* but directed to an English-speaking audience (Rodríguez Moncgal 1984, 34). Correlations can easily be established if we compare both journals' literary ideologies, or the list of the authors canonized, and novels endorsed. Emir Rodríguez Monegal, who acted as *Review*'s first director and remained as the publication's advisor till 1977, seems to be the natural link behind such continuities. For details on *Mundo Nuevo,* see Mudrovcic (1997).

10. Gerald Martin has recently considered the "boom" not only as the "product of the fiction that had gone before" but also as the "climax and con-summation of Latin American Modernism" (239).

11. Here Larsen refers to Serge Guilbaut's *How New York Stole the Idea of Modern Art. Abstract Expressionism, Freedom, and the Cold War* (1983).

12. David Rockefeller's venture was seconded by William D. Rogers, the Center's first president and former coordinator of the Alliance for Progress, William MacLeish, the executive director and former assistant secretary of state for Inter-American affairs under Franklin D. Roosevelt, and by board members René D'Harnoncourt, director at the time of the Museum of Modern Art, and Arthur O. Sulzberger, publisher of the *New York Times* (Rostagno 106–107).

13. From its beginnings in 1968, Rodríguez Monegal's voice was dominant in *Review* until his controversial resignation in 1977. Monegal's campaign questioning Ronald Christ's trip to Pinochet's Chile unleashed a massive resignation of collaborators and supporters, which eventually led to Christ's resignation in 1979, and to a redefinition of the Center's role and its journal. For details, see *Review*'s Archives and Emir Rodríguez Monegal's Papers at the Princeton University Library.

WORKS CITED

Bareiro Saguier, Rubén. "La literatura latinoamericana en Francia." *Mundo Nuevo* 30 (1969): 52–66.

Berman, Edward H. *The Influence of the Carnegie, Ford, and Rockefeller Foundations on American Foreign Policy: The Ideology of Philanthropy.* Albany: SUNY P, 1983.

Bourdieu, Pierre. *The Field of Cultural Production.* New York: Columbia U P, 1993.

Brandt, Carl D. "Letter to José Donoso." 2 Apr. 1973. *José Donoso's Papers.* The Princeton University Library, Princeton.

———. "Letter to José Donoso." 22 Oct. 1969. *José Donoso's Papers.* The Princeton University Library, Princeton.

Castillo, José Guillermo. "Letter to Emir Rodríguez Monegal." 28 Nov. 1966. *Emir Rodríguez Monegal's Papers*. The Princeton University Library, Princeton.

Castro-Klarén, Sara, and Héctor Campos. "Traducciones, Tirajes, Ventas y Estrella: El 'Boom.'" *Ideologies and Literature* 17 (1983): 319–38.

Cline, Howard F. "The Latin American Studies Association: A Summary Survey with Appendix." *Latin American Research Review* 2.1 (1966): 57–79.

Christ, Ronald. "On Not Reviewing Translations: A Critical Exchange." *Translation Review* 9 (1982): 16–23.

de Rosa, Elaine. "Center for Inter-American Relations: A Decade of Translation Service." *Translation Review* 2 (1978): 37–40.

Donoso, José. "Letter to Ronald Christ." 11 Aug. 1976. *José Donoso's Papers*. The Princeton University Library, Princeton.

———. *Historia personal del "Boom."* Barcelona: Seix Barral, 1983.

Fuentes, Carlos. "Letter to José Donoso." 11 Oct. 1977. *José Donoso's Papers*. The Princeton University Library, Princeton.

García Canclini, Néstor. *Culturas híbridas. Estrategias para entrar y salir de la modernidad*. Mexico City: Grijalbo, 1989.

Knopf, Alfred A. *Publishing Then and Now. 1912–1964*. New York: The New York Public Library, 1964.

Kutz, Myer. *Rockefeller Power*. New York: Simon and Schuster, 1974.

Larsen, Neil. "The 'Boom' Novel and the Cold War in Latin America." *Modern Fiction Studies* 38.3 (1992): 771–84.

"Magic, Matter, and Money." *Time*, 1 Nov. 1982: 82.

Martin, Gerald. *Journeys through the Labyrinth: Latin American Fiction in the Twentieth Century*. London: Verso, 1989.

McDowell, Edwin. "Publishing: A Novel's Long Trek Into English." *New York Times* 24 July 1981: 24.

Mead, Robert G. "After the Boom." *Américas* 30.4 (1978): 2–8.

Molloy, Sylvia. *La diffusion de la littérature Hispano-Américaine en France au Xxe Siècle*. Paris: Presses Universitaires de France, 1972.

Mudrovcic, María Eugenia. *Mundo Nuevo: Cultura y Guerra Fría en la década del 60*. Rosario: Beatriz Viterbo, 1997.

Rama, Angel. "Angel Rama tira la piedra . . ." *Zona Franca* 14 (1972): 15–17.

———. "Carta a *Zona Franca*." *Zona Franca* 16 (1972): 10–15.

Rev. of *A Personal Anthology*, by Jorge Luis Borges. *Time* 24 Mar. 1967. Reprinted in *Review '68*: 37–38.

Rodríguez Monegal, Emir. "Letter to Inés de Torres Kinnell (Charles Scribner's Sons)." 21 Feb. 1966a. Emir Rodríguez Monegal's Papers. The Princeton University Library, Princeton.

———. "Letter to Seymour Lawrence." 14 Oct. 1966b. *Emir Rodríguez Monegal's Papers*. The Princeton University Library, Princeton.

———. "Diálogo en Puerto Azul." *Mundo Nuevo* 20 (1968a): 93–95.

————. "The New Latin American Literature in the USA." *Review '68* (1968b): 3–13.

————. "The Boom: A Retrospective." Interview by Alfred J. MacAdam. *Review* 33 (1968): 27–33.

Rostagno, Irene. *Searching for Recognition. The Promotion of Latin American Literature in the United States.* Westport: Greenwood Press, 1997.

Sayers Peden, Margaret. "Knopf, Knopf: Who's There?" *Translation Review* 50 (1996): 27–30.

Shaw, Bradley A. *Latin American Literature in English Translation. An Annotated Bibliography.* New York: NY U P, 1976.

How the West Was Won:
Translations of Spanish American Fiction in Europe and the United States

Maarten Steenmeijer

INTRODUCTION

There are many reasons to criticize the still widely used term *boom,* coined in the sixties to cover a very complicated, multifaceted phenomenon. The main problem is that it has at least two frames of reference: it refers to the *production* and to the *reception* of Spanish American literature (in particular, the novel). But even within these frames the term is susceptible to confusion. Does, for example, the production exclusively bear on works published for the first time in the sixties, such as Vargas Llosa's *La ciudad y los perros* (The Time of the Hero), Carlos Fuentes's *La muerte de Artemio Cruz* (The Death of Artemio Cruz), Julio Cortázar's *Rayuela* (Hopscotch) and Gabriel García Márquez's *Cien años de soledad* (One Hundred Years of Solitude)? Or does it also involve works published in the preceding decades that were only "discovered" and distributed on a wide scale in the sixties (the stories of Borges and Cortázar; Carpentier's *Los pasos perdidos* (The Lost Steps); Asturias's *El señor presidente*)? As for the production, does the term exclusively apply to Spanish originals or also to translations? As for the reception, it is not clear whether the term should only be applied to the sudden increase in interest in contemporary Spanish American literature and its subsequent overnight celebrity, or if it covers as well intrinsic literary qualities and even has value as a period concept, as some scholars seem to assume.

Is this confusion reason enough to disqualify the term and to decide not to use it at all? I think one should disapprove of its use in the field of literary history, because it does not refer to intrinsic literary qualities and therefore by definition cannot be a period concept. Also, one should be aware of the reproachable tendency to reduce the *corpus* of this complicated phenomenon to the work of a small group of writers (Julio Cortázar, Carlos Fuentes, Gabriel García Márquez, Mario Vargas Llosa) and to a very specific period of time (1960–1970 or, as also has been suggested, 1965–1972). Instead, the diversity of the *boom* should be taken more into consideration. In fact, there were many *booms*. Nevertheless, the evocative power of the very term makes it suitable to refer to what was indeed a boom: the "explosively" increasing interest in Spanish American literature in the Spanish-speaking world, in Europe, and in the United States of America. It was a striking phenomenon, for in a relatively short period Spanish American literature gained sufficient prestige to be considered world literature, in spite of the weak economic position of the subcontinent, in spite of the persistent prejudices about its people and its culture, and in spite of the language barriers.

It is in this rather strict sense that I will use the term in this article, in which I propose to analyze succinctly how the introduction and establishment of this virtually unknown literature in the European and American book market took place. Where and how did it start? Where and how did it continue? Which countries set the trend and which ones followed in their footsteps? On the basis of these questions, this article studies the reception of translated Spanish American literature in Europe and the United States of America in its most spectacular, if not most important phase: the period of the introduction of the *nueva novela*. In other words, the period of the *boom*. It proposes to do so on a quantitative basis, comparing systematically the years of publications of significant translations and, on the basis of the results of this comparative analysis, examining the validity of the assumptions that have been made about the phenomenon.

THE BEGINNING

In 1951 the prestigious French publishing house Gallimard initiated "La Croix du Sud," a collection dedicated exclusively to Ibero-American literature, founded and directed by Roger Caillois. It was a courageous and important project, for it is, to my knowledge, the first systematic publishing attempt to introduce Spanish American literature to a reading public outside the Spanish-speaking world. In one sense, "La Croix du Sud" owes much to coincidence. In 1939, Roger Caillois had been invited to Buenos Aires to give a series of lectures on mythology. During his visit, he was surprised by the outbreak of the war and only returned to France following a five-year exile. In that period, he learned Spanish, became a regular contributor of the epochal review *Sur*, fell in love with its founder Victoria Ocampo and—what is most relevant here—became passionately acquainted with Spanish American literature. In the fourteenth issue of *Lettres Françaises* (October 1944)—the magazine edited by Caillois in Buenos Aires during World War II under the patronage of *Sur*—he published his versions of "La lotería en Babilonia" (The Lottery in Babylonia) and "La biblioteca de Babel" (The Library of Babel), the first French translations of Borges's stories. Borges was also the first writer to appear in "La Croix du Sud": *Fictions* was published in 1952 (Bareiro Saguier 55–56; Molloy 178–81; King 69 and 101).

In another sense, though, it was anything but a coincidence that this publishing initiative was taken in France, where the seeds of interest in Spanish American literature had already been sowed around the turn of the century, as Sylvia Molloy convincingly showed in her reception study *La diffusion de la littérature hispano-américaine en France au XXe siècle*. Molloy distinguishes three phases: "La découverte" (1900–1920), "Les débuts d'un dialogue" (1920–1940) and "Le dialogue et l'échange" (1940–). In other words, long before the *boom*, France had already "discovered" Spanish American literature. The list of titles included in "La Croix du Sud" during the first decade of its existence is a marked sign of this relatively early acquaintance with Spanish American literature: besides introducing the work of Jorge Luis Borges, Alejo Carpentier, Juan Rulfo, and Ernesto Sabato, the collection included works of authors who wrote in the traditional style that dominated Spanish American prose before the new novel changed the scene: Ciro Alegría, Gabriel Casaccia, Carlos Luis Fallas, Rómulo Gallegos, Ricardo Güiraldes, Martín Luis Guzmán, Mario Monteforte Toledo, Adalberto Ortiz, Miguel Otero Silva. Without denying the pioneering character of "La Croix du Sud" (the inclusion of Borges et al.) one cannot but conclude that in the fifties it was above all the realist vein of the *novela de la tierra* that gave "La Croix du Sud" its identity.

In this respect, "La Croix du Sud" was only innovative quantitatively, not qualitatively, for various *novelas de la tierra* had already been translated and published in the preceding decades (though not as methodically as in the fifties). It should be added that France was not the only country where translations of the *novela de la tierra* were published in the decades preceding the *boom*. The same holds for Germany, Italy, the United States and—to a lesser degree—England, as a random check concerning the publication of the translations of six classic *novelas de la tierra* shows:

	France	Germ.[1]	Italy	USA	Eng.
El mundo es ancho y ajeno (1941) (Ciro Alegría)	1946	1945	1962	1941	1942
Los de abajo (1916) (Mariano Azuela)	1930	1930	1945	1929	1930
Doña Bárbara (1929) (Rómulo Gallegos)	1943	1952	1946	1931	—
Don Segundo Sombra (1926) (Ricardo Güiraldes)	1932	1934	1940	1935	1935

Huasipungo (1934)	1938	1955	1961	1964	1962
(Jorge Icaza)					
La vorágine (1924)	1934	1934	1941	1935	—
(José Eustasio Rivera)					

According to this table, France was the first to publish the *novela de la tierra,* followed closely by the United States. In spite of this, it seems that before the *boom* "for the common reader . . . [Latin American] literature was not even a mystery nor *terra incognita*—it was an indifferent void" (Rodríguez Monegal 1969, 3). This table confirms that in the thirties there was a first attempt to inspire interest in Latin American literature in Germany (Gewecke 542–49) and that until the sixties the production of translations of Spanish American literature was rather modest in Italy.

ITINERARIES

There is broad consensus about the pioneering role of France in establishing the itinerary of the *nueva novela* (see, for example, Molloy 183; Luchting 82; Bellini 7; Gewecke 556; Wiese 116–17). The favorable conditions that made possible this privileged position include familiarity with Spanish American literature acquired in the course of this century, modest yet unique in Europe; direct contacts between writers and editors (Roger Caillois's acquaintance with the *Sur* group; contacts developed by the writers themselves, many of whom lived in Paris for a longer or shorter period); the availability of expert and enterprising translators (Couffon 224); and last but not least the relatively close and intensive contacts with the leading literary circles of Barcelona, where the legendary literary agent Carmen Balcells (the godmother of the *boom*) displayed amazing skill in publicizing the new Spanish American literature in and outside the Spanish-speaking world, and where publishing house Seix Barral initiated the epochal Premio Biblioteca Breve in 1962[2] and published many classics of the *nueva novela* in the following years, distributing them all over the Spanish-speaking world. It is hardly surprising, then, that in the sixties Barcelona earned the epithet of "capital of Spanish America."

Given their important position in the international book market, it is only fair to suppose that the United States and England also played a mediating role. It is important to add, though, that this role has been mainly attributed to the United States (Gewecke 556; Steenmeijer 1989, 87; Wiese 117). Curiously enough, however, these and similar statements about the translation *boom* have not been done on the basis of a systematic comparison but rather off the cuff or, at best, on the basis of loose facts. It would be no luxury, then, to verify these statements, proceeding in a more systematic way. It should be stressed that the subject is far too complicated to be treated exhaustively here. In fact, the elementary nature of the data presented below forces us to consider the conclusions to be no more than tentative.

The following comparative analysis concerns six countries. Besides the five countries already mentioned—United States, England, France, Germany, and Italy—I have included Holland. This country is an interesting case because of the smaller scale of its book market, its tendency to follow international trends and the fact that Spanish American literature was as good as nonexistent here before the *nueva novela* made its appearance, due to the lack of direct contacts with Spanish American literature and its very modest presence, if not absence in the academic curricula.

My analysis is restricted to ten representative authors, for the sake of clarity and pragmatism (exhaustive bibliographies are only available for some national languages). These sample cases share the following two qualities: first, they acquired an international reputation in the fifties and the sixties and, secondly, their work was translated in all six countries. They include José Maria Arguedas, Miguel Angel Asturias, Jorge Luis Borges, Alejo Carpentier, Julio Cortázar, José Donoso, Carlos Fuentes, Gabriel García Márquez, Juan Rulfo, and Mario Vargas Llosa.

The first comparison concerns the publication of the first translations of these authors in each of the countries mentioned above. In each of the ten resulting rankings the country that first published a translation of the author in question occupies the first place and gets six points; the country that follows receives five points, and so on. On the basis of these ten rankings the following table can be compiled:

1. France (53 points)
2. Italy (47 points)
3. Germany[3] (44 points)
4. United States (41 points)
5. England (39 points)
6. Holland (34 points)

According to this table, France is in fact the country where the *boom* of translations emerged. But not across the board, as can be deduced from the relatively modest difference in points. There is, in fact, a conspicuous diversity: in four rankings France occupies the first place; Germany in two, just as the United States (in one case together with England); Italy leads in one case and so does Holland. To be more specific: France was the first country to translate Asturias (*Leyendas de Guatemala* [Legends of Guatemala] 1932[4]), Borges (*Ficciones* [Fictions] 1952),

Cortázar (*Los premios* [The Prizes] 1961), and García Márquez (*El coronel no tiene quien le escriba* [No One Writes to the Coronel] 1963); Arguedas (*Los ríos profundos* [Deep Rivers] 1965) and Rulfo (*Pedro Páramo* 1958) made their first appearance in Germany; Fuentes (*La región más transparente* [Where the Air is Clear] 1960) in the United States; Donoso (*Coronación* [Coronation] 1965) in England and the United States; Carpentier in Italy (*Los pasos perdidos* [The Lost Steps] 1953); and Vargas Llosa (*La ciudad y los perros* [The Time of the Hero] 1964) in Holland.

Another relevant factor that should be taken into consideration is the time span between the publication of the original and the publication of the translation. The ranking of the sum of the resulting figures show almost the same differences between the six countries (only England and the United States have changed places):

1. France (44 years)
2. Italy (45 years)
3. Germany (59 years)
4. England (85 years)
5. United States (89 years)
6. Holland (98 years)

To check these results I have analyzed the same two samples on the basis of another comparison: the *magnum opus* of each of the ten selected authors. The titles, followed by the year of publication of the Spanish version, include Arguedas's *Los ríos profundos* (1958); Asturias's *El señor presidente* (1946); Borges's *Ficciones* (1944); Carpentier's *Los pasos perdidos* (1953); Cortázar's *Rayuela* (1963); Donoso's *El obsceno pájaro de la noche* [The Obscene Bird of the Night] (1970); Fuentes's *La muerte de Artemio Cruz* (1962); García Márquez's *Cien años de soledad* (1967); Rulfo's *Pedro Páramo* (1955); Vargas Llosa's *La casa verde* [The Green House] (1965). The comparison of the years of publication results in the following ranking:

1. France (52 points)
2. Italy (48 points)
3. Germany/United States (45 points)
4. England (43 points)
5. Holland (27 points)

Comparing the time spans between the years of publication of the originals and the years of publication of the translations of the titles mentioned above results in the same ranking:

1. France (43 years)
2. Italy (59 years)
3. Germany/United States (77 years)
4. England (79 years)
5. Holland (117 years)

The minimal differences between these four rankings suggest the following conclusions:

- France is, in the main, the country where new Spanish American literature was published first.

- The United States occupies a less significant position than expected. According to these rankings, this country was, generally speaking, slower to introduce the *nueva novela* than Italy and, probably, Germany.

- There are scarcely any differences between England and the United States. The explanation is obvious: the two countries publish the same translations. The similar positions in the rankings, however, obscure the leading position of the United States in the English-speaking world, because most translations were produced in the United States. This explains the slightly lower ranking of England in most of the rankings: not all translations were published simultaneously in the United States and England.

- The state of affairs in Germany turns out to be much more favorable than could be expected based on what has been documented on the subject thus far. In no other country has the reception of Latin American literature been studied as extensively as in Germany. And in no other country has this been done in such a (self-)accusatory tone (see, for example, Menén Desleal, Reichardt, Siebenmann 1972, Lorenz, Broyles, Wiese, Brown). Even as late as 1977 a German scholar wrote disparagingly about the "*Nichtexistenz lateinamerikanischer Literatur* in den Ländern deutscher Sprache" (Lorenz 100). In 1976 Hans Magnus Enzensberger dubbed the Germans the "last discoverers of Latin America" (Wiese 115). Maybe these severe reactions are justified as far as reception (by the German reading public and, possibly, the critics) is concerned, despite the unnecessarily harsh responsibility attributed to the publishing houses. Wiese even pretends that Germany lagged behind Holland (Wiese 118). My samples indicate, however, that Holland was far behind the other five selected countries, including Germany, which, in fact, was one of the first countries to publish new Spanish American fiction (see also Siebenmann 1972, 88; Steenmeijer 1989, 84–90).

The aforementioned examples have permitted us to determine the order in which new Spanish American fiction "conquered" the Western world. Obviously, this order doesn't necessarily imply that the countries ranked lower followed in the footsteps of the countries that lead. In theory, all countries might have "imported" the *nueva novela* independently. However, secondary sources indicate that this is very unlikely and that France and the United States played a leading role (Molloy 183; Luchting 82; Bellini 7; Gewecke 556; Wiese 116–17). Authors and works established in these two countries stood a better chance of being translated and published in Italy, Germany, England, and Holland than authors that had not been published yet in these two countries.

The leading role attributed to France is not contradicted by these case studies. In Italy and Germany, however, the role of the United States seems to have been far less important than one would have expected: most of the titles were published there before they were in the United States. Furthermore, the above rankings suggest it is not improbable that the United States set the trend for England and Holland.

In order to gain more insight in the process of trendsetting, one could take a closer look at the first translated work of the ten selected authors in each country comparing their years of publication with those in the other five countries. The choice for first translations—that is, of a work of an as yet unknown author—is not accidental, for in this case it is much more probable that a publishing house relies on decisions made by foreign colleagues with respect to this writer than in the case of a writer already published in the receiving country.

The results of this comparison are worthy of further analysis. As we have already seen, France was the first country to publish translations of works by Asturias, Borges, Cortázar, and García Márquez. Futhermore, although France was not the first to publish Carpentier (Italy: *Los pasos perdidos,* 1953), it was the first to publish a translation of *El reino de este mundo* (The Kingdom of This World) (1955). But in the remaining cases (50 percent) France was not a trendsetter: the works with which Arguedas, Donoso, Fuentes, Rulfo, and Vargas Llosa made their first appearance in France had already been published in Germany, United States, Germany, and Holland, respectively.

Although France does not provide an overarching model, there is reason enough to suppose that it was the most important one. See for example the following table, which gives a survey per country of the number of times that a first translation had already been published in one of more of the other five countries:

	Fr.	It.	Ge.	USA	Eng.	Hol.	Total
France	—	1	2	2	—	1	6
Italy	4	—	3	3	2	1	13
Germany	5	4	—	2	2	1	14
USA	6	4	4	—	1	1	16

England	7	5	5	1	—	1	19
Holland	5	5	7	6	5	—	28
Total	27	19	21	14	10	5	

France stands out in two respects: more than any other country, it had already published a significant number of the first translations of the other five countries (compare the figures in the first two vertical columns). This holds for all the countries together (see the sum totals in the last horizontal column) and for each individual country, except Holland, where France comes after Germany and the United States and shares the third position with England and Italy. Furthermore, France may not have been the leading country in six cases (see the first horizontal column), but in all of them it followed quickly after the leading countries (hence the low figures in the first horizontal column).

Another important conclusion that can be drawn from this table is that, in fact, Germany's declared culpability in ignoring literature from Spanish America is unjustified, at least insofar as its *production* is concerned. Generally speaking, the *nueva novela* wasn't introduced here later than in Italy, the United States, and England.

The data presented here induce us to call into question certain established notions about the boom and to adjust them. Generally speaking, France was in fact the first country to embrace the *nueva novela* and could, therefore, serve as an important model for other Western countries (the United States, England, Italy, Germany, Holland and, probably, several other countries in Western Europe). It is equally true, though, that France was not an omnipresent trendsetter. Contrary to what has generally been assumed in Germany and Italy, in a considerable number of cases these two countries took an independent course. The only country that can be said to have been a true follower of trends is Holland.[5] Surprisingly enough, in the United States the new narrative from Spanish America was, broadly speaking, introduced somewhat later than in Italy and, probably, Germany. Therefore, the mediating role of the United States in the boom in translations must have been less substantial than has generally been assumed.[6]

An examination of publishing and translation trends is of interest for what it suggests not only about the circulation of Latin American literature but also about the reception patterns of that literature in the various countries. Clearly the French example just mentioned suggests that the experimental nature of the new literature could be integrated more smoothly there because of the experimental aesthetic already established. The more commercial nature of publishing in the United States seems to have waited for a new product to arrive, namely, spearheaded by García Márquez's *One Hundred Years of Solitude* (see Mudrovcic in this collection). Critics have often lamented the U.S. publishing expectations of Latin American writers to solely produce novels in the magic realist mode. The reception of the new Latin American novel in Europe and the United States is not a single unified story, but a series of microhistories that reflect the reading public, cultural institutions, and the initiative of individual translators, promoters, and agents.

NOTES

1. Including translations published in Switzerland.

2. Its first winner was a young, unknown writer who was soon to become one of the central writers of the *boom,* Mario Vargas Llosa, who had competed with his first novel, *La ciudad y los perros.*

3. In view of the different spheres of influence of the two Germanies and in view of the theme of this article, I leave East Germany aside.

4. Strictly speaking, *Leyendas de Guatemala* is no *nueva novela.* But even if we exclude this book, France still was the first country to publish Asturias (the French version of *El señor presidente* appeared in 1952).

5. In the few cases that Dutch publishers set the trend, the response was anything but stimulating, as the reception of the Dutch translation of *La ciudad y los perros* shows. Holland was the first country in the world to publish a translation of Vargas Llosa's first novel (only one year after the publication of the Spanish original). Its reception was poor (the book was scarcely reviewed, and not in very positive terms) so that it is hardly surprising that Vargas Llosa's second novel (*La casa verde,* 1966) was not translated in the sixties. Only when the *boom* finally reached Holland (with the publication of the Dutch version of *Cien años de soledad* in 1972) did Vargas Llosa get a second chance. Since then, he has been one of the most translated and most appreciated Spanish American authors in Holland. The reception of García Márquez's work followed a similar course (Steenmeijer 1989, 118–21).

6. For a succinct analysis of the itinerary of the post-*boom,* see Steenmeijer 1990, 114–17.

WORKS CITED

Bareiro Saguier, Rubén. "La literatura latinoamericana en Francia." *Mundo Nuevo* 30 (1968): 52–66.

Bellini, Giuseppe. "Bibliografia dell'ispanoamericanismo italiano: le traduzioni." *Estratto da Rassegna Iberistica* 6 (1979).

Brown, Meg H. *The Reception of Spanish American Fiction in West Germany 1981–1991. A Study of Best Sellers.* Tübingen: Max Niemeyer, 1994.

Broyles, Yolanda Julia. *The German Response to Latin American Literature and the Reception of Jorge Luis Borges and Pablo Neruda.* Heidelberg: Carl Winter Universitätsverlag, 1981.

Castro-Klarén, Sara, and Héctor Campos. "Traducciones, Tirajes, Ventas y Estrellas: El 'Boom.'" *Ideologies & Literature* 4.17 (1983): 319–38.

Couffon, Claude. "La literatura hispanoamericana vista desde Francia." In Jorge Enrique Adoum et al., *Panorama de la actual literatura latinoamericana*. Havana: Casa de las Américas, 1969. 222–28.

Donoso, José. *Historia personal del "boom."* Barcelona: Seix Barral, 1983.

Gewecke, Frauke. "Fremde und Verweigerung. Zur frühen Rezeption lateinamerikanischer Literatur im deutschen Sprachraum." *Jahrbuch für Geschichte von Staat, Wirtschaft und Gesellschaft Lateinamerikas* 25 (1988): 535–62.

King, John. *Sur. A study of the Argentine literary journal and its role in the development of a culture, 1931–1970*. Cambridge: Cambridge University Press, 1986.

Lorenz, Günter W. "Zur Krise der Rezeption lateinamerikanischer Literatur in den Ländern deutscher Sprache." *Zeitschrift für Kulturaustausch* 24.4 (1974): 98–100.

Luchting, Wolfgang A. "Die lateinamerikanische Literatur und ihre deutschsprachigen Verleger." *Zeitschrift für Kulturaustausch* 27.1 (1977): 81–89.

Menén Desleal, Alvaro. "La literatura latinoamericana en los países de habla alemana." *Mundo Nuevo 55* (1971): 17–30.

Molloy, Sylvia. *La Diffusion de la littérature hispano-américaine en France au XXe siècle*. Paris: Presses Universitaires de France, 1972.

Rama, Angel, ed. *Más allá del boom: literatura y mercado*. Buenos Aires: Folios, 1984.

Reichardt, Dieter. *Lateinamerikanische Autoren. Literaturlexikon und Bibliographie der deutschen Übersetzungen*. Tübingen/Basel: Erdman, 1972.

Rodríguez Monegal, Emir. "The New Latin American Literature in the USA." *Review* 68 (1969): 3–13.

———. *El boom de la novela latinoamericana*. Caracas: Tiempo Nuevo, 1972.

Schrader, Ludwig, ed. *Von Góngora bis Nicolás Guillén. Spanische und lateinamerikanische Literatur in deutscher Übersetzung. Erfahrungen und Perspektiven*. Tübingen: Gunter Narr, 1993.

Siebenmann, Gustav. *Die neuere Literatur Lateinamerikas und ihre Rezeption im deutschen Sprachraum*. Berlin: Colloquium Verlag, 1972.

———. "Sind die Deutschen die letzten Entdecker Amerikas? Zur Rezeption der lateinamerikanischen Literaturen." In *Deutsche in Lateinamerika. Lateinamerika in Deutschland*. Ed. Karl Kohut, Dietrich Briesemeister, and Gustav Siebenmann. Frankfurt am Main: Vervuert, 1996. 297–314.

———, and Donatella Casetti. *Bibliographie der aus dem Spanischen, Portugiesischen und Katalanischen ins Deutsche übersetzten Literatur*. Tübingen: Max Niemeyer, 1985.

Steenmeijer, Maarten. *Bibliografía de las traducciones de la literatura española e hispanoamericana al holandés 1946–1990*. Tübingen: Max Niemeyer, 1991.

────. "El itinerario de la literatura hispanoamericana por el Occidente." *Iberoromania* 32 (1990): 110–18.

────. *De Spaanse en Spaans-Amerikaanse literatuur in Nederland 1946–1985.* Muiderberg: Coutinho, 1989.

Wiese, Claudia. *Die hispanoamerikanischen* Boom-*Romane in Deutschland. Literaturvermittlung, Buchmarkt und Rezeption.* Frankfurt am Main: Vervuert, 1992.

Wilson, Jason. *An A to Z of Modern Latin American Literature in English Translation.* London: Institute of Latin American Studies, 1989.

Translating García Márquez,
or, The Impossible Dream

Gerald Martin

Many Hispanists may remember when *Don Quixote* was turned into *Man of La Mancha* and "The Impossible Dream," impossible to forget, became the protagonist's signature tune. A seventeenth-century Spanish dreamer's illusions were thus corrected beyond his own author's strictures and he was recuperated for the more democratic delusions of the American Dream. One might say that he no longer did it his way. Something similar to Don Quixote's fate has befallen the work of Gabriel García Márquez, the "Colombian Cervantes."

In his case the transition has not been between elite and popular culture—his own work embodies the *transaction* between the two—but otherwise follows the well-worn but always difficult road between the "Latin" and "Anglo-Saxon" worlds, and between the Spanish and English languages. To what extent the resultant mishaps are inevitable or unavoidable is an interesting question though certainly not a new one. Undoubtedly some level of unavoidableness is inevitable. To illustrate my points I will confine the analysis to titles and to beginnings and endings.

Let us begin, then, with García Márquez's titles. No translation into English can produce the subliminal effect of those titles because English cannot reproduce the contrast between masculine and feminine gender, which is such a structuring feature of the Spanish language and, perhaps, of the "Hispanic" mentality. When we examine the whole run of García Márquez's narrative titles the effect is particularly striking because we seem to see the gradual escape from—or domination of—some female world that seems to have existed ab initio in his writerly consciousness. His first project, never finished, was a long family saga called *La casa;* his first completed novel was *La hojarasca* (1955), followed by *La mala hora* (1962) and by the pivotal story *Los funerales de la Mamá Grande* (1962). An exception to the early feminine rule, *El coronel no tiene quien le escriba* (1961), was a historical accident—though a prophetic one— because it was an offshoot of *La mala hora* and not an original project in itself. But its sense of masculine definition (corresponding moreover to a work in which the male protagonist finally defeats his long-suffering wife) foreshadowed the later works: *Cien años de soledad* (1967), *El otoño del patriarca* (1975), *El amor en los tiempos del cólera* (1985), *El general en su laberinto* (1989), and *Del amor y otros demonios* (1994). In all of these the temporal, masculine world implicitly orders and controls the natural, feminine world. Here again there was an exception to the sequence, *Crónica de una muerte anunciada* (1981), but, on the one hand, this was a belated representative of the *La mala hora* sequence and, on the other, the word *crónica* itself implicitly (within García Márquez's view of things) gives a sense of phallocentric organization to the title's implicit field of concern. (Almost all his titles involve time or history, their chronicling and their reading: "Cien *años* de soledad," "El *otoño* del patriarca," "*Relato* de un náufrago," "*Crónica de una muerte anunciada,*" "El amor en los *tiempos* del cólera," "La *aventura* de Miguel Littín clandestino," "El general en su *laberinto,*" "*Noticia* de un secuestro," etc.).

Regrettably, I repeat, none of this can be reproduced in English translation. However, I hope to illustrate succinctly the familiar truth that the untranslatable goes well beyond the matter of linguistic materiality into the—equally material?—realm of the cultural and the ideological.

García Márquez has been more read in English translation than any other writer in Spanish in the twentieth century. It seems to be generally, if tacitly, agreed that he is a master of the memorable title. Probably no twentieth-century writer has seen his work alluded to in newspaper headlines as frequently as he: if a politician goes through a tough spell, the headline, even in the English-speaking press, will be "One Hundred Days of Solitude"; if a dictator is in decline or threatened with subversion, it will be "The Autumn of the Tyrant"; and if any catastrophe at all, anywhere in the world, is deemed avoidable (and someone is to be blamed), it will be something like a "Chronicle of a Disaster Foretold." It is an extraordinary, if largely unnoticed phenomenon. Only Shakespeare can claim such widespread and instant product recognition.

We know that titles are the first and in some respects most important keys to unlocking a literary work. They are its name and identity but, unlike our own names—at least in this culture—they are also a decisive clue to its meaning. If *War and Peace* were entitled *Gone with the Wind,* and vice-versa, they would undoubtedly be different books: how different is probably a question for Borges's Pierre Menard to determine. What conclusion should we draw, then, when the titles of the works of the most widely read and possibly most widely admired Latin American writer of the twentieth century have commonly been mistranslated (I use the word recklessly)?

García Márquez, as is well known, came to world attention after 1967, when *Cien años de soledad* (One Hundred Years of Solitude) was published. For the reader's convenience I shall falsify this story some-what by dealing with titles by order of first publication in the original Spanish and not by order of translation. His first novel *La hojarasca*—rendered as *Leafstorm* in English (New York: Harper & Row, 1972; translated by Gregory Rabassa)—was published in 1955. I like the sound of "leafstorm" and I am sure that the translator did, too. How-ever, I am fairly sure that part of the reason why I like it, euphony apart, is that it exoticizes a continent that for me, more than thirty years after my first acquaintance with it, still excites me through its extreme but not total (there are still the African and Asian cases) oth-erness. It seems to me that this invented English word implies at least two concepts that hyperbolize both "leaf" and "storm," namely "jun-gle" and "hurricane." In other words, it tropicalizes the title (and the novel), and in the process distances it from us. This is unfortunate because, contrary to popular belief, García Márquez routinely normal-izes life in the tropics and generally resists all temptations of local color. But that is the first effect of this seductive invention. The second effect is to remove from the title any impact that might be considered critical or negative and any referent that might be considered social or eco-nomic. The leaves in the concept "la hojarasca" are dead leaves—leaf trash, one might say—which is the metaphor that the conservative pop-ulation of the novel's setting, Macondo, apply to the migrant workers who come and go with the rise and fall of the local economy. The cruel injustice of the metaphor derives especially from the fact that when these migrants are in the town it is because they are working and it is only when they are thrown out of work that they become something similar to the leaf trash that is discarded and burned after the planta-tions have suffered their yearly depredations. This social conflict is one that García Márquez himself lived through as a child and which he explores throughout his fiction. The word *hojarasca* (cf. José Américo Almeida's novel, *A bagaceira,* Brazil, 1928—correctly if not exotically translated as *Cane Trash*) is absolutely central to the poetics of the novel and its elegant mistranslation undermines a large part of the work's subtle politics for the English-speaking reader. Would I have retained *Leafstorm* after musing over these considerations? Maybe. But probably not.

El coronel no tiene quien le escriba was the next novel. Here the effect was the reverse: the tide was relieved of its pathetic or sympa-thetic implications. Literally meaning "The colonel has no one to write to him," or perhaps "There is no one to write to the colonel" the title was eventually translated as the dryly factual *No One Writes to the Colonel* (New York: Harper & Row, 1968, translated by J. S. Bern-stein). This underplays the character's depiction as a seventy-six-year-old orphan, abandoned by the world in general and the government in particular, but in the context of the novel as a whole no great harm is done. In this case, then, the least of all evils is the best of solutions. A hit, though not one to be paraded.

The least of all evils also extracted the title *In Evil Hour* (New York: Harper & Row, 1979, translated by Gregory Rabassa) out of the Spanish *La mala hora*. Here we revert to exoticization again, which is García Márquez's more usual fate, though in this case the form of exoticization is at first sight literary (rhetorical) rather than cultural. *La mala hora*, whose original title was to be *En este pueblo de mierda* (literally, "in this town of shit," which would have heaped an even bigger problem on the translator), is a straightforward statement, "the bad time" or "bad times" or even "evil times," with none of the literariness of "in evil hour." Nevertheless, even though this is the most prosaically realist of all this author's novels, the characters themselves tend to have a somewhat mystificatory perception of social agency and the implicitly superstitious overtones of the English title do effectively convey this. Another hit, then, though with other, different reservations.

The problem with *One Hundred Years of Solitude* (New York: Harper & Row, 1970, translated by Gregory Rabassa), surely one of the top ten titles of all time in either language, is more directly linguistic and cultural than literary. Firstly, the target language, English, has two words—solitude and loneliness—where the source language, Spanish, has only one, "soledad." This makes English "richer" in this specific case but because the translator has to choose it also, ironically, makes the result poorer because partial and particular. (This intricate phenomenon, which governs much of the relationship between the two languages, has been insufficiently studied.) In this case it also goes without saying that only one option is really feasible (*not* "One hundred years of loneliness"!) and yet "solitude" is the less frequent and the more literary of the two words in English, once again giving the uninformed reader the impression that Latin America is the home of the high-sounding and the grandiloquent. Pursuing this cultural point, "soledad" is one of the most important words and concepts in Spanish and particularly Latin American literature and there is unfortunately nothing that can be done technically to make up for the union in the Spanish word of the two basic concepts "solitude" and "loneliness," still less to mitigate the irreducible if banal reality that all three words have specific social meanings in their respective cultures.

Translating *El otoño del patriarca* into *The Autumn of the Patriarch* (New York: Harper & Row, 1976, translated by Gregory Rabassa) requires little comment except to say that even here there is a choice of the more or less literary—in this case between English and North American usage, the latter usually considering the former to be more fancy and even artificial—though the choice is also one that takes little more than a second to make: "The fall of the patriarch" would have been a translation with an ambiguity that in this specific case could truly be called catastrophic.

Chronicle of a Death Foretold (London: Jonathan Cape, 1982, translated by Gregory Rabassa) is another example of the irresistible mistranslation. Here the English title is clearly "better" than the very prosaic Spanish one, literally, "chronicle of an announced death," contrasting with the way in which the rhythmical swing of *Cien años de soledad* finds little echo in the English version. Yet the effect is, first, to make the title again more literary in several ways, including word order; second, once more, to bespeak a Hispanic "world" of destiny, superstition, and—yes—romance whose direction is the very opposite of García Márquez's intention in this superbly subtle and ambivalent work. The point of the word *anunciada* (announced) is to imply that the death is not unavoidable (or inevitable: more of this below), whereas the primary meaning of "foretold" tends to imply the opposite. That which is announced is by definition known; that which is foretold, much less so. Well, the whole point of the novel is to portray a death that everyone could have prevented and nobody did prevent and to inquire how and why this could have happened. To say that a death is foretold is to imply a quite different concept of destiny—that of the characters—than the version the author himself propounds. Here the whole novel is, in one sense, lost. Would I have given another title? Probably not. Particularly as the evidence of the use of this title in newspaper headlines around the world seems to contradict my assertion, suggesting that in this case at least (the argument would not hold for *Leafstorm*) García Márquez's audience has managed to read the right meaning—forewarned or pre-announced—into the title on the strength of the rest of the novel; and even those newspaper readers who have not read his book will implicitly understand that the phrase is a literary reference and will therefore further understand that they must "make allowances."

I would like to linger somewhat less briefly on *El amor en los tiempos del cólera,* whose English title is unavoidably *Love in the Time of Cholera* (New York: Knopf, 1988, translated by Edith Grossman). There are losses. The Spanish, as usual, is more factual, indeed more historical: the switch to the singular, "the time" instead of "los tiempos," inevitably signifies literariness, rhetoric, the search for dramatic effect, and also again conveys a sense of destiny, which is what "we" (most native speakers of English) "expect" from Hispanic culture and Hispanic writers though not of course what they themselves are trying to communicate to us. On another matter, the word *cólera* in Spanish is the normal word for anger (though in that case feminine in gender), whereas choler in English is so archaic as to barely signify one of the uncontrollable phenomena that García Márquez wishes to run through his title (love, time, disease, passion).

Here, though, I would like to stray a little beyond the title, though no farther than the beginning and the ending of the novel. (No twentieth-century writer has more of a sense of an ending or, indeed, of a beginning, than García Márquez; nor is any more repetitive than he in this respect.) Few examples could be found of the act of translation having a more decisive impact upon the destiny of a work than the translation of the beginning and more particularly the ending of *El amor en los tiempos del cólera,* though, as will be seen, the effect involved is merely a more dramatic version of phenomena we have already examined. The English version begins: "It was inevitable: the scent of bitter almonds always reminded him of the fate of unrequited love." One might think that the ingredients are already sufficiently "Latin"/ "Romantic"—though beware: García Márquez is writing a parody—for the translator to be cautious. Anything that can be done to reduce this effect should be done. One example would be to use "unavoidable" instead of "inevitable." Would I have done so? Probably not. But the fact remains that, as with the word "soledad," Spanish only has one option in everyday use and English has two; and unavoidable is not only the more concrete word but is clearly, in this case, the meaning intended by García Márquez. Here is a doctor doing a practical job; as he sets about it a concrete sense perception materially brings about an emotional association; whereas the word *inevitable,* combined with "bitter almonds" and "unrequited love," has us quickly beginning the beguine at the very start of a novel whose true intention is to explore and critique notions of romantic love and its conventionally perceived relation to sexual passion. Is it inevitable that we use the word *inevitable?* Probably. Unavoidable is just *too* prosaic.

But this is just the beginning, so to speak. The end of the novel is much more of a problem. If we return for a moment to *No One Writes to the Colonel,* we will see an example of a novel whose last word, as in a poem, bears the weight of the entire novel and simultaneously redefines it, every last word of it, we might say. When his despairing wife asks the stubborn colonel what, if he will not sell his dead son's fighting cock, they will now be able to eat, he replies: "Shit." Here the fortunate translator has no problem. The associations of "mierda" and "shit" coincide substantially in both languages and even the expression "to eat shit" translates solidly and smoothly. This is not the case with *Love in the Time of Cholera,* a novel whose last substantive phrase also retrospectively redefines the entire book—only, unfortunately, more so in English than in Spanish:

> The Captain looked at Fermin Daza and saw on her eyelashes the first glimmer of wintry frost. Then he looked at Florentino Ariza, his invincible power, his intrepid love, and he was overwhelmed by the belated suspicion that it is life, more than death, that has no limits.

"And how long do you think we can keep up this goddamn coming and going?" he asked. Florentino Ariza had kept his answer ready
for fifty-three years, seven months, and eleven days and nights.
"Forever," he said.

Unfortunately, that is not what the Spanish says. Spanish has a
much used, more or less exact equivalent of "forever," namely "para
siempre," but what García Márquez uses is "toda la vida," most usually
translated by "for the rest of our lives." Since its literal meaning is "all
of life," there is admittedly a secondary implication going beyond "our
lives" to "all life" and therefore to "forever"; but there is also, of course,
an incoherence in proposing to go on beyond the rest of our lives to all
of life. In short, the translation, which makes the novel end on one
word, like *No One Writes to the Colonel,* abolishes the materiality of
García Márquez's phrase in favor of a word that inevitably suggests the
Platonic idealism "typical" of Latin culture, especially when it refers to
love. Yet this novel, like most of García Márquez's oeuvre, is concerned
precisely to question the Quixotic illusions inherent both in romantic
love and in the obsessive pursuit of power. It treads a dangerous line
between seriousness and parody and finally opts for seriousness, for
concreteness, for what is rather than what might be, the human and the
collective rather than the unspecifiable abstract.

Nevertheless, "for the rest of our lives" is *too* concrete, *too* precise,
too limited. Here the Spanish phrase has more meanings than any English phrase can supply. Here we lose. But García Márquez loses more; he
loses almost everything. If it were not the end of the novel I, had I been
the translator, would unhesitatingly have put "For the rest of our lives";
but it *is* the end of the novel and I can't quite make up my mind. The
result, in any case, is that the English text helplessly confirms the book as
a high-class soap opera, proof that the Latins still prefer impossible
dreams to concrete reality, proof even that impossible dreams really can
and do come true. Yet as a serious artist García Márquez, as mentioned
above, is concerned to explore this entire problematic, not to draw conclusions about it. Ultimately he is what Timpanaro would call a Leopar-
dian pessimist; his philosophy follows Gramsci's slogan, borrowed from
Rolland and paraphrased: "Pessimism of the intellect, optimism of the
will." No serious work of his could end by juxtaposing the words "life"
and "forever"; on the contrary, "death" and "forever" is the normal for-
mula, posited and—if possible—resisted, as earlier in this same paragraph, but not denied. "Forever" is what Florentino Ariza would have
said when he was nineteen years old but his readers have learned a lot in
half a century. Not least that life does not last forever but death does.

This brief review of a few problems arising from translations of
García Márquez illustrates yet again that what Jakobson called "creative transposition," which is what all translators of novels are seeking

when they turn one long string of words into another long string of words, has very definite limits. Titles and endings, on which writers inevitably bestow close attention and great intensity, routinely present even the best translator with problems that are insoluble. For translation itself remains the best example of the fact that all communication is imperfect, a necessary but impossible dream.

Translating Vowels,
or, The Defeat of Sounds:
The Case of Huidobro

José Quiroga

vowel: one of a class of speech sounds in the articulation of
which the oral part of the breath channel is not blocked and
is not constricted enough to cause audible friction.

Not all linguistic codes choose to represent vowels in writing. Ferdinand de
Saussure recalls in his *Cours de linguistique générale* that the Greeks
assigned a sound to each letter in contrast to other codes that generally represented only the implosion or interruption of sounds in consonants.
Because the Greeks divided the spoken chain into homogeneous acoustic
phases, in them we can find the origins of our present-day vowels. The
transfer from sound to text was done, with few exceptions, on an equal
basis: a sound was equivalent to a written representation. In this transfer,
vowels are the purest images of translation: a glyph, a letter, that stands for
pure sound with no friction. These translations from sound to text, their
gaps and their economies, are my point of entry for examining the ambiguities and paradoxes in the translation of a poem that has no original language and whose last section is composed only of vowels. I am referring to
Vicente Huidobro's *Altazor o el viaje en paracaídas* (1931) and to Eliot
Weinberger's translation, published in 1989 by Greywolf Press.

Altazor implies a certain route or passage, a progression, a course,
a parallel movement that shapes the source and the target into specular
constructions that read and comment on each other, to the extent that
the target poem—*Altazor*—comments on the fallacies of the original,
which is a poem about the death and the rebirth of language. This route
or passage that I see in *Altazor* and in its translation is precisely a
vocalic, frictionless transfer from consonants, to vowels, to translated
vowels, that parallels the passage from sound into text that I referred to
in Saussure's Greek examples. *Altazor* is an emblem for how, when Latin
American experiments in sound are translated into English, vowels
become words, sounds become typography.

Latin American poems seem to stand on the verge of sound and text, between an oral and a written tradition. This is especially evident in the poetry of the avant-garde, in which sound appears as welcoming the "sublime," the place where language or text apparently goes back to an oral foundation in order to achieve a certain kind of unity between sound and sense. In Latin America the desire for this perfect symbiosis is related to the longing for an original language, the repository of all perfect meaning, somehow grafted onto or under Spanish. Sound represents the attempt to go back to a "primal scene" of the tradition, to a nostalgia for the plenitude of orality. In Luis Palés Matos's *Tun tún de pasa y grifería,* for example, what seem to be random sounds are actually meaningful words. The Afro-Caribbean vocabulary serves a dual function: it is at once rhythmic and signifying, it encompasses the categories of sound and meaning. The agrammatism of the Spanish obscures the grammatical sense that is being played out in a different language, somewhere else, in the space of nostalgia or plenitude. Another example could be César Vallejo, whose poetry is composed of written, legal formulas that have permeated the life and culture of the Andean civilization. In several of Vallejo's poems, it is obvious that the idea of the text is founded upon a previous elimination of sound, so that his poetry is already a translation and therefore a necessarily fragmentary language. I would argue that his grammatical dislocations are necessarily attempts to go back to an orality that is paradoxically rescued by means of text.

Huidobro's *Altazor, a Voyage in Parachute,* is a long poem in nine cantos written by the Chilean poet from 1919 to 1931, as a commentary, critique, or point of closure for the Latin American and European avant-garde. *Altazor* is self-consciously a poem about literature, about the poet and about poetry, about text and about sound. Huidobro, who wanted to conquer the arena of the Parisian avant-garde, stands as an allegorical fable of Latin American poets trying to belong to the center of culture, and his poem is an excessive monument and epitaph to his grandiose desires. For twelve years, Huidobro collaged or collated a series of Cantos into a poem with a dim but nevertheless visible thread: a voyage in parachute that becomes soon enough a voyage in and through language, as if language were the fabric of the parachute itself, the means of and the reason for a work of language falling or decomposing, ascending or restructuring itself until, at the end of Canto VII, the reader is left with an apparently random, syllabic, or vocalic series.

> Campanudio lalali
> > Auriciento auronida
> Lalali
> > io ia
> i i i o
> Ai a i ai a i i i i o ia

This paradoxical, vocalic end to this random collection assembled over ten or twelve years can be interpreted in two ways: either as the end of language as such (from sense to nonsense, from communication to privacy, from public and conventional to private and hermetic) or as the beginning of a new language (since the series is formed precisely by using the letters "Ai a i ai a i i i i o ia," a series that resembles the sound of the Spanish word *ahí* or *allá*). Even though ultimate meaning is unassailable by both design and purpose, Huidobro seems to say that language is permanently here and elsewhere.

Before commenting on Weinberger's translation of *Altazor,* a further point should be made about Huidobro's poem. For *Altazor* is truly a work with no original language. Its Preface was published in *La Nación,* in Buenos Aires, in 1925, as a translation of "Altazur," itself a fragment of a long poem called "Voyage en Parachute." Two more sections were published in transition (Paris, 1930) as a "Fragment d' Altazor," and in *Favorables Paris Poema,* the review edited by César Vallejo and Juan Larrea in Paris. When Huidobro published in Spain, in 1931 *Altazor o un viaje en paracaídas,* and added "A Poem in seven Cantos, with a preface," the previous "voyage en parachute," becomes a shadow that hangs over the text, especially since the word-plays in the "original" version presented in 1931 in Spanish, show traces of a French original as if French were the tain of its mirror. This is evident in the famous passage of the "rossignol," written in French, in which the rules of the game are more important than the conventions of codified language:

> mais le ciel préfère le rodognol
> son enfant gaté le roregnol
> le romignol
> le rofagnol
> rosolgnol
> le rolagnol
> rossignol

The same game appears in the Spanish version of the poem published by Huidobro in 1931:

> Pero el cielo prefiere el rodoñol
> Su niño querido el rorreñol
> Su flor de alegría el romiñol
> Su piel de lágrima el rofañol
> Su garganta nocturna el rosolñol
> El rolañol
> El rosiñol

Huidobro's self-translation keeps the game and the sound of the bird's name but actually creates a new bird, a "rosiñol," which does not exist in Spanish except as an allusion to the almost homophonic "ruiseñor." Huidobro translates following the rules of the game and the rules of sound, the musical scale affixed to a nonexisting word is more important than sense, so that Huidobro's connection between sound and sense privileges sound. The English translation by Weinberger, however, restores the perfect equation between sound and sense, since *ruiseñor* (the word alluded to in the Spanish "original") is nightingale, in English. Therefore, and with a well deserved bow to Keats, Weinberger translates:

> But the sky prefers the nighdongale
> Its favorite son the nighrengale
> Its flower of joy the nighmingale
> Its skin of tears the nighfangale
> Its nocturnal throat the nightongale
> The nighlangale
> The nightingale

The place where sound and text blur the distinctions between original and target is in Weinberger's simple, elegant, and meaningful translation of the last Canto. Vowels are, in Huidobro's essentialist notion, at once the origin and the purest element of sound: an imperfect point of closure that is also a point of passage. Vowels represent the purity of sound as marker and at the same time written deferral of identity (hence the play upon *ahi* or *alla*). Weinberger had to face what is perhaps the simplest yet most difficult problem for a translator, for Huidobro defied him to translate pure sound from one system on to the other, when the letter itself (the vowel) does not guarantee that the sound will actually be translated:

> Lalalee
>   Eeoh eeah
> ee ee ee oh
> Aheee ah ee ahee ah ee ee ee ee oh eeah

Yet the first revelation of Weinberger's translated vowels as Huidobro's essentialist fantasy is ultimately based not upon sound, but upon a convention that in turn needs to be doubly represented in order to be rescued back into sound. For in order to translate the conventional representation of sound, another arbitrary representation—the (h)—must be added on to the letter. The "a" sound is transformed into "ah" as word, while at the same time the (h) is added on to the vowels but the content, the meaning of the word that Huidobro wanted to create, allude, or represent as origin (ahí or allá) is lost in English. Contrary to all other translations, sound is reproduced but possible meaning is lost. Weinberger translates against translation: sounds can be translated into words, but words can never become sounds and words once again.

I should illustrate this with a simple diagram:

lack of original	"original" language	translation
	1) shows traces of a second, implied original	1) rebirth of language in different code
	2) theme is destruction and rebirth of language	2) the closure of the original becomes typography therefore
		3) the pretension of the source (sound as beginning and end, even the possibility of having sound in writing) is debunked

If, as Walter Benjamin has explained, translation uncovers hidden meanings within the originals, the translation of Latin American poetry has, in many cases, uncovered questions that the poems, poets, or critics themselves are sometimes too reluctant to ask. I wonder if it is not too presumptuous to use Weinberger's simple conversion of sound into typography as a clue to a much needed interpretation of the tradition as a whole, and see in a new light the fruitful experiments with concrete poetry of Haroldo de Campos and others, since translation seems to be a particularly crucial concept for Latin American literature. What Weinberger's translation of Huidobro's rootless poem shows is that, before being translated into another language, say, English, or French, or German, Latin American texts are already translations of a previous source that in itself questions the notion of original. From Columbus's encounters with native Americans to Mario Vargas Llosa's *The Storyteller,* Latin America writes itself as an uncanny palimpsest in which the nostalgia for an oral tradition furnishes a polemical undercurrent of ambivalent desires. From el Inca Garcilaso's careful translation of the mainly oral poetry of the lost empires, to Pablo Neruda's prophetic retelling of a still nameless nature in *Canto general,* some of the most important texts actually have as founding principle and argument a mediation between two systems—the oral and the written—in which the grammar of the text itself attempts to convey the seemingly alien, a-structural grammar of the singer of tales. In this central combination of sound and text, the text becomes a translation of itself, and words obscure and at the same time reveal the tain of their own surface, generally by means of grammatical dislocations—the triumph of the text is then built upon the failure of the mimetic rendering of sound. Although I have chosen to examine it in the context of Huidobro, I have alluded to the fact that the operation takes place in three distinct systems: the Afro-Caribbean black, the Andean, and the cosmopolitan avant-garde context of Huidobro's Paris. The translation of Huidobro's ambiguous closure is not permitted into another system, which actually freezes the voice by the power of the consonant. The text is the revelation of aporia: the non-resolution of a problem as resolution, the moment of textual difficulty opening itself up as the tensionless passage of vowels with no friction. For Latin American texts install themselves precisely on this aporia between systems that reveal the coexistence of different modes of thought—be it text and sound or Western modes of rational thinking with other, non-Western modes.

What Weinberger purposely has done in his translation of the last Canto of *Altazor* is illustrate the passage that I talked about in the beginning. By transforming a sound poem into a concrete text, he has rendered time into space, because in order to transfer the characteristic sound they possess, vowels surrender voice to typography and open themselves to new and different possibilities. From voice to typography, from presence to absence, Latin American literature, that project created in the eighteenth and early nineteenth century, still manifests its founding aporia in the 1930s with texts that aspire to a certain kind of plenitude in sound. Translation somehow resolves the aporia as narrative fallacy, as if the aporia were but a creative and rhetorical stance, the poems already having buried their sound into a structure that can only be gleaned by an alphabet of letters and meaning. For me, Weinberger's silent and muting [h] stands as a metaphor for the translation of Latin America. It is the silence of a consonant paradoxically recovering, while at the same time signaling, the defeat of sounds.

WORKS CONSULTED

Benjamin, Walter. *Illuminations*. New York: Harcourt Brace Jovanovich, 1968.

Huidobro, Vicente. *Altazor. Temblor de Cielo*. Ed. René de Costa. Madrid: Ediciones Cátedra, 1986.

———. *Altazor, or A Voyage in Parachute*. Trans. Eliot Weinberger. Saint Paul, Minnesota: Graywolf Press, 1988.

Saussure, Ferdinand de. *Cours de Linguistique Generale*. Publié par Charles Bally et Albert Sechehaye. Paris: Payot, 1966.

The Indigenist Writer as a (Mis)Translator of Cultures: The Case of Alcides Arguedas

Edmundo Paz-Soldán

INDIGENISM/REGIONALISM'S TRIP

Latin American writers have always been obsessed with representing the Other, (mis)translating the Other's language and culture in order to assimilate him or her better within the search for the complex identity of a country or the continent.[1] Perhaps this obsession has nowhere been so evident as in the *mundonovismo* of the early part of the century, which came to full maturity with the regionalist writers of the twenties. This movement attempted to renew Latin American literature by positioning itself against a vision of *modernismo* as an aesthete's escape from reality; while *modernismo* was the inauthentic voice of the continent, regionalism saw itself as a founding myth, as the authentic, essential, autochtonous expression of the culture.

We know now that regionalism and its important subgroups—*indigenismo,* for example—were the expression of an urban middle—or upper-middle—class which, in their attempts to describe the reality of the continent, ended up refashioning it according to their own dreams and fears. Whoever looks for the Other in regionalist novels will only find traces of themselves; the rest will be the problematic result of the regionalist's trip to the essence, an Other that says more about the writer's temperament or sociocultural background than about the Other himself or herself, a (mis)translated Other who has been done violence to, and whose "cultural forms or concepts or indigenous practices are recuperated . . . via a process of familiarization . . . whereby they are denuded of their 'foreignness,' even, perhaps, of their radical inaccesibility" (Dingwaney and Maier 4–5).

The Bolivian Alcides Arguedas (1879–1946) is the quintessential example of the writer as (mis)translator of cultures. Thanks to his critical position regarding the "exoticism" of the modernist poets, and to his insistence on the need to create a national literature through the representation of Spanish-American reality, he was from the beginning fully associated with *mundonovista* currents.[2] His regionalist vocation is already present, albeit in a rather crude fashion, in *Wuata Wuara* (1904), a first novel that deals with the rape of an Indian woman in a hacienda in the Bolivian highlands, and with the subsequent Indian uprising against the white owners; his mature vision comes to fruition in *Raza de bronce* (1919), one of the four or five truly classic indigenist novels.

Arguedas wrote after the 1899 indigenous uprising of Zárate Willka. This rebellion reawakened in urban society a fear of the Indian which had always been present since colonial times, and unleashed rhetorical and physical abuse against the Indian in the early part of the century, a period baptized by the historian Danielle Demelas as that of "creole darwinism."[3] The indigenism of the day, led by Alcides Arguedas, tried to assimilate the Indian into the national imaginary and thus reconstitute this imaginary altered by Zárate Willka's uprising (García Pabón 126–27). Applying popular strands of late-nineteenth-century racialist European thinking to understand the Indian and scientifically legitimize urban prejudices about him, and mixing it together with a revelation of the unjust conditions of indigenous life and work in the haciendas of the Bolivian highlands, Arguedas is a key writer in the construction of a poetics of indigenism/regionalism.

According to his poetics, the essence of national identity, the conflictive nucleus where the future of the nation is defined, can only be found outside the cities, in the countryside (the plains, the jungle, the highlands). The classic indigenist/regionalist writer is an urban subject who travels to the countryside in order to have a more comprehensive view of the nation, and to legitimize his/her vision through a direct knowledge of non-urban reality. This trip does not have the romantic connotations that a similar exploration could have had throughout most of the nineteenth century. The writer is more like an amateur ethnographer, a *démodé* positivist who takes advantage of his/her superior position of power and constitutes the culture being translated as an Other culture, "fixing" it, making it "static and unchanging," and, paradoxically, giving it a place in history: an inferior one in a "teleological, hierarchical model of civilizations" (Niranjana 3). This approach to a regional reality, however, can never fully abandon an urban place of enunciation. The attempt to solve the national question only repeats discursively the contradictions inherent to an ethnically and culturally heterogenous society.[4] Writers such as Alcides Arguedas or the Colombian José Eustasio Rivera always had an excentric, "from-without" vision of the countryside.

The regionalist trip has its formal projection in narrative structure. The most well-known novels, such as Rivera's *La vorágine* or Gallegos's *Doña Bárbara*, narrate the trip of an urban witness—the narrator, the main character—to a rural referent. They often begin by letting the reader know that a trip of that nature has just taken place, as in Matto de Turner's *Aves sin nido (Torn from the Nest)* (1889), where we are told in the second chapter that the Marins "had taken up temporary residence in the village" (9). This structural need to narrate the change of geographical space and what happens afterward permeates the logic of translation at work in the whole process: urban culture is not only where the novels' audience is located, it is also the matter from which the literary representation of the countryside is built. As we will see in Alcides Arguedas's *Wuata Wuara* and *Raza de bronce,* the language of the Aymara characters, the glossary of words from the indigenous languages used in the novels, even the description of the landscape in urban terms, testify to the writer's impulse to make familiar what is foreign, exotic, Other.[5]

WUATA WUARA

The narrator of indigenist novels is, like the writer, excentric to the Indian world: he is the only narrative authority, and the Indian referent is seen through the prejudiced mediation of the scientific discourse of degeneration. The Indians' language is translated into Spanish: in the contact between languages, the narrator's almost wholly absorbs the other.

The logic of translation is operative at several different narrative levels. Even though there are no profound interferences into the morphological and syntactical structures of Spanish, there are lexical variations and borrowings at the basic level mentioned by Martin Lienhard in *La voz y la huella*.[6] In *Wuata Wuara,* Quechua words referring to food, clothing, animals, or particular characteristics of Indian life in the highlands, are set in italics, and some are accompanied by their Spanish translation in parenthesis: "Over the *patajati* (bed) of mud and on top of *kesanas* of dry and yellowish cattail, three dirty and tattered children lay, their faces blackened by dirt" (Sobre el *patajati* (lecho) de barro y encima de *kesanas* (tendido) de totora seca y de color amarillento, estaban recostados tres chiquillos sucios y haraposos, de caras ennegrecidas por la mugre) (372–73).[7] If the novel as a literary genre can be understood in Latin America as a laboratory of production of cultural and linguistic integration models in very heterogeneous societies, indigenist narrative, in its classic period (1910–40), fully privileges Spanish, and demarcates with typographic signs—italics—its separation from indigenous languages. Quechua words are set apart, deviate from the Spanish official norm. It is not until José María Arguedas that indigenist literature attempts to artistically recreate Quechua syntax in the structure of Spanish itself, fusing both languages although still privileging Spanish.[8]

Discursive practices are at their most powerful when least noticed. It is certainly a convention accepted by almost every writer and reader that the non-Spanish speakers of the Latin American novel have to speak in Spanish; the novel, after all, is an urban genre, and its readership belongs to the Spanish-speaking middle and upper-middle classes. However, it is a measure of the power of convention, and the power of a state language to dictate the rules of the game, that a movement such as indigenism, so obsessed with finding the identity of the nation and representing its "autochtonous reality," can so easily simplify the linguistic heterogeneity of the indigenous population.[9] Even though A. Arguedas warns us in the prologue that *Wuata Wuara* is a novel of "indigenous mores" ("costumbres indígenas") (361), it seems to overlook speech, since the Indian characters always speak Spanish. At most, there is a word sprinkled here and there; using perfect Spanish syntax, Agiali says to Wuata Wuara: "Then you are going to be more beautiful than a seagull flying from the nest for the first time" [Pues has de estar más hermosa que una *keulla* (gaviota) que por primera vez sale a volar a su nido] (364). Arguedas's "imagined community" is not the whole nation; it is its Spanish-speaking inhabitants, or a "translated nation."[10]

But the Other not only speaks in Spanish; he or she also thinks in Spanish the thoughts that urban people think the Other thinks. Bakhtin saw the novel as a genre whose main virtue was to open itself up to a polyphony of voices, to let its language be constituted through the competition among different languages, each of them with its own ideological weight.[11] In *Wuata Wuara*, there is a constant confrontation between whites and Indians; however, there is no dialogism in the Bakhtinian sense, since it seems that the narrator's racist ideology has been internalized by the Indians. Although the colonized is always contaminated by the ideas and images of the colonizer, and he/she can easily be an accomplice in the dissemination of a society's hegemonic model, Arguedas's crude way of dealing with the issue affects the novel's verisimilitude.

Choquehuanka's thoughts about the Indian, a mixture of long-standing racial prejudices in the Andes and the discourse of degeneration filtered through the work of Gabriel René Moreno, Bunge, Gobineau, or LeBon, are seen also, with very little change, in *Pueblo enfermo* (1908), the long essay in which he devised a racialist (and positivist) construct to explain the backwardness of Bolivia and the Spanish-American continent. According to Choquehuanka,

> la vida de las razas estaba expuesta a seguir las mismas variaciones que la vida de los hombres, y eran aquéllas fuertes en la edad viril y miserables en la juventud, y se le hizo que acaso la suya llegaba a los lindes en que se pierde la personalidad de una raza y sólo se conserva la agrupación informe de seres ligados entre sí apenas por afinidad de costumbres. (372)

the life of races was destined to follow the same variations of the life of men, and they [i.e., the life of races] were strong in the virile age and miserable when young, and he thought that perhaps his was reaching the limits were a race's personality is lost, and what remains is the amorphous group of beings linked with each other just by affinity of customs.

Arguedas projects into Choquehuanka's discourse various fantasies of the creole imaginary. One of them is related to the impossibility of Indian participation in the project of national modernization, which is seen as a sort of an apartheid by mutual agreement; the Indians, says Choquehuanka, "did not demand that their rights be respected, because they well knew they would never be paid attention to . . . eternally exploited by the bosses, they did not have ambition for power, nor did they want a victory in any sense. They wanted peace, tranquility, to be left alone with their barbarism . . ." ([n]o exigían el respeto de sus derechos, porque bien sabían que jamás serían atendidos . . . eternamente explotados por los patrones, ni ambicionaban el poder, ni tampoco querían el triunfo en ningún sentido. Ellos querían paz, que los dejasen tranquilos, que les permitiesen vivir con su barbarie . . .) (406). Another fantasy justifies stereotyped Indian qualities on the abuses they receive from whites: the Indian "is suspicious and distrustful; he has distrust in his blood, he has it and transmits it by heredity, and he is ferociously atavistic, because in him gravitates the hatred accumulated by many generations dead by the savage despotism of whites" ([e]s receloso y desconfiado; la desconfianza la tiene metida en la sangre, la lleva y la transmite por herencia y es feroz por atavismo, porque gravita en él el odio acumulado de muchas generaciones muertas bajo el peso del despotismo salvaje de los blancos) (371).

Atavism, a scientific concept developed by late-nineteenth-century European science, and which purported to explain the existence of primitive traits in modern individuals,[12] is essential to Choquehuanka and Arguedas's understanding of the Indian. Even though the Bolivian author ethically justifies the Aymara rebellion, the way the rebellion takes place, with grotesque scenes of cannibalism, emphasizes on the other hand the Indian's inferior status as a human being. These scenes, of course, remind the reader of the Zárate Willka uprising, in which some acts of cannibalism were commited by the Indians against a batallion of voluntary upper-class soldiers from the city of Sucre. According to the anthropologist Eric Langer, Indian cannibalism can be thought of "as an 'occasional' ritual associated with rebellion and violence" (184). If the whites symbolically devour the Indian by taking over their lands, abusing them physically, and denying them the most elemental civil rights, the relationship is inverted through the cannibalistic ritual: it is now the Indian who, literally, devours the white man. What takes place in the novel is not connected at all, as Langer suggests, to a defense of land and ethnic identity. Rather, the predominant feeling is one of instinctive revenge, and underscores what *Wuata Wuara* really is: a moralizing message from Arguedas to his own class. If the white landowners do not learn to "educate" their desires, the Indian's primitive, uncontrollable fury will overwhelm them and, literally, devour them. The atavistic Indian, caught in the grid of modern science, was a credible threat to them.

RAZA DE BRONCE

Raza de bronce, Arguedas's fourth and last novel, is a reelaboration of *Wuata Wuara.* It was published in La Paz in 1919, and with a definitive edition in 1945.[13] Arguedas was conscious of his obsessive dedication to *Raza.* In the final note to the definitive edition of the novel, he writes with pride:

> Este libro ha debido en más de veinte años obrar lentamente en la conciencia nacional, porque de entonces a esta parte y sobre todo en estos últimos tiempos, muchos han sido los afanes de los poderes públicos para dictar leyes protectoras del indio, así como muchos son los terratenientes que han introducido maquinaria agrícola para la labor de sus campos, abolido la prestación gratuita de ciertos servicios y levantado escuelas en sus fundos. (348)

> This book must have affected, over more than twenty years, the national conscience, because from then until now, and especially lately, there have been many efforts from the public powers to dictate laws protecting the Indian; landowners as well have introduced agricultural machinery to work their fields, have abolished the free services rendered [by the Indians] and have built schools in their fields.

By representing the landowners' abuses, Arguedas, according to his own reading, helped make the landowning and political elite more aware of the Indians' plight. Even though the novel is a fundamental part of the debate on the "Indian question" which took place in Bolivia during the first half of the century, it is very difficult to estimate the degree of influence of a literary work in the changes that take place in any given society. As Cornejo Polar writes, the note shows "naiveté or opportunism [and] . . . imposes a new reading code and modifies the tragic sense of the text into another which is encouraging and optimistic" (ingenuidad u oportunismo [e] . . . impone un nuevo código de lectura y modifica el sentido trágico del texto en otro más bien alentador y optimista) (198–99).

The process of resignification of *Wuata Wuara*'s plot takes place in *Raza* with essential elements added to it and omitted from *Wuata Wuara,* in form as well as content. All of *Raza*'s first part is new. Most of the excesses of the discourse of degeneration are attenuated, perhaps because now there is some distance from the 1899 uprising. The biological/racialist rhetorical condemnation of the Other—the Indian and the *mestizo*—gives way to a less explicit and more ambiguous rhetoric, which both metaphorizes the Indian as a member of the strong "race of bronze," and condemns him/her as a premodern, superstitious being. The burden of the critique rests now, as it has been since *Pueblo enfermo,* on the *mestizo.*

Arguedas deviates in *Raza* from the basic paradigm of the trip from the city to the countryside; this time, the trip takes place within the rural world: Agiali and two other Aymaras from Pablo Pantoja's hacienda travel from the highlands to the valley in order to sell their products. The critic Teodosio Fernández suggests that this trip is Arguedas's "pre-text" to show the geographic, agricultural, and ethnic diversity of the region (521). By representing this diversity, Arguedas emphasizes the heterogeneity of each sociocultural universe: the uniform, homogeneous Indians of *Wuata Wuara* have been replaced by Indians who are very distinct from each other.

In Arguedas's fiction, the highland and the valley form a matrix of binary oppositions. The valley is the place of abundance, of agricultural richness; the highlands are the "yermo," the territory in which nature, with its droughts and floodings, furiously overwhelms the Indians. As in all regionalist novels, most notably in Rivera's *La vorágine,* men are shown as minuscule entities intimidated by the immensity of nature.[14] In *Raza,* the Andean peaks "terrorized and filled with anguish the spirit of the poor *llaneros.* They felt despicably small, powerless, weak. They were afraid of being men" (aterrorizaba[n] y llenaba[n] de angustia el ánimo de los pobres llaneros. Sentíanse vilmente empequeñecidos, impotentes, débiles. Sentían miedo de ser hombres) (68).

Nature has an operative function in the novel: it determines the characters' identity and the nation's "essence." Arguedas differentiates the Indians' identity deterministically, according to the place they belong to, be it the highlands or the valley. The harsh nature of the highlands has as a correlate an Indian who is hardened, distrustful, austere, and who has to be carried away by his/her most primitive impulses in order to survive in an inhuman environment. In contrast, the more generous nature of the valley creates a more benevolent Indian, somebody who suffers less and therefore is less of an animal. The first Indian from the valley that we encounter in the novel is very different from the melancholic Aymaras; he is seen walking by the road "whistling a happy tune" (silbando una tonada alegre) (21). He thinks that the Aymaras "are usually thieves," and they do not prove him wrong (21).

There is something, however, which all the Indians have in common: they are superstitious, premodern, that is, prerational beings. They are afraid of a cave that overlooks Lake Titikaka, and believe that dark spirits live within it. When the river takes Manuno away, they say it was predicted by Chulpa, the community witch. And when a drought threatens the lake, Choquehuanka decides to make an offering to its divinities. The scene of the ceremonial offering is representative of Arguedas's eccentric view of Aymara culture. Choquehuanka and the main authorities of the community catch fish; they open the fishes' mouths, and insert in them a coca leaf and drops of alcohol, pronouncing a magic spell that asks the fish to be fruitful so the Indians' hunger can be sated. As soon as the ceremony is over and the Indians leave the lake, the narrator ironically describes what happens to the fish; seagulls and ducks "whirled and gave acute shrieks around the poor fish, drunken and hurt, and they swooped with noise of fondled beaks and wings, in order to devour the fish that had the mission to reproduce themselves to sate the hunger of the 'very poor men'. . ." (revoloteaban lanzando agudos chillidos alrededor de los pobres peces ebrios y lastimados, y se abatían, con ruido de picos y alas sobadas, a devorar los pescados que llevaban la misión de reproducirse para aplacar el hambre de los 'pobrecitos hombres'. . .) (144–45).

To be sure, Arguedas made an effort, if many times misguided, to translate the Indian language and culture for an urban audience, and thus incorporate the Indian into the national imaginary. He wanted to be as far away as possible from the modernists caricatured by him in the character of Suárez. Suárez cannot see reality because he, "[s]aturated to the bones with certain modernist readings, was obsessed with enchanted princesses of medieval legends, elves, fauns and satyrs" ([s]aturado hasta los tuétanos de ciertas lecturas modernistas, estaba obsesionado con encantadas princesas de leyendas medioevales, gnomos, faunos y satiros) (294). Being a *mundonovista* meant for Arguedas attempting to realistically describe the customs and cultural practices of the Indians. A realistic Indian, however, does not necessarily mean an Indian closer to reality than the one represented by the Indianists or the *modernistas*. Arguedas's (mis)translated and (mis)understood Indians show the impossibility of bridging the gap between heterogeneous cultures in Bolivia, and thus the tragic fracture of the nation.

Arguedas had many presumptions about what an urban audience may find alien. He put in parenthesis a Spanish translation of the non-Spanish words used throughout the text, such as "quena (flauta)," or "vizcachas (liebres)"; he attempted to clarify the difference between "laikas (brujos)," and "yatiris (adivinos)"; he incorporated sometimes a basic explanation of Indian cultural practices in the flow of the text, as in: "[The Indians] were practicing *acullico,* that is, the three of them chewed coca leaves in silence, impassive and mute, lost in their deep rumination" ([Los indios] practicaban el *acullico,* es decir, mascaban coca los tres y permanecían silenciosos, impasibles y mudos, como abstraídos en su onda cavilación) (16, italics in the original); "the comrade, who was on his service week (pongueaje)" (el compañero, que hacía su semana de servicio *[pongueaje])* (19, italics in the original). The translation of words that indicate a cultural peculiarity of the society being translated generally results in a simplification, in one way or another a mistranslation. Does the Spanish word *adivino* mean the same as "yatiri"? Or, as in an example given by Lienhard, do the Mesoamerican *cues* (indigenous sanctuaries) mean the same as "pirámides" (pyramids) or "templos" (temples) (97–98)? In the translation process, a society's complexity can be simplified, sometimes by linguistic limitations, sometimes by the translator's mistakes and prejudices. In the Andean context of the early twentieth century, Arguedas's (mis)translations can be understood as a sort of performative act in which the national fracture is acted out.

Surely for Arguedas's Bolivian urban readers, cultural practices such as *pongueaje* and *acullico* were easily understood and did not need to be translated. Why translate them, then? Arguedas's meticulous attempt at translating the Aymara world, which varied and evolved in the different editions of *Raza,* is also due to the fact that for him, as for the regionalist writers in general, the urban audience was not only the national audience but the Spanish American and peninsular reading public as well. Arguedas's oscillation in some matters of translation shows his purpose of addressing more than one urban audience at the same time. In the first edition of *Raza,* published in La Paz in 1919 and with a local readership in mind, one reads, for example, "brujos y *yatiris*": there is no translation of *yatiris.* In the 1924 edition, published in Valencia, Spain, and with a peninsular and Spanish American readership in mind, one reads: "brujos *(yatiris)*"; now both words are equivalent.[15] "Khara," in the 1919 edition, becomes "mestizo *(Khara)*" in 1924. More frequent is an inversion that subtly shows the degree of familiarity with some words Arguedas may expect from his readers: "*pongo* (sirviente)," in the La Paz edition, becomes "sirviente *(pongo)*" in the Spanish edition. Angel Rama has perceptively commented on this, indicating that the use of two different lexical codes at the same time (e.g., the glossaries of the regionalist novel) is a form that survives from Colonial times (50–51). This exercise, which turns the "man of letters" into a translator, certifies, for Rama, "the lettered man's conscience of being exiled at the borders of a civilization whose vital center (and its reader as well) is in the European metropolis" (la conciencia del letrado de que está desterrado en las fronteras de una civilización cuyo centro animador (cuyo lector también) está en las metrópolis europeas) (52). The Aymara world travels to the city and further travels abroad via Alcides Arguedas; caught up in local and global processes, the Indigenist/regionalist novel constructs this world as an Other to the nation, and attemps to fully subsume it.

But not all the words are translated by Arguedas, maybe because he could not always find an equivalent, or perhaps he thought these

words had already been incorporated by the Spanish language. *Mijis?*
Macamacas? Chipas? What is alien cannot fully be included within
Arguedas's culture and language.[16] One, then, remembers Choquehuanka's reasons when authorizing the Indian revenge against the
white oppresors: "to open between them and us deep abysses of blood,
so that hate latently lives in our race, until it [our race] is strong and
dominates or is defeated by the ills" (abrir entre ellos y nosotros *profundos abismos* de sangre, de manera que el odio viva latente en nuestra raza, hasta que sea fuerte y se imponga o sucumba a los males)
(344, my emphasis). Arguedas's optimistic final note cannot erase the
tragedy of *Raza de bronce,* in which two cultures battle it out in the
Andes, and the powerless one is incorporated in the national imaginary, albeit never in full fashion. The "deep abysses" that separate
whites from Indians guarantee the misunderstanding, the mistranslation, and sometimes the impossibility of translation. Could Arguedas
have done it otherwise? Could the classic indigenist writers? Maybe.
But then, perhaps they may not have been writing about and from
fractured imagined communities.

NOTES

1. Throughout the chapter, I will use the term *translation* in the wide sense
given to it by contemporary critical ethnography, and which is aptly summarized
by Dingwaney and Maier: "translation is not restricted to . . . linguistic transfer
alone; translation is also the vehicle through which 'Third World' cultures (are
made to) travel—transported or 'borne across' to and recuperated by audiences
in the West" (4).

2. For a critical overview of Alcides Arguedas's work, see my doctoral dissertation: *Alcides Arguedas y la narrativa de la nación enferma* (U. of Califor-
nia-Berkeley, 1997). See also the essays collected by Antonio Lorente Medina in
the critical edition of *Raza de bronce.*

3. See Demelas's "Darwinismo a la criolla." For Zárate Willka's uprising,
the best account is still Condarco Morales.

4. See, in this regard, Cornejo Polar's *Escribir en el aire,* esp. 194–207.

5. This impulse is also shared by traditional ethnography. James Clifford
has studied in *The Predicament of Culture* how much ethnography is "enmeshed
in writing" (25), and how ethnographers attempted to "translate" another culture to make it understandable in the terms of the ethnographers' own culture.

6. Lienhard mentions three basic procedures of modification of one language when in contact with another: the inclusion of words of the other language in order to describe a particular reality (borrowing); the recreation of a
concept from the other language (semantic copy, or translation); and the appropriation of a concept from the other language through a semantic restructuring
of an existing word (resemantization) (97–101).

7. Translations are mine.

8. In "La novela y el problema de la expresión literaria en el Perú," José María Arguedas defended Spanish as a "legitimate means of expression of the Peruvian world in the Andes" (174). At the same time, he said he used Spanish as a "primary element which needed to be modified . . . until turning it into [my] own instrument" (170). In the process, he knew that "something is lost in exchange for what is gained" (173).

9. Niranjana, following Pierre Bourdieu and also quoting him, says that symbolic domination reproduces the social order by mixing recognition with misrecognition: "recognition that the dominant language is legitimate . . . and 'a misrecognition of the fact that this language . . . is imposed as dominant'" (32).

10. I am, of course, referring to Benedict Anderson's often-quoted concept of the nation as an "imagined community."

11. See his "Discourse in the Novel."

12. The most well-known proponent of atavism was the Italian criminologist Cesare Lombroso, who believed the criminal was a biological throwback. Atavism, however, lost its specificity and soon was used to include modern man. See Herman.

13. There is also a 1924 edition, published in Spain with significant changes to the 1919 edition.

14. *La vorágine*'s ending is paradigmatic of man's losing battle with nature in regionalist novels. After trying to find Cova and his comrades for some five months, the Colombian consul in Manaus sends a telegram to the government, which ends by saying: "The jungle devoured them!" (385).

15. I have not consulted the original 1919 and 1924 editions. I have used Lorente Medina's edition of *Raza*, which shows all the variations of the text throughout its different editions.

16. Antonio Lorente Medina provides, in his edition of *Raza*, footnotes with many translations of words left untranslated by Arguedas. The critical task of illuminating the many layers of a manuscript contributes this time, however involuntarily, to a process of familiarization of the Indian world of the novel, initiated by Arguedas and left incomplete by him.

WORKS CITED

Anderson, Benedict. *Imagined Communities. Reflections on the Origin and Spread of Nationalism*. Rev. ed. London: Verso, 1992.

Arguedas, Alcides. *Raza de bronce*. 1945. Ed. Antonio Lorente Medina. Madrid: Colección Archivos, 1988.

———. *Wuata Wuara*. 1904. *Raza* 357–422.

Arguedas, José María. "La novela y el problema de la expresión literaria en el Perú." 1960. *Yawar Fiesta*. Buenos Aires: Losada, 1977. 165–74.

Bakhtin, Mikail: "Discourse in the Novel." *The Dialogic Imagination*. Ed. Michael Holquist. Tr. Caryl Emerson and Michael Holquist. Austin: U of Texas P, 1981. 259–422.

Clifford, James. *The Predicament of Culture: Twentieth-Century Ethnography, Literature, and Art*. Cambridge: Harvard UP, 1988.

Condarco Morales, Ramiro. *Zárate, el "Temible" Willka*. Second ed. La Paz: Renovación, 1982.

Cornejo Polar, Antonio. *Escribir en el aire: Ensayo sobre la heterogeneidad socio-cultural en las literaturas andinas*. Lima: Horizonte, 1994.

Demelas, Daniele. "Darwinismo a la criolla: el Darwinismo social en Bolivia, 1880–1910." Tr. Giancarla de Quiroga. *Historia Boliviana* I/2 (1981): 55:82.

Dingwaney, Anuradha, and Carol Maier, Eds. "Introduction." *Between Languages and Cultures: Translation and Cross-Cultural Texts*. Pittsburgh: U of Pittsburgh P, 1995. 3–15.

Fernández, Teodosio. "Las tensiones ideológicas de Arguedas en *Raza de bronce*."Arguedas, *Raza* 519–35.

García Pabón, Leonardo. *La patria íntima: Alegorías nacionales en la literatura y el cine de Bolivia*. La Paz: CESU/Plural, 1998.

Herman, Arthur. *The Idea of Decline in Western History*. New York: The Free Press, 1997.

Langer, Eric. "Native Cultural Retention and the Struggle for Land in Early Twentieth-Century Bolivia." *The Indian in Latin American History: Resistance, Resilience, and Acculturation*. Ed. John E. Kicza. Wilmington: Scholarly Resources, 1993. 171–96.

Lienhard, Martin. *La voz y su huella: Escritura y procesos de interacción cultural 1492–1989*. 1990. Third Ed. Lima: Renovación, 1992.

Matto de Turner, Clorinda. *Torn from the Nest*. 1889. Tr. John H. R. Polt. New York: Oxford UP, 1998.

Niranjana, Tejaswini. *Siting Translation: History, Post-Structuralism, and the Colonial Context*. Berkeley: U of California P, 1992.

Rama, Angel. *La ciudad letrada*. Hanover: Ed. del Norte, 1984.

Rivera, José Eustasio. *La vorágine*. 1924. Ed. Montserrat Ordoñez. Madrid: Cátedra, 1990.

Borges, the Original of the Translation

Walter Carlos Costa

"... the most humble of all tasks."
"That of the translator? Yes, but one of the most beautiful."

—Borges to María Esther Vázquez

Translation seems to play an essential role—much more important than is generally supposed—in the creation and development of culture, nationally as well as individually. The greater or lesser autonomy of a culture seems connected to the way in which it incorporated in the past—and handles in the present—elements imported from elsewhere, in a word, to its politics of translation. Some civilizations seem to translate more and better than others, the usual examples being Rome in antiquity and Western Europe and Japan in modern times. The process is obviously complex and includes periods of greater and lesser activity, with phases of massive importation followed by development of their own local literature and subsequent exportation of it. Periods of crisis and of loss of self-confidence tend to register an increase in translations.

A similar process can be observed in individual writers. Practically all writers, in the West and elsewhere, who found their voice did so, in some form, through translation. In Hispanic letters the great renovators were always tied to foreign literatures: Cervantes, who "translated" the literature of Renaissance Italy, Huidobro, who "translated" the poetry of the French avant-garde, Lezama Lima, who incorporated a vast and heterogeneous foreign library. Even in the "most literary of countries," translation was essential to the formation of the following major authors: Voltaire (English writers), Baudelaire and Mallarmé (Poe), Nerval (Goethe), and Proust (Ruskin). As we approach the twentieth century we observe writers practicing translation not just in a broad sense (like Cervantes) but in the strict sense: the German Romantics systematically translating the great literature of other countries,[1] Pasternak translating Shakespeare. Translation begins to function as a site of apprenticeship and testing of topics and forms.

Jorge Luis Borges inscribes himself, then, in a long tradition that preceded him and that continued after his appearance on the stage of world literature. The fact that he contributed in a powerful way to the renewal of writing in Spanish starting from the inspiration of English-language writing does not differ greatly from the cases of Machado de Assis or Fernando Pessoa. His use of philosophical and historical sources is not, to be sure, a novelty in world literature. What makes Borges's case truly singular is the scale on which he operated, more typical—in volume, worth, and impact—of a group of writers, a literary school or even an institution than of a single writer working alone. Borges worked with so many texts from so many traditions that he gives the impression of having read and been acquainted with everything, which is certainly not the case, as Daniel Balderston has shown with precision.[2] A writer obviously does not need to be erudite—the erudition of great writers such as Shakespeare and Keats seems to have been rather precarious—but it is interesting that in the case of Borges his erudition makes educated people uncomfortable and his critics feel the obligation to mark out the limits of his knowledge, which otherwise would be frightening for its breadth, diversity, and depth.[3]

Despite the evident limits of his references, Borges's use of the legacy of world literature is unique. One possible explanation for his extraordinary achievement is in the intelligent and flexible use he made of the possibilities of translation. In fact, Borges not only assimilated and made use of foreign literatures but also acted as a true cultural advocate for both his country or language and for humanity. How this could occur in the case of what he called a "mere Argentine" is what I will now explore.

One of the main difficulties of a writer from a peripheral country such as Argentina is the relative poverty of the national cultural system. Writers in the United Kingdom, the United States, or France have access to practically any material they might need in their native language: sufficient material to develop their writing, to find models and sources on topics of interest. In other words, they can count on a legion of precursors.

A related phenomenon is that translators in the dependent countries spend much of their time translating texts that are of poor quality and which make little contribution to national culture. In contrast, a few translators in the more powerful countries end up having a greater impact on their culture, and sometimes on that of other countries, simply by having concentrated on texts that are of greater cultural importance. Borges's effort to bring to Spanish-speaking readers some of the texts that he considered important ended up stimulating new translations of these authors. In the final years of his life his selections from the universe of literature began to have influence even in what was considered important in the hegemonic countries and, in consequence, brought about changes in what could be considered the canon of world literature. This fact is unheard of in the history of Hispanic letters.

The intellectual in a dependent country has special difficulties. He or she must simultaneously help found a tradition and establish his or her personal place within that tradition. The first need often leads him or her to a problem that is well known among Spanish American and Brazilian writers: didacticism, that is, the temptation to renounce the search for something unique (always an uncertain thing if one is concerned about results) in favor of a pedagogical stance: to bring into national culture what has been already done in other languages and cultures. If a writer in a peripheral country dares to do more and to speak to the world he or she will probably be attacked for being alienated, elitist, and insensitive to the situation of cultural poverty suffered at home. Such figures are often seen as a-national or anti-national, as has occurred with Machado de Assis, Guimarães Rosa, Clarice Lispector, Lezama Lima, and, perhaps for good reason, with Borges.

The radical difference between Borges and these other innovators is that he did not merely transcend local limits by following the example of great foreign writers, but that he recreates in his work the privileged conditions that existed in the dominant countries, in an idiosyncratic but nevertheless quite eloquent way. Thus, he did not only not hide the sources that he made use of in the process of making himself into an international figure but he made them explicit as a central element of his esthetic. This gesture of exploration of dominant culture, which might have been viewed as a proof of subordination, is instead transformed into an affirmative gesture of autonomy. At the same time that he learns from foreign models he teaches a lesson to those foreign literary systems, giving them a new and original version of their own unexplored riches. And translation will be a key, if not indispensable, instrument in this process.

Translation will be essential for Borges's literary project for a very simple reason: if it is true that a large part of his readings were done in English, an equally large part were of authors from other cultures, especially Western and Asian classics. In contrast, the overwhelming majority of his writings were in Spanish. Translation was always an instrument for inserting what he read into what he wrote.

Borges's readers know that paradox is one of his favorite ways of expressing his thought. Paradox has two features that are especially useful for Borges: it draws attention because it makes the reader confront a proposition contradictory to the ideas surrounding it and it is formally elegant because it is organized through parallelism. Through paradox he explained his assimilation of works written in languages that he did not know, through translations:

F. S.: Haven't you ever felt a kind of remorse when reading the Greek classics in translation?

J. L. B.: No, I used to think about this the same way I thought about Arabic. Not knowing Greek and Arabic allowed me to read, so to speak, the *Odyssey* and *The Thousand and One Nights* in many versions, so that this poverty also brought me a kind of richness. (Sorrentino 87–88)

Exactly how does this transformation of "poverty" (being dependent on translations, he means, is not always trustworthy) into "richness" (to use translations to get better acquainted with the original work)? Here Borges used a method that is practiced more or less spontaneously by specialists: the comparison of various versions. Thus, Martín de Riquer uses the English, French, and Italian translations in his edition of *Don Quixote* to clarify passages in Cervantes's text that are ambiguous today. The great difference is that while specialists show an interest that we could define as topical, Borges is interested above all in the text as a whole. Some examples will serve to define Borges's method, which is at the same time original and effective—and is as revolutionary now as it was when he wrote.

The most obvious are those key texts of world literature written in Greek and Asian languages and which form basic references of Borges's universe, such as the *Iliad,* the *Odyssey,* and the *Arabian Nights.* While many modern writers probably haven't read even a single version of these works, Borges carefully read various versions of them in English, French, and German. Through the various rewritings he comes to a sort of supra-text of these works and is able to imagine the possible variants, even those variants that are produced by an ancient Greek reader (or listener) of Homer or an Arabic speaker of the *Arabian Nights.* Through the incessant reading of multiple translations a transcendent instance is created, of which the original is just one version, despite being the first in the series.

It is probable that Borges used this method with various masterworks of world culture the originals of which were not written in Spanish, English, French, and German, the modern languages that he read best. This happened with many Greek works and with those from Asian languages, as in the case of the *Zohar,* which he says he read in various editions in English and German (Ferrari 99).

What is most surprising about this is that it did not diminish his desire to learn the languages in which these works were written, as is demonstrated by his learning Old Norse and, at the very end of his life, Japanese. It is also important to note that the learning of languages was always linked for Borges to the effort to come closer to texts and understand their processes of composition and ways of functioning. With great pragmatism, he does not only incorporate the procedures he learned in this way into the writing of his own work (as many others have done) but he makes these processes explicit in the creative work and in a great number of didactic texts, which took the form of reviews, anthologies, and interviews.

Borges is intellectually tolerant in a country, a continent, indeed in a world, where it is often difficult for opposite or even merely different points of view to coexist. In relation to questions of translation this is particularly true. In contrast to many translators and theorists of translation,

Borges is characterized by tolerance, self-irony, and pragmatism, stances that complement each other to form the profile of a skeptical theorist and critic of translation who celebrates the power of translation.

In the same way that he seemed not to remember his own texts well, confusing at times *Ficciones* and *El Aleph,* so countless times Borges denied having been the author of certain translations. It was perhaps a way of resisting our cultures' obsession with the author and authority and the relative lack of interest in a text's suggestive level, for him what is truly important.

Here Borges assumes a position that is the diametrical opposite of authors such as Lawrence Venuti, one of the most influential present-day scholars of translation studies. Venuti has demonstrated in a well-documented and convincing way that the dominant mode among translators in English-speaking countries has been a forced subordination (imposed by publishers, by the ideology of the time, or perhaps self-imposed by the translators) to normative practices.[4] Venuti asserts the "visibility" of the translator in order to produce a translation that is foreign-sounding and that introduces into the system of reception some new elements of the original text as well as idiosyncratic traces of the translator, reasserting a tradition whose greatest representatives are Schleiermacher and Benjamin.

Borges, essentially skeptical and attentive to the lessons of history, takes a much more cautious position. Instead of granting the translator the status of author, as Venuti and a growing number of translators and scholars of translation would do, Borges seems to consider the ambiguous status of the translator in the same light as he considers the ambiguous status of the author, an indirect but emphatic way of affirming that the two concepts overlap, the author being in many senses a translator and the translator to varying extents an author. The opposing positions are explained by the very different concerns that move Borges and Venuti, the first being fundamentally interested in the vicissitudes of the text and the latter in the vicissitudes of the translator.

Thus, in a famous essay, "The Enigma of Edward Fitzgerald" (in *Other Inquisitions*), Borges affirms that Fitzgerald found his destiny as a writer through a foreign text. Borges is less concerned with fidelity to the Persian original or with Fitzgerald as translator than with the notable fact that a text that presents itself as a translation managed to enter the English canon. The case is stranger still in that Fitzgerald had failed as an author and as a translator and succeeded as an adapter: though Borges does not use the word, it is obvious that *The Rubaiyat of Omar Khayyám* is more an adaptation than a translation. Rather than defending translation as a profession of the translator or fidelity to the author, Borges is drawn to Fitzgerald through his view of the literary text as Platonic type.

The same could be said of his evaluation of Galland's version of the *Arabian Nights.* According to Borges, the Galland translation was the most important one for a series of reasons that does not include fidelity, since he calls it "the worst written of all, the most dishonest and weakest, but . . . the best read" (*Selected Non-Fictions* 93). The praise of "creative and felicitous infidelity" extends also to the translations of Mardrus and Burton, at the same time that Borges criticizes the unimaginative fidelity of the German translators of the *Arabian Nights*. His explanation is that the French and English translators succeeded in bringing their native literatures into the language of the translation while the German translators limit themselves to philological rigor.

My hypothesis is this: Burton's and Mardrus's translations, and even Galland's, must be viewed as the *consequence* of a literature. Whatever their virtues or defects may be, they are works that presuppose a rich prior process. In a way, the almost endless and inexhaustible nature of English literature is present in Burton, who brings together the harsh obscenity of John Donne, the huge vocabulary of Shakespeare and Tourneur, Swinburne's tendency toward the archaic, the crass erudition of the seventeenth-century writers of treatises, the energy and vagueness, the flair for storms and magic. In Mardrus's joyous paragraphs Flaubert's *Salammbô* coexists with La Fontaine, the *Manequim de Vime,* and the Russian ballet. In Littman, who was as incapable of lying as George Washington, the solemnity of the Germans is only too evident, and the result is very poor in contrast. Germany's encounter with the *Arabian Nights* should have been more productive.

Borges, unlike those critics who look only for errors or the new theorists of translation who argue for the visibility of the translator, seeks out translations that reveal aspects of the original that were present in a virtual way but that can only fully appear when two conditions are met: that the language has produced diverse literary forms and that the author brings these forms into the translated work. That is why Borges at the end of his essay imagines what Kafka might have produced if he had tried his hand at a translation of the *Arabian Nights:* "Chance has played at symmetries, contrasts, digressions. What might a man—Kafka—do if he organized and intensified this play, remade it in line with the Germanic distortion, the *unheimlichkeit* of Germany?" (*Selected Non-Fictions* 109).

But Borges does not always defend a translator's license or infidelity as a sufficient strategy for the production of a new text that harnesses the energy of the original. He frequently argues that in certain cases the "literal" solution is the most productive, as with the translation that Burton gave of the original title of the *Arabian Nights,* the *Book of the Thousand Nights and a Night* (*Selected Non-Fictions* 96).

At times he prefers an intermediate position, such as he says he chose in his translation of Whitman's *Leaves of Grass:*

Whitman's language is a contemporary language; hundreds of years will pass before it is a dead language. Then we will be able to translate and recreate it in full freedom, as Jáuregui did with the *Pharsalia* or Chapman, Pope and Lawrence with the *Odyssey*. In the meantime, I see no other possibility other than the one I have chosen, which oscillates between a personal interpretation and a resigned sense of rigor. (Whitman 22)

Here Borges makes his typical use of paradox, defending a position that is the exact opposite of that taken by the majority of specialists for whom more ancient texts will cause their translators the most problems. Borges's idea is that an ancient text free itself, so to speak, of its author, allowing the translator to exercise his or her creativity fully; similarly, he also argues the seemingly strange idea that some texts "defeat" their translators, as happens with *Don Quixote* and the novels of Dostoevsky. For him the force of certain texts is a consolation to the translator who is unsure of having done a good job, as he says in the prologue to his selections from *Leaves of Grass:*

> One fact comforts me. I remember many years ago attending a performance of *Macbeth;* the translation was every bit as bad as the actors and the gaudy set, but I left the theater undone by the passion of tragedy. Shakespeare had opened a way for himself; Whitman will do the same. (Whitman 22)

The conviction that certain authors forge a path seems to have guided his work as an anthologist. In his many anthologies and collections the text and the authors occupy the central place, not the translators. There is a peaceful coexistence of texts translated by Borges with translations by others, good, bad, and indifferent. Borges seems to have trusted that once the text or its author gained acceptance, if the translation presented problems it would be redone.

Borges's contradictions and paradoxes resist definitive conclusions about translation but suggest a number of important contributions. By putting translation at the service of his literary project, Borges gave little importance to translation in itself, his attitude shifting from ignorance to negligence. If, on the one hand, he defends the role of the translator, on the other, in his various collections, he tends to pass over the role of the intermediary without whom the text in Spanish would not exist.

Thus, in his book *Prólogo con un prólogo de prólogos,* all of the translated texts for which he wrote a preface appear without a mention of the translators unless he translated them himself. This was probably a decision by the publishers, but in the prefaces he makes no mention of the process and the problems of translation. It seems impossible that he could have been indifferent to the difficulties and pleasant surprises that formed part of the translation of authors as varied, in different languages, and as demanding of their translators, as Shakespeare, Gibbon,

Lewis Carroll, Melville, Whitman, and Kafka—all canonical authors—or the less canonical Wilkie Collins, Marcel Schwob, and Attilio Rossi.

Clearly, Borges's principal interest is in the general quality of the texts, not in their importance as "fixed" texts with a given set of properties. He was apparently not interested in how the Spanish-language translators dealt with the untranslatable wordplays of Shakespeare or Lewis Carroll or the elaborate syntax of Carlyle. For his purposes in his book of prefaces what seems important is to publicize the imagined worlds of Shakespeare and Henry James, of Collins and Kafka. With translations that pay attention to what matters most, Borges doesn't bother to comment on their status as translations: the important thing is that they are available in Spanish.

His attitude is different in relation to some other texts, translated by authors who matter to him, including his own translations. In the preface to the book of prefaces he makes reference to two memorable titles of translations, in which the translators brought into the target language something of the word-order specific to the original language, among them the "Cantar de los cantares [Song of songs] as Luis de León writes" (Borges, *Obras completas* 4:13).

To put it another way, Borges adopted an attitude that is not so much programmatic as pragmatic. Instead of proposing a method of translation he develops that method in his translations; that is, instead of forming a school, as the German Romantics or the Brazilian concrete poets did, Borges preferred to use what he saw as readable translations, just as he used texts that he considered important. Just as he never encouraged anyone to write the way he did so he never urged anyone to translate as he did.

A typical illustration of this is his relation with the U.S. translator Norman Thomas di Giovanni, with whom he worked for three years in Buenos Aires. Emir Rodríguez Monegal notes that this collaboration resulted in Borges becoming the co-author of the translations, but never an English-language author per se. His rather Victorian handling of English contrasted with di Giovanni's very different handling of the language, resulting in translations that are quite strange at times (Rodríguez Monegal 413). Monegal's critical assessment of these translations is echoed in passing by Daniel Balderston, who wrote in 1986: "The English translations are widely scattered, uneven in quality, and by no means complete" (xxv).

It remains curious that a declared Anglophile was translated mostly by North Americans, for the most part university professors, who produced scholarly translations that at times were distinct and distant from Borges's style of fiction. With the exception of the poetry, which seems to me to have become more poetic in English than in Spanish, Borges's work has been translated into English in ways that stress a natural and normal style more than the linguistic transgressiveness that characterizes

the Spanish originals. Nevertheless, Borges never criticized his translators, perhaps because he knew (as a good student of literary history) that
readers and critics would demand new translations that would be commissioned in due time.

Frequently in Borges the best ideas appear as *boutades*. This happens for instance in the affirmation that translation often *improves* the
original. This notion is related to another, repeated frequently throughout his work, that time often *improves* some works, or parts of them.

Here we find a surprising equation: if the passage from a text in one
language to another text in a different language has something in common with the passage of a text through time, this means that translation
and time act on texts in similar ways. The passage of time means, among
other things, the passage of readings that, above all in the case in which
those readings are recorded, modify the text.

Borges also considers on several occasions the crucial problem of the
possibilities of a language and how they are used in literature. As
always, his vision is pragmatic and flexible, that of an observer attentive
to the facts and not simply a follower of a conventional opinion or of
fashion. In contrast to those who see "the language" as something fixed
and given, Borges separates the possibilities of a language from how
writers make use of it. His direct knowledge of some Indo-European languages and indirect knowledge of many others leads him to sketch out
a theory (that he never really develops) of linguistic possibility. But
Borges never fully separates language from culture, as when he praises
English and French translations for their incorporation of techniques
that had been elaborated in the course of their literary histories.

One of the strongest and most original points of Borges's thinking
on translation is his assessment of the relative possibilities of English and
Spanish. His long familiarity with texts in both languages and, certainly,
his long practice of reading translations and of translating inform his
commonsensical position, sometimes so different from the conventional
thinking, which became an important tool in his own writing.

In contrast, it is worth noting how different his position was from
those defended by Norman Thomas di Giovanni and by Mario Vargas
Llosa, both of whom are representative of normative ideas about translation. Di Giovanni, for instance, comments on the "measure and economy of [Borges's] style," which he says is radically different from the
florid rhetoric that he claims is dominant in Spanish and closer to English models (Sorrentino 128–29). Vargas Llosa, similarly, argues that
"Spanish is a wordy language, bountiful and flamboyant" (Di Giovanni
112). Neither Vargas Llosa nor di Giovanni makes a distinction between
the language and the literary tradition, nor do they notice that there is a
long tradition of economic and concise expression in Spanish—in
Lazarillo de Tormes and the poems of Fray Luis de León and, more
recently, in Juan Rulfo and Juan José Arreola. In Portuguese, this tradi-

tion, which similarly is not the dominant one, runs from Gil Vicente and Machado de Assis to Graciliano Ramos and João Cabral de Melo Neto. Borges's view of the advantages and disadvantages of Spanish and English is much more precise and more flexible. He says, for instance, in one interview: "The Spanish language tends to the abstract, English to the physical, and its common physical expressions tend to be untranslatable. In Spanish there is a difference between two verbs of being [*ser* and *estar*] that is not frequent in other languages" (Vázquez 73).[5]

There is an important difference between Borges's strategy and that of other innovators in the field of translation such as Ezra Pound and the Brazilian concrete poets Augusto and Haroldo de Campos. In their practice they represent three ways of handling the translated text that we could classify as follows. Augusto and Haroldo de Campos, although they declare themselves disciples of Pound, in their practice as translators are closer to the tradition of the German Romantics, theorized by Schleiermacher and later by Walter Benjamin. They opted for putting their linguistic knowledge and poetic talents at the service of the authors they considered innovators within world poetry. In so doing, they forced the limits of literary Brazilian Portuguese, attempting to incorporate the techniques they found in foreign authors. The result was a true school of poetic translation in Brazil. Pound incorporated some elements of foreign poetic works into his own work, without being as concerned with linguistic knowledge. The result was often closer to the adaptation of the Edward Fitzgerald variety than to translation properly speaking. Borges, in contrast, chose an original way of working. Like Pound, he incorporates elements of the original into his work, but these elements are minor features of the original and respond to a wide variety of different textual models. Thus, these texts, sometimes direct translations, sometimes translations from other translations, help him create a new type of text, in which those elements are an important but subordinate part.

At the same time, his translations of complete texts fulfill a different function and responded to his efforts to help them reach new readers (or sometimes were commissioned by publishers). He was not concerned in these translations with following the original author's poetics, instead impressing his own style on the texts. It is not surprising, then, that he should at times have denied his own authorship of these translations, despite the textual evidence to the contrary.

It is no coincidence, then, that translation is central to Borges's *modus operandi*. His is a poetics of rereading and rewriting, essential to every project of translation. Borges was one of the writers who explored most fully the practical and theoretical aspects of translation. He gave a new dignity to the translated text in general, and not only to great translations. His critical and theoretical contribution is of the highest importance, containing many lessons that can be studied and extended. His work as a translator is perhaps more important in terms of his own work than in terms of that of the authors whom he translated. He broadened the use of translated texts but seems to have made only a paltry contribution to the kind of translation that brings techniques developed in other languages into literary Spanish, in contrast to the German Romantic school or that of the Brazilian concrete poets, the tradition that is defended at present by theorists of translation such as Henri Meschonnic and Lawrence Venuti. In Borges's theory and criticism, which is present in all of his work, we find the seeds of new modes of translation that future generations can cultivate.

Translated by Daniel Balderston and Marcy Schwartz

NOTES

1. In Berman (1995) we find a careful exposition of this grandiose project.

2. "Indeed, it could be argued that Borges did not invent anything. He worked with the detritus of a culture, shuffling and picking through through the shards. The ruined culture is that of Europe: the fragments of the cultures of Islam, India and the Orient are those brought back by plundering imperial missionaries, governors and merchants. Borges was, as he would say himself, unsurpassingly ignorant of Arabic, Hebrew, Farsi, Sanskrit, and Chinese, and only slightly conversant in his later years in Japanese; his knowledge of these cultures is to a large extent drawn from the infinite pages of the *Encyclopaedia Britannica* and the manuals of Buddhism, Persian and Chinese literatures and the like that he cited so often. His learning was indeed encyclopedic, but often at several removes from its subject" (Balderston, xv).

3. For instance, it is striking that Brazilian literature barely figures in Borges's work, even that of the writer most like him—Anglophile, ironic, urbane—Machado de Assis.

4. Venuti notes how little importance translated work has in the publishing world of the United States and the United Kingdom.

5. The point to which Borges's famous concision derived from English models is worthy of debate. Besides the various Spanish models mentioned, it should be noted that many of the English writers that Borges admired could be characterized not as concise and economical but as baroque. Rodríguez Monegal, in his turn, notes that Alfonso Reyes influenced Borges's attempts to be "succint and direct" (197).

WORKS CITED

Balderston, Daniel. *The Literary Universe of Jorge Luis Borges*. Westport: Greenwood, 1986.

Berman, Antoine. *L'Épreuve de l'étranger: Culture et traduction dans l'Allemagne romantique*. Paris: Gallimard, 1984.

Borges, Jorge Luis. *Borges on Writing*. New York: Allen Lane, 1974.

———. *Obras completas*. Madrid: Emecé, 1996.

———. *Prólogo con un prólogo de prólogos*. Buenos Aires: Torres Agüero, 1975.

———. *Selected Non-Fictions*. Ed. Eliot Weinberger. Trans. Esther Allen, Suzanne Jill Levine, and Eliot Weinberger. New York and London: Viking, 1999.

Di Giovanni, Norman, ed. *In Memory of Borges*. London: Constable, 1988.

Ferrari, Osvaldo. *Diálogos*. Barcelona: Seix Barral, 1992.

Highet, Gilbert. *The Classical Tradition*. New York and Oxford: Oxford University Press, 1976.

Lambert, José. "Traduction." *Théorie littéraire*. Ed. Marc Angenot, Jean Bessière, Douwe Fokkema, and Eva Kushner. Paris: Presses Universitaires de France, 1989.

Rodríguez Monegal, Emir. *Borges, una biografía literaria*. Mexico City: Fondo de Cultura Económica, 1986.

Sorrentino, Fernando. *Seven Conversations with Jorge Luis Borges*. Trans. M. Zlotchew. Troy: Whitston, 1982.

Vázquez, María Esther. *Borges: imágenes, memorias, diálogos*. Caracas: Monte Avila, 1977.

Venuti, Lawrence. *The Translator's Invisibility: A History of Translation*. London: Routledge, 1995.

Whitman, Walt. *Hojas de hierba*. Ed. and trans. Jorge Luis Borges. Buenos Aires: Lumen, 1969.

Puga's Fictions of Equivalence:
The Tasks of the Novelist As Translator

Vicky Unruh

María Luisa Puga's novel *Las posibilidades del odio* (Mexico 1978) narrates six versions of life in postcolonial Kenya embodied in characters whose shifting relationships to an enduring colonialist order are shaped by their individual circumstances of race, class, tribal origins, and gender. With the rapidly changing city of Nairobi in the 1970s as a site of convergence for its stories, the novel highlights the uneasy task facing a diverse human group on the verge of (re)articulating its own identities. In the face of this daunting undertaking, immense accumulations of enmity—the possibilities of hatred—are recast as powerful sources of a community's potential. The work has been interpreted as an allegorical commentary on persistent colonialist structures of Mexican society; as an exposition of the more personal histories underlying the chronological lists of twentieth-century Kenyan historical events that precede each of the six accounts; and as the fictional prototype of a postcolonial world characterized by an enduring experience of foreignness.[1] I would argue as well, however, that the novel generates a nuanced meditation on the problems of translation, through a thematic portrayal of the role of linguistic politics and multilingualism in the formation of postcolonial subjectivity and through the singular linguistic conditions of its own telling. In a narrative world inhabited by speakers of numerous Bantu languages, including Swahili as the lingua franca, and of English as the language of (post)colonization and pedagogy, *Las posibilidades* conceives of language as an index of social hierarchies, as a path to upward mobility and power, and, in the characters' search for a linguistic home, as the fault line between identity and difference. A strong impetus for communication, on the other hand, weaves through all six stories, whose characters embody the desire for connection and rootedness implicit in "idiomas que no fueran extranjeros" (189). In this vein, the narrative provides multiple cues of its own self-conscious conception as a translation, not only because this novel in which characters speak Swahili, English, Kikuyu, Abaluya, Akamba, and Italian is written in Spanish, but also because the work

194

constructs an implicit novelist-as-translator whose presence highlights the thematics of translation. Specifically, the novel examines the problems inherent in the equivalence of distinct linguistic and cultural experience that the act of translation implies, the tensions accruing to a translation founded on such an apparently democratic spirit of interchangeability, and the challenges and responsibilities of a novelist who undertakes translating a cultural-linguistic reality that is not her own. The narrative unfolding of these issues in *Las posibilidades* points to the significance of such an inquiry as well to the post-1968 Mexican literary culture in which Puga's first novel emerged.

Each of the six tales in the novel privileges the characters' personal optic through first-person accounts or internally focalized free indirect discourse. The first section presents the racist monologue of a white Kenyan safari guide who laments to an unidentified tourist his displacement at the hands of both the ex-colonials and black Kenyans. In the second story, we hear a black Kenyan indigent's emotionally muted, interiorized account of his marginal life, first as an orphaned outcast in his Nandi tribal village, then as a fugitive from both the Mau Mau and district leaders, and finally as a one-legged beggar on the streets of Nairobi. In the third section, José Antonio, a young, upper-middle-class Mexican hires Jeremiah, a lower-middle-class, Abaluya student to be his tour guide to the Kenyan coast. Through shifting focalization, the story documents their uneven efforts at friendship. In section four, Mr. Matiolo, an anxious and solicitous Akamba office manager, who has internalized the colonialist world view, is fired because he misunderstands his supervisor's English instructions. In part five, a British expatriate, out to prove that superiority is only a "truco," describes an elaborate plot to manipulate black Kenyan students to revolt. Part six presents the novel's most intricate story, the novella-length *Bildungsroman* of Nyambura, a young woman of the dominant Kikuyu tribe. Her tradition-bound mother dies when Nyambura is a child, her upwardly mobile Christian father works as an engineer for the Voice of Kenya, her older brother dies from a beating following anticolonialist student protests, and her younger brother prepares for a career in the emergent tourist industry. As a postgraduate student in Rome who is writing a thesis on Kenyan history, Nyambura, with her British lover Chris as interlocutor, pieces together the story of her fragmented life. She ultimately rejects a possible interracial marriage and "la nacionalidad flotante" to return to Kenya and "escribir lo mío" (283).

Characters in all six stories inhabit a multilingual scene that constantly requires them to experience the world through shifts from language to language. But we do not fully understand that we are to read the novel itself as a translation until well into Nyambura's story. Here Chris reacts with surprise to her racist verbal assault when she observes that his "payasadas" in response to her requests for emotional space typify somebody whose grandfather was not a slave. The narrator records his reaction: "Uúchale *(o el equivalente)*. Chris quedó suspendido en total sorpresa" (243–44, my emphasis). With the parenthetical "o el equivalente," the narrator not only underscores the fact that Chris and Nyambura aren't conversing in Spanish (they speak English to one another), but also conveys that their words are reaching us through the agency of a translator whose textual presence the parenthetical expression embodies. This presence is subsequently reinforced when Nyambura incorporates into her life-account a conversation at the university in Nairobi with a Mexican woman she had met at a lecture on African literature. The woman had explained that she wanted to write a story about Nairobi, and although Nyambura reports having resisted her overtures of friendship, on the eve of her return from Rome to Kenya, she observes that she would now be more than ready for this cross-cultural dialogue. A subtle shift of Nyambura's interlocutors in the novel's closing pages—she is by now speaking about Chris rather than to him—suggests the conversation may well have come to pass and encourages readers to merge the authorial figure of the Mexican woman and the narrating translator of the words we have been reading. The fact that Puga herself lived in Kenya for a year and a half while her then husband worked for the United Nations gives the work's implicit novelist-as-translator an autobiographical air that reinforces this reading.

The construction of the work's narrator as a translator produces a series of effects. In her work on cultural identity and the politics of transmission, Sherry Simon observes that, in contrast to a traditional goal of producing a seamless work in which the translator's hand is imperceptible, recent translation studies—and here she draws on the work of Gayatri Spivak—posit the necessity of foregrounding the "complexity of agency in translation" (142) by rendering visible the figure of the translator. Translators, she affirms, "actualize prevailing attitudes toward Otherness," and are "fully engaged in the literary, social, and ideological realities" of their time (137). In this vein, Puga portrays the translators in *Las posibilidades,* the narrator and several characters, as agents with their own histories, agendas, and prejudices. In search of correspondences between postcolonial Kenya and her own national experience, for example, the Mexican writer-translator pours out her own story to Nyambura (who is uncomfortable and unresponsive), revealing her own middle-class roots, her feminism and anticolonialist politics, and her aversion to most things "gringo," American or English. Similarly, in the novel's third story, Jeremiah's class and ethnic differences from the other Africans they meet determine how much and how accurately he translates for José Antonio.

If these characters and their world constitute the "original texts" that *Las posibilidades* is translating, moreover, the meeting between the Mexican woman and Nyambura embodies an uneasy encounter between a translator from one cultural reality and the unyielding material she will translate from another. Translation research, Simon argues, shows that, "because there is no total equivalence between cultural systems, the alignment between source and target text is necessarily skewed" (136). In this spirit and notwithstanding the narrator-translator's search for the precise counterpart of *uúchale,* the meeting between the Mexican writer and Nyambura accentuates instead the absence of correlations and is charged with tensions accruing from Nyambura's unwavering reluctance to "jugar a la igualdad"—the game that such equivalency would imply—and the writer's simultaneous confession of her inability to perceive fully the reality she wants to portray: "pero veo y veo y no entro" (276). Thus, the meeting constitutes the "necessarily skewed" encounter between source and target text, between Nyambura's emerging life story and the Mexican writer's account, as on the one hand the Mexican speaks far too much and on the other Nyambura offers up very little. This uncomfortable rendezvous of incongruities, with its fluctuating balance of power, is paralleled in the mobile narrating agency telling Nyambura's story: a gradual shift in dominance from the free indirect discourse to a more direct account in Nyambura's own words. In the context of these narrative moves, we may re-read the novel as a translated text that construes translation as a laborious task in which there are no neutral participants, no facile assimilation or equivalencies, and no value-free democratic process of cultural communication.

The characters' ordinary linguistic experiences exemplify this concept of translation, as we may read each of the six tales in part as the story of its protagonist's difficult relationship to language. Spivak has argued that translators of works from postcolonial societies must come to terms with the internal intricacies of these worlds and strive to understand the ways in which meanings are produced within them.[2] As the translator of a culture that is not her own, Puga's narrator works to convey the imposing linguistic complexity of the cultural experience she is interpreting. In each story, language emerges as the site of character traiting, an outward cue that provokes self-defining acts of assimilation or differentiation. The white Kenyan provides a particularly ironic counterexample to the narrator's approach. As a kind of cultural translator himself, a safari tour guide, he affirms without apology—"claro está" (12)—that he understands no African language but he still claims to know Kenyan blacks well. They are "parte normal del paisaje," he explains, as he transforms his own linguistic ignorance into a primitivist portrayal of people who, to his mind, communicate with "sonidos que emiten cuando discuten entre ellos" (11), emit "una especie de halo negro," and are enveloped in "una aureola llena de silencio" (13). As a trilingual black Kenyan (Abaluya, Swahili, and English), Jeremiah makes more sophisticated linguistic observations, but he, too, decodes the identity of others through language cues subject to misreadings. Thus, his Mexican traveling companion José Antonio presents a particular challenge when they first meet: because his English is clearly not British, Jeremiah decides he is from the States. Similarly, in the British nuns' boarding school, Kikuyu students isolate Nyambura because her good English makes them question her Kikuyu roots.

Elaborate code switching among black Kenyans further complicate these linguistically grounded acts of inclusion and exclusion, as characters pull class or ethnic rank on one another through language. In a world in which mastery of English leads to promotions, Mr. Matiolo provides the most obvious example. Because he is poorer than his friend and fellow Akamba tribesman, Julius, he has had fewer English classes and thus loses his job. The upwardly mobile Julius, on the other hand, who normally speaks to Matiolo in their native Akamba, switches to the more widely understood Swahili or to English when he puts him down in front of non-Akamba co-workers and friends. In a similar spirit, but on a more gendered note, as a child, Nyambura's brother Ngongo speaks English to their father when he wants to exclude Nyambura, who at that point speaks it less well, or their mother who doesn't speak it at all. Switching codes to assume a temporary identity, Jeremiah lets the Swahili truck driver who gives them a ride think that he and José Antonio are American tourists, and, speaking less than perfect Swahili, he learns far more about the man's views than he would have by revealing himself as an Abaluya.

While in such scenes the novel implies that a colonized people's multilingualism can be resourcefully mined for survival or temporary advantage, it also portrays characters in an anguished search for an elusive, translation-free linguistic home, an integrated sense of place and self through language. The English expatriate inciting revolt provides an instructive counterexample: his project includes the explicit resolution not to learn a Kenyan language precisely because the consequent assimilation could undermine his plan. But the Nairobi beggar and Nyambura, who occupy opposite ends of the novel's social spectrum of black Kenyans, offer the most penetrating examples. When he first appears on a city corner near the Nairobi Hilton, the permanently exiled beggar has long since abandoned speaking at all. Surrounded by a mélange of local and international languages and harboring accumulated cultural knowledge, he has little access to the means for communicating his experience: "no tenía a quien decirlo. Ni hubiera sabido como decirlo" (40). Still, he decodes the language of the footsteps around him, distinguishing rich from poor, black from white, through the differentiating sounds of their shoes and feet on the pavement (37). In his isolation, moreover, the language he hears around him—"mil frases, gestos, manos, tonos de voz y un ruido en torno que más parecía un arrullo" (25)—inscribes the only participatory space for which he actually yearns: "cerraba los ojos para retener sus voces todo el tiempo posible" (34). By the time she arrives in Rome, by contrast, Nyambura has mastered to varying degrees Kikuyu, English, Swahili, and Italian. But as either an exile or an initiate in all four of her languages, Nyambura finds integration in none. In contrast to the English imposed by her father and teachers, she recalls the Kikuyu spoken to her mother as "normal" (189). In boarding school, however, she learns among other Kikuyus that she knows little about the cultural practices inscribed in her "native" language. She eventually becomes most at home in Swahili—"ese lenguaje que había aprendido a amar en grupo y con esfuerzo y que ahora era el suyo" (208)—but when she arrives in Rome, she finds refuge from her halting Italian in English, the very language that, in the mouths of the nuns, she had experienced as "pedazos de palabras incomprensibles" (225). Nyambura's most powerful insight comes with the recognition in Rome that the sense of rootedness found in an unwritten space of origins—"de cielo sin construir, de calles sin trazar"—or in "idiomas que no fueran extranjeros" will always elude her (189).

In communicating this kind of experience, the task for Puga's novelist-as-translator, then, becomes the transmission of a linguistic reality that is itself neither fixed nor open to easy reading. Nyambura's experience through all of her languages, in fact, epitomizes what Homi Bhabha, in his account of "hyphenated cultures" as the site of the "incommensurability" of the worlds they connect (218), has called "living in the midst of the incomprehensible" (235). The fact of not understanding—what they see and, above all, what they hear—is the single experience shared by all of the protagonists in Puga's novel. Like the translator with a resistant text, they continually labor to "imagine" what lies behind another's words, as when Mr. Matiolo struggles to decipher instructions, the beggar hears impenetrable words whirling around him, Jeremiah tries to conjure up Mexico as José Antonio describes it, and Nyambura strives to interpret the Mexican woman's tone and gestures and to "imaginarse el cuerpo de esas palabras" (274). Thus, the characters' hyphenated linguistic activity, spanning diverse linguistic registers, serves less as a communicative bridge between worlds than as a sign of their cultures' "untranslatability," in Bhabha's terms, and, in Walter Benjamin's, of the intrinsic foreignness of all languages (75). In this vein, we can more fully appreciate the irony of the narrator-translator's parenthetical, self-revelatory move in "Uúchale (o el equivalente)" (243). In foregrounding the process of translating-by-equivalence, the narrator has conspicuously selected a word that has no actual equivalent in English, the language spoken by the character who emits it. Simon has noted that some contemporary translators leave expletives untranslated because they are anchored in contexts (140). Like many expletives, *uúchale*, which is uniquely Mexican both morphologically and in its usage, harbors site-specific etymological intricacies that a translator could illuminate only with a lengthy footnote. Thus, the narrator-translator of *Las posibilidades* draws our attention to the process of translation with a word that is essentially untranslatable and whose conditions for meaning in another language must be carefully negotiated by its user. This choice communicates as well not only the narrator's grasp of the estranging linguistic experience of those who inhabit the world she is translating, but also her identification—specifically as a translator and as a writer—with that experience.

The selection of an expletive such as *uúchale*, moreover, foregrounds the communicable power of a word that derives less from its actual semantic content than from its material force. In this spirit, Nyambura, too, focuses on the palpability of words, which she often experiences as material embodiments of inequality, for example when she realizes that "history" for the nuns means the history of white men: "las palabras . . . comenzaron a llamarle la atención. Eran curiosamente desiguales. Cuando se referían a la realidad de África, pasaban por encima, como aviones, como nubes; cuando se centraban en Inglaterra, descendían hasta los individuos, los tocaban, se multiplicaban en mil y mil detalles convincentes y vivos" (251). Puga's novel, in fact, portrays language as so incommensurable with character experience that fleeting moments of cross-cultural communication emerge, like the expletive *uúchale*, somehow beyond the quotidian task of language to mean. Thus, Jeremiah and José Antonio experience their most connective moment as they watch the "diálogo amoroso" between a young boy and his ball on the beach: "Un lenguaje universal mediante la pelota que . . . entendieron al instante" (91). In the same spirit, although Nyambura fails to "imagine" fully the meanings emerging from the Mexican woman's words, she does identify with something she recognizes beyond them: "a ratos percibía algo familiar—no en las frases, sino más bien una como sensación que le flotaba en la cara a la mexicana" (274). The Mexican writer in turn searches for a way to communicate in her story of Nairobi something that lies outside of the words she can't find: "una silueta que haga sentir esa extrañeza, rabia o miedo" that she senses in the city (276). These endeavors at cultural bridging beyond words point to the longing implicit in all translation for what Benjamin called the "inaccessible realm of reconciliation and fulfillment of languages" (75). But even as the novel strives for that reconciliation, it always returns, like Nyambura, to the necessary foreignness of words, whose barriers one could bring down only in passing: "Palabras. . . . Soltarlas. . . . Se evaporaban solas y las fronteras caían y el aire fresco entraba, pero luego . . . había que trazarlas otra vez, erigirlas para cubrirse" (241).

With the tasks undertaken by its internal novelist-as-translator, then, *Las posibilidades* documents acts of cultural and linguistic bridging that, while formidable, dispiriting, and always partial, are not unproductive.[3] In looking to connections beyond words, in fact, the work stresses the potential creative power of translation. Jeremiah discovers, for example, that when he translates for José Antonio he not only finds "otras maneras de ser africano," he actually creates new things: "En muchos casos inventaba, claro" (87). This conception of translating as inventive evokes Bhabha's portrayal of the hyphen in hyphenated cultures not only as a site of incomprehensibility but also as a place where—and here he is quoting Salman Rushdie—"newness enters the world" (227). Thus, the novel works to represent a community that, through its participants' "language *in actu*," as Bhabha characterizes translation (228), assumes the arduous process of (re)inventing its own modes of expression.

Through its focus on translation, then, we may read *Las posibilidades del odio* as the story of a (post)colonized community seeking its persistently elusive sense of linguistic place. This theme also illuminates how the novel speaks to Puga's own cultural contexts. Just as Nyambura returns from Rome to Kenya to "escribir lo mío" (283), Puga, who in 1968 had left Mexico for Europe and then Africa, returned in 1978 to undertake her own project as a writer of prose fiction.[4] The work of young Mexican novelists of Puga's post-Tlatelolco generation has been characterized by its attention to "unstable identities" (Brushwood) and by its moves to "recupera(r) la mexicanidad sin gritar nacionalismos" (Sefchovich 226). In a sometimes critical dialogue with established notions of "lo mexicano," these writers, as Danny Anderson has argued, make evident "the struggle in process in Mexican culture" and foreground that "every construction of reality is motivated by particular interests" (17). In this context, Puga's focus on linguistic fragmentation and hierarchies in Kenya points to her subsequent attention to language in Mexico, as she came to argue that language deprivation is a common factor in colonized societies (*Itinerario* 23). These views were shaped as well by her long-standing interest in Mexican cultures outside of the capital. After her return to Mexico, Puga, who had grown up partly in Acapulco and Mazatlán, Sinaloa, traveled widely and lectured on literature in provincial Mexico and situated some of her fiction in regional contexts. Drawing on her experience with Mexico's regional diversity and echoing the Kenyan experience of "living in the midst of the incomprehensible" (Bhabha) that her first novel embodies, she has argued that in Mexican schools, which promulgate the language of the elite, "nos hacíamos nación dentro de la incomprensión" (*Itinerario de palabras* 22–23). She has also evoked her Acapulco childhood with its "mil sonidos incontrolados" as a linguistic mélange that for readers of *Las posibilidades* calls to mind the dissonance enveloping the Nairobi beggar: "su hablar costeño, casi africano. El inglés de los turistas. El español de los comerciantes gachupines (muchos venidos de La Habana), y el italiano o el alemán de algún despistado avecinado ahí" ("El escritor" 16). In a pedagogic tour through provincial Mexico in the '80s, moreover, Puga lobbied for students to find their own languages, not through the standardized, erudite Spanish of the classroom but through a confrontational "conquista del derecho de expresarse exactamente desde quienes son" (*Itinerario* 34). The matter-of-fact, relaxed vernacular quality of Puga's own fictional style—inscribed in *uúchale* and its equivalents—manifests precisely this kind of expressive agenda. In this vein, Anderson has demonstrated that Puga's prize-winning novel *Pánico o peligro* (1983) constitutes its protagonist's complex struggle to "identify (with) a language of her own" (19) and, in the face of exclusionary notions of *mexicanidad,* to "give voice to identities and realities previously excluded from the cultural conversation" (24). *Las posibilidades del odio* embodies a fitting apprenticeship for these larger projects. In the guise of her novelist-as-translator, Puga confronts the linguistic complexity of another world. As when Jeremiah translates Africa for José Antonio, this confrontation brings into sharper focus her own encounters with the foreignness of words—like those of her early childhood, "desprovistas de sentido" ("El escritor" 15)—and with the cultural and linguistic perplexities that shape individual and community experience in a late-twentieth-century Mexican world.

NOTES

This chapter is dedicated to my colleague Danny Anderson, with gratitude for our continuing conversation.

1. See, respectively, Acevedo-Leal and Bradu, Reckley, and González Abellás. Reckley draws her analysis from the fact that each section of the novel is preceded by a continuing list of historical events that, in its totality, takes the reader from 1888, the year of the formation of the British East Africa Company, to 1973, when postcolonial Kenya became the site of the United Nations Program for the environment. For more comprehensive studies of Puga's fiction, see de Beer and López's *Historia, escritura e identidad.*

2. See "The Politics of Translation" in Spivak's *Outside in the Teaching Machine.*

3. On this point, I take issue with Debra Castillo's otherwise perspicacious reading of Puga's novel. While she does not focus specifically on language, Castillo regards the work in part as an account of its own failure in "speaking about Africa to Africans as well as Latin Americans" with anything more substantial than the "tourist guide's superficial platter" (250). I believe that the translation thematics I am foregrounding point to the work's more sanguine, though guarded, view of cross-cultural conversations.

4. On the autobiographical elements in Puga's fiction, see López's "Autobiografía interminable."

WORKS CITED

Acevedo-Leal, Anabella. "El reconocimiento de la realidad a través de la alteridad en *Las posibilidades del odio.*" *Monographic Review/Revista Monográfica* 8 (1992): 223–28.

Anderson, Danny J. "Cultural Conversation and Construction of Reality: Mexican Narrative and Literary Theories After 1968." *Siglo XX/20th Century* 8.1–2 (1990–1991): 11–30.

Benjamin, Walter. "The Task of the Translator." *Illuminations.* Ed. Hannah Arendt. Trans. Harry Zohn. New York: Shocken, 1969. 69–82.

Bhabha, Homi. *The Location of Culture.* London and New York: Routledge, 1994.

Bradu, Fabienne. *Señas particulares: Escritoras (Ensayos sobre escritoras mexicanas del siglo XX).* Mexico City: Fondo de Cultura Económica, 1987. 118–35.

Brushwood, John S. *La novela mexicana (1967–1982).* Mexico City: Grijalbo, 1984.

Castillo, Debra A. *Talking Back: Toward a Latin American Feminist Literary Criticism.* Ithaca: Cornell UP, 1992.

deBeer, Gabriella. "Maria Luisa Puga." *Contemporary Mexican Women Writers.* Austin: U of Texas P, 1996. 11–57.

González Abellás, Miguel Angel. "Jugando con estereotipos: Los extranjeros y la identidad nacional en México y el área del Caribe hispano, 1978–1993." Diss. U of Kansas, 1997.

López, Irma M. "Autobiografía interminable: La novelística de María Luisa Puga." *Texto-Crítico* 3.4–5 (1997): 73–82.

———. *Historia, escritura e identidad: la novelística de María Luisa Puga.* New York: Peter Lang, 1996.

Puga, María Luisa. "El escritor que uno quería ser." *Ruptura y diversidad.* By María Luisa Puga et al. Mexico City: UNAM, 1990. 15–19.

———. *Las posibilidades del odio.* 2nd. ed. Mexico City: Siglo Veintiuno, 1985.

Puga, María Luisa, and Mónica Mansour. *Itinerario de palabras.* México, D.F.: Folios Ediciones, 1987.

Reckley, Alice. "The Historical Referent as Metaphor." *Hispania* 71.3 (1988): 713–16.

Sefchovich, Sara. *México: País de ideas, país de novelas: Una sociología de la literatura mexicana.* Mexico City: Grijalbo, 1987.

Simon, Sherry. *Gender in Translation: Cultural Identity and the Politics of Transmission.* London and New York: Routledge, 1996.

Spivak, Gayatri. *Outside in the Teaching Machine.* London and New York: Routledge, 1993.

Translation in Post-Dictatorship Brazil:
A Weave of Metaphysical Voices in the Tropics

Else Ribeiro Pires Vieira

This is the use of memory:
For liberation . . .
History may be servitude,
History may be freedom

—T. S. Eliot, *Little Gidding*

After the 1964–1983 military dictatorship in Brazil, an intense activity of translation, which, in Peircean terms, makes the past known to present memory, gave sharper contours to the period's complex interplay of simultaneity and anachronism. In the "advances and retreats of these complicated and not at all naive 1980s" (Messeder 70), it is perhaps not surprising that the fictitious linearity and homogeneity imposed by the authoritarian regime would be substituted by a more complex and delinearized history. More specifically, translated English metaphysical poetry, actively circulating during this period, introduced an alternative past that entered into dialogue with the epigonic history narrated by Brazilian memoirist literature, vigorously produced in that decade by political exiles returning to the country. Through their autobiographies, they also initiated a dialogue with the younger generation; conversely, as Sussekind remarks, memoirs represent a form of vampirization, by the younger generation, of the other's historical experience (1985, 55). Poignantly, the former militant Alfredo Syrkis establishes the connection between the rehabilitation of historical memory and the transmission of experience:

> We made a lot of mistakes and the validity of the moral gesture does not attenuate the dimension of that defeat, which cost many dear and valuable lives. I believe it is important to recover these memories and transmit them especially to this new generation appearing in the 80s. The transmission of experiences is not easy, their assimilation even less so. But today's social movement itself is broader, deeper, richer and more mature. (Syrkis 4)

Another cultural and literary event of great importance further delineated this scenario of dialogues with voices from the past: in 1985, the debate on postmodernism reached the confused political-cultural scene of the New Republic (Hollanda). Postmodernism, in its eclecticism, displays a "tendency to loot the 'imaginary museum' of successive styles, cannibalizing the past" (Rouanet). From the mid-1960s, the *Antropofagia* (Cannibalism) movement of the 1920s was also revitalized through critical rereadings of works.

Translating England, reading Brazil: this interweaving of voices from different times and countries leads to questions of what and who is translated, and why and how it is translated. Arguing that translation is a sign that aids in the reconstitution of an era's cultural mosaic, I shall explore areas of permeability between English metaphysical poetry translated in Brazil and some Brazilian texts produced between 1978 and 1991. This period covers the beginning of democratization after the military dictatorship, the establishment of the New Republic, as well as the years following this crucial historical transition, whose panorama suggests a growing exchange with international culture and, more specifically, a publishing boom in the translation of poetry.[1] Alongside the romantic William Blake, John Donne, the best known metaphysical poet, "the poet of love and death," was the most translated name of this transition period. In the attempt to understand the meanders of Brazilian cultural history at such a conjuncture, a Heideggerian speculative thread weaves the fabric of this text: what historical experiences made Brazil share discourses with the apparently alien frame of reference of the English metaphysical poets?

Such a hermeneutic orientation further enables the hypothesis that such translation was productive of a deeper consciousness of history. Thus, in what follows, I shall exemplify ways in which, in post-dictatorship Brazil, the sharing of discourses with an alien yet convergent history can be seen as a process of coming to terms with the traumatic wounds of the national history such as mandatory silence, obliterated cultural memory, physical and psychological torture. For this purpose I shall use Jorge Luis Borges's notion of precursors as a way of examining the dialogue between cultures without the rivalry inherent in the study of influences. Arguing that writers create their own predecessors and that their work modifies our conception of the past and the future, Borges suggests the element of freedom and volition involved in such a choice. The recognition of the voice of an author in texts of other literatures and periods also refers, according to him, to affinities of form, tone, or mentality. A similar situation occurs in the perception of a work in a certain way as prefiguring another. As Brazilians attempt to break free of the psychological enclosures of dictatorship, what echoes do they find amongst the chosen seventeenth-century precursors? How does the strong analytical emphasis of metaphysical poetry interact with the more factual testimonies of the political exiles?

The metaphysical vein makes a strong presence, for example, in Brazilian popular music. In 1978, Caetano Veloso sings, in Brazilian rhythms, John Donne's poem "Elegy: Going to Bed" translated by Augusto de Campos. Caetano Veloso recreates metaphysical poetry in other novel ways. We detect an intertext from *Hamlet* ("the world is out of joint") in the refrain of the opening song of *Circuladô*, a CD that he produced in 1991: *alguma coisa está fora de ordem / fora da nova ordem mundial* (something is out of order/ out of the new world order). In this particular song, "Fora da ordem," Caetano takes advantage of the metaphysical poets' perception of life's disjunctions to read the contemporary national history. The sense of disjunction belongs to the English seventeeth century, but through a convergence of historical horizons, it becomes Brazilian, because here *em Sampa de onde mal se vê quem sobe a rampa/ tudo parece que é ainda construção e já é ruína* (in São Paulo from where you hardly see who goes up the ramp/ everything seems to be under construction and is already a ruin). This movement of insertion of world history into Brazilian cultural space, which limits the universality of the archive, is followed by a reverse movement that has the history of Brazilian culture as its starting point. The sense of disjunction in *Hamlet* expressed in the refrain, initially sung in Portuguese, takes on universal dimensions when it is finally translated back into English, French, Spanish, and Japanese. It is Brazilian culture that now crosses the borders, re-universalizing in other languages Brazil's own historicity.

In his introduction to his translation of John Donne's work, Paulo Vizioli highlights the contemporaneity of the metaphysical poets, noting "a vigorous dualistic expression that foretells all the cultural and spiritual fragmentation of the world we live in" (in Donne 12). From Jauss we raise the hypothesis that the Brazilian historical horizon of the 1980s has certain analogies with the historical horizon of the metaphysical poets: they are two worlds in a state of perplexity, two worlds that oscillate from one extreme to another, two worlds of cultural polarization—on the one hand, the literature of death as the maximum negation of the physical and, on the other, an erotic literature celebrating sexual pleasure. Wordplay catches this dualism that few periods of history have shown so clearly as the 1980s in Brazil: through the gaps of near-homophony *('a meta física dos metafísicos')*, Augusto de Campos foregrounds a physical objective *(meta física)* within metaphysics (metafisica).

Alex Polari Alberga, in the epigraph to the work of Alfredo Syrkis, *Os carbonários: memórias da guerrilha perdida* (The Carbonari: Memoirs of a Lost Guerrilla War), emphasizes, for example, the precarious-

ness of interrupted lives, lost illusions, and open wounds, for a generation that finds present support in fragments of the past's search for
ideals—these are the elements that are emphasized, for example:

> Our generation had little time
> It started at the end
> But our search was beautiful
> Oh darling, how beautiful was our search!
> Even with so many lost illusions
> Even with so many broken illusions
> Even with so many splinters of dreams
> With which even today
> We cut ourselves[2]

John Donne, however, never wrote his memoirs; this was left to his
biographers. A torturous childhood and adolescence, in a world in which
death surrounded him at every movement, the abandonment of faith
under the pressure of historical circumstances and its resulting conflicts,
the pragmatic adoption of Anglicanism have caused his biographers to
call Donne's work "the art of apostasy" (Carey). In an extensive historical study of Donne, John Carey raises significant points for my argument
on the convergence of horizons in the England of the seventeenth century
and the history of the 1960s and 1970s in Brazil that was recovered in
the 1980s. "The first thing to be remembered about Donne is that he was
a Catholic; the second is that he betrayed his faith" (Carey 14). Sharing
with the Brazilian former exiles the impossibility of professing a faith, we
may recall the repressive measures that culminated in the military
regime's Institutional Act No. 5 of 1968, which legalized censorship and
drastically reduced Brazilian citizens' individual liberty and civil rights.
Donne also maintained up to a certain time a profession of faith under
the aegis of anti-Catholic legislation. To be a Catholic in Elizabethan
England was not impossible, but it was difficult and risky. Catholics were
prohibited from taking part in political life and from entering universities; heavy fines were levied for failure to appear at Anglican rites;
Catholic seminarians were considered traitors if they remained in the
Queen's realm; spies reported on where Masses were celebrated; the
houses of Catholics were invaded and looted; Catholics were blackmailed
and intimidated; threatened Catholic families fled, ending up homeless or
seeking refuge on river boats; Catholic prisoners were tortured and many
of them executed (Carey 15–18). The *Divine Poems and Sermons* already
presuppose the apostasy suggested by Carey; even so, Donne's paradoxes,
according to David Daiches, suggest an anguished intensity of man's relations to power, in the specific context of the religious conflicts in England
(Daiches 366). Death emerges in his well-known "Divine Poem X" as a
powerful presence that he fights tenaciously if only conceptually.

To describe England, to read Brazil. John Donne, the poet of love and death, as Paulo Vizioli summed up, transmits to Brazil his sense of the disjunction of life, sharing his universe with the former exiles's tortuous experiences narrated in the early 1980s. The portrait sketched by Carey of a world of prohibitions and political and religious intimidation mirrors, across the Atlantic and three centuries later the experiences of former Brazilian exiles, who were persecuted for the "heresy of Communism," a world of censorship and prohibitions, where the ideals of the young regarding a more just society were shattered. Brutally interrupted projects, indelible scars, texts that are never erased—these are recorded in memoirs published in Brazil especially in the late 1970s and early 1980s.

Brazil lives in 1985 a particularly acute consciousness of history—a fleeting history that writes itself in the interstices between death and intense love. In this most significant year, Donne was the most translated poet but other metaphysical poets also carry on a dialogue with the Brazilians experiencing notable oscillations and polarizations as history once again points to new projects and ideals recovered but brutally interrupted. In January, the country witnessed a political campaign to elect the first civilian president since the military dictatorship, a campaign that deeply affected the population emotionally. The victory of Tancredo Neves was hailed in Brasília by an immense crowd, in the most spontaneous of demonstrations. While Fafá de Belém sang the national anthem in the background, in a climate of rehabilitation of national symbols, Tancredo Neves "metaphysically" announced in his speech: "with the ecstasy and terror of having been the chosen one, as Verlaine would say, I deliver myself to the service of the nation." In April of the same year, the newspaper headlines throughout the country displayed the grief of Brazilians following the death of the new president. "Metaphysically," the clapping of hands amidst tears marked the end on April 21 of the man who just a few short months before had been chosen to lead the country in its most joyful and peaceful popular movement of political change. The metaphysical poets intimated to Brazilians that life is frighteningly ephemeral, that death awaits us at every moment. Long live the intensity of love—*carpe diem*—is the message John Donne would bring to Brazilians in the scenario of 1985, as would another English metaphysical poet, Andrew Marvell.

In the work of this other Donne, the poet of erotic love, death emerges as a consciousness of the fleeting nature of time together with a hedonistic urge to take advantage of the present moment, as in "Elegy XIX: Going to Bed." The conception of death as *una vox dormienda,* as in Catullus, associated with an exhortation of *carpe diem,* as in Horace, are noteworthy in Marvell's work, as is seen in his famous poem "To His Coy Mistress." A desire for the intensity of love is expressed in hyperboles. For example:

An hundred years should go to praise	Mil anos para contemplar-te a Testa
Thine eyes and on thy forehead gaze;	E os Olhos levaria. Mais duzentos
Two hundred to adore each breast;	Para adorar cada Peito,
But thirty thousand to the rest	E trinta mil para o resto

is transposed into a cold, realistic vision of death:

then worms shall try	Os vermes hão de por à prova
That long preserved virginity,	Essa comprida Virgindade,
And our quaint honour turn to dust,	Tua fina Honra convertendo em pó,
And into ashes all my lust:	E em cinzas meu Desejo. A Cova
The grave's a fine and private place,	É ótimo e íntimo recanto. Só
But none, I think, do there embrace.	que aos amantes não serve de alcova . . .
(Marvell 334–35)	("À amada esquiva," de Campos
	1978, 170–73)

The words of the English metaphysical poets resonate with the Brazilian writers' in the scenario of 1985, when memoirs remain popular and the best-seller among political books that year was *Brasil nunca mais* / "Torture in Brazil," a survey on torture in the country during the period of repression. In the same year, in his nineteenth book, *Agrestes / Rustics*, João Cabral de Melo Neto for the first time emphasizes death as an insidiously creeping presence in the urban scene:

é porque a morte nos sepulta	it's because death buries us
sem perguntar, à força bruta,	without asking, by brute force,
nas organizações urbanas	in the urban organizations
traçadas em copacabanas,	outlined in copacabanas,
de onde o vivo volta sedento	from where the living return thirsty
e o morto é a fresta no cimento.	and the dead are the cracks in the cement.
(143–44)	(my translation)

Conversely, Carlos Drummond de Andrade chose that year, 1985, to publish two of his works of poetry that had been set aside for a long time: *Amar se aprende amando* / (Love is Learned by Loving), and *Amor, sinal estranho* / (Love, Strange Sign). The theme of love in its cosmic dimensions, all-powerful and imbuing life with the stuff of poetry, is presented to the public as an epigraph to the book *Amar se aprende amando*:

"O amor que move o sol,	"Love that moves the sun,
Como as estrelas."	Like the stars."
O verso de Dante resplandescente,	Dante's resplendent line,
e curvo-me ante a sua magnitude.	and I bow before its magnitude.
. . . Ouso insinuar,	. . . I dare to insinuate,
sem pretensão a contribuir	with no pretension to contribute

para que se desvende o mistério amoroso:	to the unravelling of love's mystery:
Amar se aprende amando.	Love is learned by loving.
Sem omitir o real cotidiano	Without omitting the daily real
também matéria de poesia.	also the material of poetry.

(my translation)

In the strange realism of Donne's poem "The Flea," for example, the erotic in everyday life, under the watchfulness of death, is drawn into an imaginative fantasy. In the words of Augusto de Campos, Donne "can arrive at incredible discoveries, even the feat of poeticizing that which is unpoeticizable" (Campos). "The Flea" combines passion and logical reason in an unconventional expression of love:

It sucked me first, and now sucks thee,	Tendo sugado a mim, e a ti depois,
And in this flea our two bloods mingled be;	Nela se mescla o sangue de nós dois;
Thou know'st that this cannot be said A sin, nor shame, nor loss of maidenhead.	Sabes que isso não pode ser chamado Defloração, vergonha, nem pecado.

(trans. Vizioli 1985, 21)

As Antonio Cícero and Jorge Salomão comment in their "Manifesto Supernovas," poetry of love and death, poetry of love in the poeticizing of daily life, also made use of science as material for making poetry. The seventeenth century in England, the 1980s in Brazil—two heterogeneous yet converging worlds that unconventionally express love interweaving poetry with science (in Messeder 171).

In Reformation England, John Donne, an innovative poet, had also broken with the Petrarchan tradition and the conventions of pastoral poetry, introducing into poetry images taken from scholastic sources such as astronomy, astrology, and mathematics. No English poet after the middle of the seventeenth century would use a mathematical instrument in a love poem, as Donne did. In a comparison of João Cabral de Melo Neto's poem, *"Estudos para uma bailarina andaluza"* (Studies for an Andalusion Dancer), and Donne's "A Valediction: Forbidding Mourning," Augusto de Campos points out the "ingenious," "metaphysical" proximity of the two poems: in João Cabral, the proximity between the tapping of the dancer's legs and the telegraph; in Donne, the souls of the two separated lovers are compared to the legs of a compass (de Campos 128).

By way of conclusion, I would like to stress that Brazilian culture did not merely recycle forms developed from foreign sources. Rather, the voluntary act of choosing one's predecessors through translation at that time contributed to borders opening up to re-embrace both the national and the international. Dialogues between post-dictatorship Brazilian poets and English metaphysical poets follow a complex course, at the same time as they shape the contours of a history that interweaves two metaphysical worlds in the tropics—two worlds whose historical and political ideology is delineated by reading between and through the lines—in intertextuality.

Text translated by Thomas Laborie Burns

NOTES

1. Between 1978 and 1991, seven anthologies specifically of metaphysical poetry were among a total of twenty-four books of English poetry compiled and translated in Brazil, together with several anthologies of Russian, French, German, North American, and Spanish-language poets.

2. The poem is from *Inventário de Cicatrizes* (Inventory of Scars), by Alex Polari Alberga, cited as an epigraph in Syrkis.

WORKS CONSULTED

Andrade, Carlos Drummond de. *Amar se aprende amando: poesia de convívio e de humor*. Rio de Janeiro: Record, 1985.

Borges, Jorge Luis. "Kafka y sus precursores." *Jorge Luis Borges: Obras Completas 1952–1972*. Buenos Aires: Emecé Editores, 1989. 2: 88–90.

Campos, Augusto de. "A meta física dos metafísicos." *Verso, reverso, controverso*. 2.ed. rev. São Paulo: Perspectiva, 1978.

———. *John Donne—o dom e a danação*. Rio de Janeiro: Noa, Noa, 1977, reprinted in *O anticrítico*. São Paulo: Companhia das Letras, 1986.

Carey, John. "Apostasy." *John Donne: Life, Mind, and Art*. London: Faber and Faber, 1981. 15–36.

Daiches, David. *A Critical History of English Literature vol. 2: Shakespeare to Milton*. London: Secker & Warburg, 1960. 366.

Donne, John. *John Donne: o poeta do amor e da morte*. Intro., trans., notes Paulo Vizioli. São Paulo: J.C. Ismael, 1985.

Hollanda, Heloisa Buarque de. "Introdução." *Revista do Brasil—Literatura Anos 80* 2.5 (1986): 28–53.

Marvell, Andrew. "To His Coy Mistress." *The New Oxford Book of English Verse. 1250–1950*. Ed. Helen Gardner. London and New York: BCA, 1972. 334–35.

Melo Neto, João Cabral de. *Agrestes*. Rio de Janeiro: Nova Fronteira, 1985.

Messeder, Carlos Alberto. "O Novo Network Poético 80 no Rio de Janeiro." *Revista do Brasil—Literatura anos 80* 2.5 (1986): 66–81.

Rouanet, Sérgio Paulo, "A Verdade e a Ilusão do Pós-moderno." *Revista do Brasil-Literatura anos 80* 2.5 (1986): 28–53.

Sussekind, Flora. *Literatura e Vida Literária: Polêmicas, Diários & Retratos.* Rio de Janeiro: Jorge Zahar, 1985.

Syrkis, Alfredo. "Pre(pos)fácio." *Os Carbonários: Memórias da Guerrilha Perdida.* 7th ed. São Paulo: Global Editora e Distribuidora Ltda, 1981.

Bodies in Transit:
Travel, Translation, and Gender

Francine Masiello

Geography is only the apparent form—purely superficial—
of exile.

—Héctor Bianciotti

In *El río sin orillas* (1991), Juan José Saer, a long-time resident of
Paris, offers a tender account of his native Argentina, told from the
perspective of estrangement and return. Saer opens this book with a
description of his arrival in Buenos Aires. As the plane descends
toward Ezeiza airport, the writer's eye drifts over the landscape and
falls upon the River Plate, a marker of *patria* and home. This river
becomes symbolic of the monumentality of the exile's return, a flow of
the nation's past running through the writer's mind. Yet the aerial
vision inspires a second thought: the minor presence of Argentine culture in the global order of things. Unlike Occident and Orient, whose
past, according to Saer, "hierve de héroes, de sabios y de tiranos" (25),
Argentina is only a latecomer to the banquet of major nations. From
the monumental to the minor, he constructs a nostalgic legend about
the *patria* in order to translate Argentine territory for an audience
residing abroad.

Saer's account seems decidedly anachronistic here, hardly offering
a disruptive voice in today's transnational map, scarcely entering the
global postmodern that suppresses all ties to nation. In fact, in *El río
sin orillas*, he depends on travel back to the homeland to erase contradiction and fault, to systematize internal discourses to the rhythm
of a single language. This approach repeats the regionalist or sentimental aspects of the neoliberal experience, but in other late-twentieth-century works, landscape and subjectivity find alternative styles
of representation.

Contrast, then, the gaze of Saer to that of Luisa Futoransky, another
Argentine who shares Paris as the exile's home. She writes in a volume
of poetry:

Un país es tu nombre
y la ácida violencia con que acude una palabra
a tu indefensa boca de viajero.
Es un mapa con un río cuya desembocadura y
nacimiento
se unen, curiosamente, en el punto exacto de la tierra
que desea abonar tu osario.

(*Partir, digo* 1982, 13)

If Saer announces the River Plate as "un río sin orillas," Futoransky turns her attention instead to the liquid borders of language and the crossing flows of the imaginative realm. She studies the convergence of mythologies surrounding our fixed illusions of nation, more a question of hybrid modes of desire and our perceptions of the inadequacies of fixed place and form. This late-twentieth-century perspective moves bodies through a river of language, constructing an alternative global map from nomadic, female wisdom.

Futoransky describes this condition as the work of a "contrabando hormiga," a gesture not based on monumentality, but on the supplements of minor resistance. The contraband traffic mocks the power of official myth and attacks its subjugating forces. And for Futoransky, the contraband discourse is mounted on the practice of translation, an acknowledgement of the transformational magic of language that helps the foreigner negotiate difference. In this way, her poetry and prose are situated outside of Argentina; she congregates Africans, Asians, and Jews as examples of persons displaced, all tied together in a theater of misreadings and errors in linguistic reshaping.

For this reason, Futoransky emphasizes the presence of the dictionary in her writings; she supplies stage directions for reading prose; she celebrates the cabalistic "abracadabra" that creates the illusion of magic through language; she plays with tongue twisters that both resist translation and integrate polyglot traditions. These are cues that help the foreigner to overcome the anxiety of displacement, to negotiate what Futoransky describes as "las humillaciones intransferibles que producen los idiomas de los otros, el sentido de encontrarse aún más ajena y exilada—si cabe, todavía—por ser sapo de otro pozo" (1986, 105). In the process, she exposes the language of State that classifies immigrants and "others," prescribing rules of behavior and identity to fix the exile in a particular location in politics or history.

It is no surprise, then, that the author mixes prose and poetry in her books, that she trades citations and original thought, that she offers multiple translations of a single phrase, that she links translation to castration. In *De Pe a Pa*, she writes: "piensa que te piensa le pasó por la cabeza repetidas veces una palabra que conoce en inglés, bastante horrible de sonido y por lo que con ella cabe asociar: *pro-cas-tri-na-tion; Laura, basta de procastrination,* que viene a ser una castración por postergacíon producida por la pereza y la vacilación. Pavada de rima ¿verdad?" (1986, 14). The flawed translation (an intentional slip in her move to English?) allows the author to touch a submerged reading about the violations of language; but the translation also opens to facile rhyme, a true castration of meaning in verse. Exercises in translation are linked to a mutilation of form; they express the foreigner's loss in the absence of a linguistic pact; they remind us that translated culture enacts a violence upon female bodies. This even has a reach in the travelogue account that the writer provides of her new surroundings. Futoransky, who spent the early years of the Proceso first in Japan and then in China, reads Chinese culture, for example, through state medical services for women, in particular to practices of abortion, sterilization, and controlled sexual pleasure; "el Estado en suma, te pide tu virilidad o tu femineidad por un plato de lentejas," she writes (*Son cuentos chinos,* 119). But the trade is not merely economic; it produces sexual knowledge. It is a way to acknowledge repression and to admit the possibility of desire.

Like Futoransky, other intellectuals prompt speculation on the violence of linguistic difference and propose cartographies of desire that often confuse our base understanding of home and nation. The travel mode becomes a way to test the constraints of law, to put in doubt all original discourse, to study the effect of the mask of language on subjectivity and expression, to bring in focus relationships of sameness and difference. Writing from the perspective of exile, María Negroni in *Islandia* (1991) questions the authenticity of the traveler: "Primero se pone una máscara" (23), she explains. Principal to the texture of her volume is the mark of translation and doubleness; how to speak from the position of exile, how to speak through language belonging to others, how to collect different experiences under the banner of epic poetry. For Negroni, writing is an act of impostorship tied to translation and exile from power. Her book is written in the halting language of one who is forced to speak a foreign tongue; she stammers in a voice of halting self-affirmation. "En despoblados, en intervalos pulsa la travesti sus poemas" (71). Negroni's project is to capture "Su Robinson narrar en femenino" (59) at the price of normal syntax and grammatical rule. The surprising violations of linguistic norms call our attention to the outsider's dilemma in writing, they remind us of her estrangement from the language of home.

This kind of travel tracks an alternative route of return to Argentina; it leans toward a *mapa mundi* that reorganizes relationships between North and South, East and West, familiar and distant landscapes. It tests the boundaries of home and foreign, it charts the course of racialized bodies, it registers bilingual and dissonant voices; and, finally, it crosses the voyage of self-exploration with reflections on sexuality and translation. The following texts by Griselda Gambaro, Graciela Safranchik, and María Moreno bring us closer to this problematic.

TRANSLATION AND EXILE

The convergence of rivers and tongues, already signaled in these introductory pages, becomes the focus of Griselda Gambaro's attention in her recent dramatic work, "Es necesario entender un poco" (1996), as she delves into the space of no man's land, on board ship from China to France. Here, she questions the relationship among men of unequal linguistic power. Basing herself on tales of Jesuit missionaries in eighteenth-century China, Gambaro tests one's tolerance to difference and the capacity of language and translation for recording this range of experience. The problem is enacted by the figure of Hue, a Chinese translator and scholar who is taken by a Jesuit to France and driven into ultimate bondage. Despite his skills at translation, his failure to understand the language of colonial rule relegates him to the asylum where he is forced to join in the theatrical projects of the Marquis de Sade. The Asian man is a victim of his linguistic and racial difference, a victim of non-understanding.

Hue inaugurates his commission on ship en route to France. The sea emerges as the sustaining metaphor of his translation practice but now, an agitated sea stirs bodies and tongues; for Hue, it creates the illusion of letters that dance on the page and signals that the body, as translating machine, cannot withstand the waves of movement. If Hue cannot read or decipher once he begins his travel from home, the priest who escorts him insists on the fixity of signs and the facile transparency of language. In this respect, the ocean voyage triggers a cultural conflict that will end with Hue's enslavement; when he arrives in France, the *letrado* will become a *lacayo*. Griselda seems to tell us that colonial mastery determines meaning in language. Moreover, the struggle for interpretative rights, to borrow Jean Franco's phrase, becomes—in the seat of colonial command—a matter of physical force; the whip and the prison ultimately control language and our access to meaning. Translation is a matter of power.

Several things have to be noted here as phenomena of Argentine literature today. In their move through the Orient (and I use this word with a certain irony, of course), Argentine writers pick up on a fascination for otherness and use the distance between cultures to explore the construction of meaning, to explore their own conditions as "other" in the society in which they live. It is not surprising, therefore, that the Orient should occupy the site of so much contemporary Argentine writing. Witness only Diana Bellessi's *Tributo del mudo* (1982), dedicated in part to the image of an abandoned concubine and high priestess of Tao who was later put to her death; Mercedes Roffé's apocryphal book, *El tapiz* (1983), supposedly written by Ferdinand Oziel, a Sephardic Jew from Morocco; or the recent issues of *Tokonoma,* a contemporary Argentine journal directed by Amalia Sato and devoted to Japanese literature translated into Spanish. And in order not to allow us to think that the Oriental flame is only a feminist writer's passion, we should also remember César Aira's *Una novela china* (1987), Daniel Guebel's *La perla del emperador* (1990), or Juan Gelman's obsession for Sephardic language and poetic traditions as witnessed in *Dibaxu* (1994). This is not a return to the *modernista* configuration of the Orient as in the works of Rubén Darío, but a call for a project in translation that resists official maps of meaning drawn on the North/South axis. Julia Kushigian has spoken eloquently to the project of contemporary orientalism in Latin America as a way for writers to affirm and preserve their own sense of self vis-à-vis the construction of the "other." She also describes the "active polyglossia of the Orient" as a way to "overcome a fusion of opposites" (1991, 14). But the Orient, I want to claim, is not only a site from which to enact a debate about the limits of the "real"; it offers a site to emphasize voice over form, performance over fixed beliefs. The Orient brings together relations of translation and power, of translation and erotics. As his male protagonist falls in love with a cross-dresser and double agent posing as diva in Chinese opera, David Hwang in *M. Butterfly* paradoxically observes that Asia was an ideal site to search for a "real man" (1988, 6). In the Latin American context, in the Argentine context in particular, the Orient also opens to a discussion of sexuality and the state, this time in the context of translation.

Contemporary literature devoted to this theme invites us to ask about the foreign challenges presented to the politics of gender. It invites us to reconstruct categories of masculine and feminine once removed from the North/South lens. It also allows us to think of the cross of languages that tests any global truth, to examine the secrets of state that foreclose the exile's voice.

TRANSLATION AND EROS

The translational dilemma often evokes subjects who fail to enter arenas of power. But the presence of the translator also allows us to speculate on representational form and eros. Like the other women writers to whom I have alluded, Graciela Safranchik relies on this situational motif, this time, through Akinari, a Japanese translator in search of the ideal woman. Her novella, *El cangrejo* (1995), is about Akinari's search for a woman called Miranda, whose name evokes that of Prospero's daughter and all the problems of colonial oppression through language that Shakespeare proposed in *The Tempest*. It is also a way to link the erotic to the dynamics of translation.

Safranchik's novel posits translation as a central metaphor of the book. It is not surprising, therefore, that this novel is focused on a Japanese figure removed from his native land; in an unnamed foreign country, he plays the role of the outsider who must make sense of language and form. As in the original folio of *The Tempest* where Miranda (and not Prospero) teaches Caliban to speak,[1] in *El cangrejo* Miranda's presence inspires Akinari to struggle with language and form. These acts of translation and interpretation also offer the possibility of change in Akinari himself: "Soy una crisálida," he says early on in the novel (8). Akinari assumes the names of the authors whom he translates. As if to negotiate between water and land, between different constructions of life and desire, between different temporal moments separating him from his writer of choice, he takes the name of "El Cangrejo" as one of his writerly disguises. A convergence of form and text, of the beauty of image and one's comprehension of meaning, and—in a mythological sense—of the convergence of masculine and feminine as the basis of a rebirthing, *El cangrejo* engages the distances that separate image and identity. At the same time, it explores the gap between culturally disparate subjects.

Safranchik mobilizes our wisdom about bilingual and translational divides. Akinari's father was a Japanese professor of languages, his mother an "equilibrista de la palabra" (68–69), and Akinari himself takes the title of "el bromista, el gran farfullador" (69). Yet Akinari's mother was a foreigner in Japan; her language skills were derived from her role as an outsider in a distant country. These parental bilingual necessities are thus imposed on the hero; Akinari, an outsider himself, living in an unnamed country outside of Japan, inherits a passion for translation, a different approach to intimate relationships and to history and form. He thus works out the soul of "el otro Akinari," a modern rendering of an ancient author dating from the age of the shogun (20), but he also teaches Japanese and corrects the written work of his students. His work with language always reflects a translation sensibility that passes through time and nation, but it also allows him to construct different versions of self.

Does the translator give an exact dictionary account of experience? Or does s/he cultivate distortion in order to construct an object of love? The only clarity we have comes at the close of the novel, when Akinari embraces Miranda and the narrative of translation comes to an end. This is not a simple love story, but a metaphor about the expression of desire. Akinari studies the ways in which aesthetic and erotic meanings are produced from the translational act, from the spatialization of oppositional values, from a conflict of cultural ideals. But he also tells us that the limits of sexual knowledge are produced from a crisis in language. Sexuality becomes the testing ground for the translator's exercise in self-representation.

The late twentieth century may evoke the *modernista*'s imagined voyage to the Orient in our last *fin de siglo;* more importantly, it now provides a way to raise the question of otherness from the perspective of the translator. Interestingly enough, Gambaro and Safranchik screen out the feminine voice and focus, instead, on a masculine figure as protagonist and writer. In a move toward impostorship of the kind noted earlier by María Negroni, the shift of gendered voice builds in the necessity for a sustaining mask in the act of literary translation.

In a recent volume of essays, *Lo propio y lo ajeno* (1996), poet and critic Diana Bellessi speculates on the effects of translation: "Es la traducción un esfuerzo de alteridad. Alteridad del cuerpo respirando la música de otra lengua y en la estricta particularidad de una voz que la habla" (1996, 29, included in this volume). She repeats the words *doble esfuerzo, eco, amor, misterio* throughout her text in order to prepare for her charge, a readiness to transform and create: "otra cosa de aquella rosa plena de sentido que el original ofrece." Bellessi notes the simultaneous efforts of mimetic respect and disavowal through translation. This is a pact between lovers, poets allied in a common project, but when— we might ask—does translation announce the inadequacy of language or even absence and loss? To address this darker aspect, I want to conclude by turning to an acrid postmodern text by María Moreno.

TRANSLATING LESBOS

In *El Affair Skeffington* (1992), Cristina Forero writing under the pseudonym of María Moreno mocks the claims of the United States and Europe to any original culture; she toys with the projects of recuperating sources and of advancing an "authentic" voice. The vehicle for this irony is found in the exercise of translation. *El Affair Skeffington* tells of the discovery of a collection of poems written by Dolly Skeffington, described as a North American expatriate in the Parisian literary gatherings of the 1920s. The pretext of this anecdote allows Moreno to revisit what she calls the scene of Paris-Lesbos and the cast of characters and conventions that define high modernism as we know it.

We quickly realize that Dolly Skeffington wrote under pseudonym; for that, she is likened to Pauline Tarn who took the pen name of Renée Vivien, or Judy Gerowitz who later became known as the artist, Judy Chicago. It is then an additional irony that author Cristina Forero takes the pen name of María Moreno. In the world of doubleness that becomes symbolic of writing itself, Moreno/Forero echoes the doubleness of "Paris-Lesbos," sustaining cloaked identities and secret liaisons, and an ambivalent regard of sexuality that was the hallmark of Paris in the 1920s. This doubleness is everywhere, at once fluid and defiant. It describes the group of women stewed in modernist broth; at the same time, it announces the screen or disguise that belongs to language, literature, and translation. This doubleness directs the reader to the pact between eros and writing, to the floating identities that contribute to the unstable idea of the "author."

"Será cuestión de burlar al padre, ocupando su lugar, ahora de per-
vertido" (11), explains the narrator. Not only is the description of Paris-
Lesbos an assertion of sexual choice and authority in writing, but for the
polyglot world of the exiles, it is a matter of rebellion and perpetual
movement. In the poem, "Aguas," one of Dolly's supposed texts, a narrator writes: "Tu petite soeur fluye como el agua / subiendo desde el
fondo de la tierra" (99). Same-sex love is always in movement, at once
source and actualization, another gesture against the monumentality of
landscape and national form; it posits an alliance toward the search for
alternative meanings.

In the early pages of her text, Moreno parodies the voice of the serious scholar who would pretend to identify sources and dates, bringing
the tools of textual criticism to the service of modernist literature in
English. She thus tracks the author's confused biography and the publication record of the twenty-eight poems, linking the texts to sources
such as Margaret Anderson's *Little Review* or events in Greenwich Village, but she also presents Dolly's poems about the outsiders of this distant culture: Chicanos in Los Angeles, gay men in World War II, and
lesbians in love in Boston. The trick, of course, is as old as literature
itself; what is worth our attention here is the linking of translational
practice and sexual pleasure. For the unspeakable of lesbian love,
Moreno explores what cannot be said: she devotes attention to sameness and difference, she takes her readers on an odyssey through prohibited territory and language, she tests asynchronicities against conventional literary order, she toys with traditional concepts of
authorship and the genres that have excluded women. At the same
time, she reminds us that the memory of all sexual pleasure is in itself
an act of translation, a repositioning of discourses that creates the illusion of access to what is out of reach or unknown.

In the ambiguities of Paris-Lesbos, a woman's attraction to a man
and or a woman is the starting point for this endless quest. In the long
run, it is joined to one's will to surpass any allegiance to nation. This
linkage comes forward when Moreno pokes fun at the fixed definitions
of sexuality sustained by Victoria Ocampo:

> Siempre me fascinó la belleza femenina pero el lesbianismo ha sido una
> tentación o una comarca desconocida para mí. "El hombre fue mi
> patria," bramaba en otra parte (aunque estuviera allí), Victoria
> Ocampo, y Nina Hamett cantaba por los cafés de la *rive gauche:* "Nos
> fuimos a la Argentina/ donde todos los hombres son maricas." Tal vez
> para las mujeres norteamericanas e inglesas que hicieron de Paris una
> exhumación de Lesbos, también el hombre fuera su patria, sólo que
> ellas estaban exiladas. (13)

From the known maps of charted pleasure, we then move out of fixed
terrain; lesbian sexuality in this instance is a condition of exile. It pro-

duces a need to speak beyond *padre* and *patria,* to announce the insufficiency of any single language, to engage the noncorrespondence of images belonging to flawed translation.

Moreno's book, of course, reminds us of the fiction of all writing authority. The false manuscript, the multiple languages, the shifts between Buenos Aires and Paris upset any stable idea of voice, sexual preference, and place. But it is also a book that reminds us of the infinite flows of meaning set in motion by sexuality and language. Translation, in this context, shows us an economy of mismatched signs whose single truth is difference. It presupposes an unresolved conflict between source and copy in the same way that the image of Dolly is organized around the double:

> En la vida de Skeffington el dos insiste: nació en 1892, llegó a París en 1922, tiene dos nombres, dos objetos de orientación sexual, dos formas de expresión: la escritura—dos estilos, dos géneros, y una suerte de arte conceptual. (41)

In addition the text is made available in Spanish by the intervention of the translator Delia, who interprets the words of Lily Tate as she tells what she knows of Dolly. Delia translates from English to Spanish to explain the nature of Dolly's love for her girlfriend Gwen:

> lo que más raro me parecía de mi abuela y Gwen cuando yo era chica era la manera que tenían de apoyarse la una sobre la otra. No se parecía a la forma de tocarse entre dos hermanos o entre madre e hijo, era . . . un . . .
> Se hizo un silencio y luego Lily Tate y Delia hablaron rápidamente en inglés. Era bastante aburrido hasta que Delia, que no parecía estar traduciendo dijo ¡jolines!, pero Lily permaneció absolutamente inmóvil buscando la palabra perdida. Su mutismo era la angustia de los otros, no la falla de ella. Parecía tener todo el tiempo del mundo. Como si se tratara de una propuesta didáctica Pilar, Lola, Marga, Marisa y Mary Murci se lanzaron a tirar palabras, respetando los turnos y a gran velocidad: "abrazo," "cruce," "encimamiento," "abroche," "a lo siamés," "abotone," "acople," "soldadura," "costurón." Lily Tate habló y Delia tradujo "engarce." "Podrías haberlo dicho tú," dijo Lola pero Marga seguía mirando la piedra y Lily continuó hablando a través de Delia. (51)

Finally, the narrator confesses the intense love of the pair is best defined by absence. In this encounter, individuals lose their constituting identities; no longer separate, they enter a zone that is marked by the impossibility of complete translation.

Elusive, lost, or transformed once again; the slippage of translation becomes the equivalent of a kind of sexuality that escapes the codes of speech. Translation fails to coordinate identity and desire, to breach the gap between representation and the intensity of female passion. In effect, *El affair Skeffington* signals our blind faith in the communicational truths of language; equally important, it signals the failure of translation to move tongues between different forms of experience. As a result, then, the inability to name passion between women unhinges our critical knowledge; it is as futile as defining literary history without taking account of women. Moreno makes fun of the pretentious categories that govern the academic mind; she puts to test the translational process that fails to link language and sex. She also reminds us that what one suppresses or forgets in one language can be a starting point for discussion in another.

Traditional descriptions of the translation experience explain the dialogue between self and other, the transformations of the source text, the recollection of genealogies, the links between past and present. But these women writers suggest that translation is constant disruption, referring in the final instance to a crisis of identity and power. I opened this article with mention of Saer, who described the River Plate as "un río sin orillas." But the interrogations of contemporary women draw our attention to the undefined edges of language and land that fails to define us, not to the river itself. "[C]omo una compuerta que cede espacios, respiración" (1), writes Alicia Genovese in her recent volume, significantly titled for our purposes here, *El borde es un río* (1997). Contemporary women writers such as Genovese will constantly draw attention to the flow of the margins rather than the river itself. They remind us that slippage and displacement are the soul of translation; these gestures render one's condition as eternally "foreign," even within the limits of home, but they also leave women writers unbound by the rules of correspondence belonging to literary law.

NOTE

1. For a splendid discussion of Miranda's voice in *The Tempest* and the problem this poses for feminist literary theory, see Joanna O'Connell (1995).

WORKS CITED

Aira, César. *Una novela china.* Buenos Aires: Javier Vergara, 1987.

Amati-Meffier, Jacqueline. *The Babel of the Unconscious. Mother Tongue and Foreign Languages in the Pschoanalytic Dimension.* Madison, CT: International University Press, 1993.

Bellessi, Diana. *Tributo del mudo.* Buenos Aires: Tierra Firme, 1994.

——— . *Lo propio y lo ajeno.* Buenos Aires: Feminaria, 1996.

Futoransky, Luisa, *Partir, digo.* Valencia: Editorial Prometeo, 1982.

———. *De Pe a Pa (o de Pekín a Paris)*. Barcelona: Anagrama, 1986.

———. *Son cuentos chinos*. Buenos Aires: Planeta, 1991.

Gambaro, Griselda. "Es necesario entender un poco." *Teatro 6*. Buenos Aires: Ediciones de la Flor, 1996.

Gelman, Juan. *Dibaxu*. Barcelona: Seix Barral, 1994.

Genovese, Alicia. *El borde es un río*. Buenos Aires: Tierra Firme, 1997.

Guebel, Daniel. *La perla del emperador*. Buenos Aires: Emecé, 1990.

Hwang, David. *M. Butterfly*. New York: Penguin-Plume, 1988.

Kushigian, Julia. *Orientalism in the Hispanic Literary Tradition: In Dialogue with Borges, Paz, and Sarduy*. Albuquerque: U NM P, 1991.

Moreno, María. *El Affair Skeffington*. Buenos Aires/Rosario: Bajo la luna nueva, 1992.

Negroni, María. *Islandi*. Murcia: Colección Carabelas, 1991.

O'Connell, Joanna. *Prospero's Daughter: The Prose of Rosario Castellanos*. Austin: University of Texas Press, 1995.

Roffé, Mercedes. *Ferdinand de Oziel, "El Tapiz."* Buenos Aires: Tierra Baldía, 1983.

Saer, Juan José. *El río sin orillas*. Buenos Aires: Alianza, 1991.

Safranchik, Graciela. *El cangrejo*. Buenos Aires/Rosario: Bajo la luna nueva, 1995.

De-facing Cuba:
Translating and Transfiguring
Cristina García's *The Agüero Sisters*

Israel Reyes

The recent popularity of U.S. Latina/o literature has occasioned the peculiar phenomenon of translating texts into Spanish that were originally written in English, texts that describe the experiences of Latin American immigrants who had already made the journey from one language into another. Many of these texts, particularly those written by Cuban American and Puerto Rican writers, narrate the past as a point of departure, a life begun in Spanish but remembered in English. One such translated novel, Cristina García's *The Agüero Sisters,* begins with a murder in Cuba, whose surreal consequences emerge later in the United States. When make-up maven Constancia Agüero wakes up one day in Miami to find that the face of her murdered mother has replaced her own, a Cuban past returns to de-face the American present as it imposes its lines and curves on the features of the exiled generation. Similarly, Alan West's Spanish translation, *Las hermanas Agüero,* is a refraction that does not completely occlude the English text it rewrites. However, the translation of Latina/o texts from English into Spanish transfigures the relationship between language and memory, creating a warped circularity that retraces a literary tradition but does not necessarily return to a point of origin.

In the title we already foresee the dual linguistic register in which García's text operates. The Spanish surname, Agüero, within the English title places us squarely in a Cuban American reality where Spanish and English often flow into each other, sometimes creating the unique locutions known as "Cubanamericanisms."[1] Even more telling of how the novel will proceed is that *agüero* translates into augury, omen, or presage.[2] An *agüero* can signal good or bad luck, as in the commonly used *buen* or *mal agüero*. A popular idiomatic expression is *un pájaro de mal agüero*—a bird of ill omen—that refers to a person, thing, or real bird whose appearance precedes calamitous events. The pages of García's novel flutter with dozens of birds, which appear just when a disaster is about to strike one of the members of the Agüero family. However,

García's *agüeros* look in more than one direction. They function as signs in the sense that they circulate within an economy of history and memory, between that which has passed on and that which lives on. Language, then, is the currency of that exchange.

The novel opens with a "Prologue" set in the past, September 8, 1948, to be exact. The reader, and no one else, witnesses a murder: Ignacio Agüero, Cuban ornithologist, shot his wife, Blanca, when they were alone on an expedition in the Zapata Swamp. At first, Blanca proceeded as she would have on any other expedition for endangered species of birds, but she heard a noise behind her and saw an extremely rare species of hummingbird. When she turned around, her husband had already taken aim, not at the bird but at her. Carrying his wife's body back to the nearest village, he "began to tell his lies" (García 5).

And thus the novel begins to tell the story of Constancia and Reina, the Agüero sisters, who were quite young when their mother died and only vaguely remember her as we see their present-day lives unfold in Cuba and the United States. Reina, an electrician, lives in revolutionary Cuba and Constancia, exiled in the '60s, goes from New York to Miami with her husband, Heberto. Eventually these two sisters are reunited in Miami, and Constancia makes a journey back to Cuba to recover a part of her past, but not before death, disaster, and all manner of marvelous realities occur in a narrative that jumps from the past to the present through a series of intermingling texts.

The novel is divided by place and voice, moving from Cuba to New York and Miami, and following the lives of Constancia, Reina, Dulcita—Reina's daughter—and other family members. Throughout the fragmented narrative, we read, presumably along with Constancia, a long letter in which Ignacio Agüero tells his life story and admits his guilt in the murder of his wife. After learning that her father had buried an old trunk of his personal belongings back in Cuba, Constancia returns to her place of origin only to have her image of her parents—and herself—completely transformed. In this fictive journey García rewrites the return to the island that Lourdes and Pilar undertook in *Dreaming in Cuban,* and it becomes quite clear that this first narrative lays the groundwork for much of the plot and characterizations that appear in *The Agüero Sisters.* Both texts tell the story of a family divided by politics, religious belief, generational conflict, and the miles that separate Cuba from the United States. Both novels also depict a return to Cuba that eventually marks a transition in the lives of the exiled generation, a difficult but necessary realization that the Cuba of yesterday exists neither in Cuba nor in modern-day Miami, where several generations of Cuban exiles nostalgize[3] their inevitable return to pre-Castro Cuba in the post-Castro future.

To say that García simply rewrites *Dreaming in Cuban* in *The Agüero Sisters* would be a short-sighted critique; we must consider literary translation to be a representational endeavor that crosses not only from one language to another but across the boundaries of texts. Recent studies in translation have developed the notion of refraction to describe how texts find their way into popular discourse or into other texts belonging to divergent literary genres. André Lefevere defines refracted texts as those that have passed into the corpus of a literary tradition by way of multiple rewritings; a comic book version of the Bible, for example (Lefevere 13). Because we know so many of the "classics" only through their multiple refractions, should we finally confront the "original," our familiarity with the canon is offset by an alienating misrecognition: "And yet, for many years, that perception *was* the classic for us, and for many readers it is the closest they will ever get to a classic they think they know rather intimately" (13).

In many ways, *The Agüero Sisters* is a refraction of several Latin American texts, including García's previous work. Many similarities arise in a comparison between *The Agüero Sisters* and Alejo Carpentier's *Los pasos perdidos* (The Lost Steps), particularly the journey back to a homeland that the novels' exiles undertake. While Carpentier portrays a literal and figurative journey back to the source, a shedding of cultural baggage and entry into the womb-like space of the jungle, García problematizes that return to the original. When Constancia Agüero travels to Cuba to sift through her late father's belongings and uncover the murderous secret behind her mother's death, she finds an estranged familiarity in her surroundings. Cuba has been refracted and fragmented so repeatedly that Constancia ponders whether her memories of Cuba are more a result of her exile than of her ever having lived there. And yet, for so many Cuban exiles, that "original" Cuba resurfaces continuously with a nostalgic song played on the radio, with every *cafecito* sipped on Miami's Calle Ocho, and with the sound of dominoes clacking together.[4] The desire to return to that Cuba sets in motion the multiple refractions of the homeland that, inevitably, create an original that was never there.

Further refractions occur when traveling from one culture and language to another, not only in the act of translating a text, but in a text whose remembrance of things past happened to have occurred in a language that lies outside the text's dominant grammar. Discussing translation's continual reference to a pure original, an "intact kernel" of truth, Jacques Derrida, in *The Ear of the Other,* says that

> [t]he desire for the intact kernel is desire itself, which is to say it is irreducible. There is a prehistoric, preoriginary relation to the intact kernel, and it is only beginning with this relation that any desire whatsoever can constitute itself. Thus, the desire or the *phantasm* of the intact kernel is irreducible—despite the fact that there is no intact kernel. (115)

That "*phantasm* of the intact kernel" is as much the exile's yearning for Cuba as it is Alan West's translation of García's novel. "Translators," as Suzanne Jill Levine says, "upon escaping the mother tongue in order to serve another language, experience exile in their own language, and share with exiles an expanded cultural context that gives them a privileged view of their original language's limitations" (Levine 1). West, an exiled Cuban himself and a bilingual poet, translates what, in English, is supposed to be a memory of what happened in Spanish. Does García's text lend itself to Spanish translation because, supposedly, so much of the characters' memories and dialogues occur in Spanish? A good translation does not try to find precise equivalencies when going from one language to another; rather, it refracts and re-members a text so as to write over—or de-face—the original. If we were to read West's text first, the "original" García novel could be considered a strange version of its translation, even as it remains slightly visible under the texture of its refractions.

As early as the translation of the epigraphs, we see how West's transformative poetics reconfigures the features of the English original so that it is almost unrecognizable, but not quite. García epigraphs her novel with two quotations, one from Octavio Paz in Spanish, the other from Hart Crane in English. West leaves the Paz quotation intact, but instead of translating the lines by Crane, he replaces them with a Spanish poem of his own, titled "Andar, Arder." Crane's poem tells of the power of memory:

> Forgetfulness is white—white as a blasted tree,
> And it may stun the sybil into prophecy,
> Or bury the gods.
> I can remember much forgetfulness.

Is the Spanish translation of a Latina text such as García's a way of remembering forgetfulness, or is it returning the exile to the home of her mother tongue? English is so much a part of the Latina/o experience (for many U.S. Latinas/os it is the mother tongue) that a return to Spanish is not a return to the original, just as West's translation of the Crane poem produces another poem entirely:

> ¿Quién habla?
> Habla el río, espejo de la memoria.
> ¿Qué se olvida?
> La entraña, la voz, el fuego.
> ¿Dónde nace el fuego?
> ¿En la lengua, la sombra, el sueño?
> ¿Por qué nos miente el sueño?
> Para que la palabra no zozobre.
> ¿Qué nos mira cuando morimos?
> El destello, el agua, la sobra.
> Cuando habla el hueso
> La carne calla.

I will not endeavor to translate this poem, as my critique is already a refraction of this particular text. However, I will comment on how West combines elements of the Paz epigraph—*"Hablar/Mientras los otros trabajan/Es pulir huesos . . ."*—with what he de-faces onto the lines by Crane. West's series of questions and answers already evokes a form of dialogue, much in the way his translation speaks to and from García's novel. He reads Paz's lines on the futility of language when there is work to be done, the way words scintillate with death as they polish bones, and he traces these ideas over Crane's words about memory and forgetfulness. The result is his own poem that does not necessarily reproduce either of the previous two. And yet, all the elements from the lines by Paz and Crane are recognizable in West's translation of them. Although he has completely written over the Crane poem—he has de-faced it—we can partially discern its shape underneath.

Consequently, West's translation of García's novel de-faces the Latina text as it writes over the previous migration from Spanish into English. The Spanish past remembered in English is now refracted into Spanish, but this refraction does not constitute a fragmented past now made whole, a return to an "intact kernel" that is self-evident and true. That bygone Cuba of yesteryear that lingers in the memories and cultural practices of every Cuban exile and subsequent generations of Cuban Americans exists as a memory in English. The main character in *Los pasos perdidos* returns to Latin America after years of life in the United States only to have the atavistic Spanish rush in on him as soon as he lands at the airport. Constancia, on the other hand, finds upon her return to Cuba that her Spanish is outdated and clumsy, not only because it is a holdover from the 1950s, but because it has already come into irrevocable contact with English.

The Spanish is not completely occluded, though, as García's text makes clear when she intersperses Spanish words and phrases throughout the English text. *"Bueno, mi amor,* you are long past the age of illusions," Reina says to her daughter Dulcita when they are still in Cuba (García 38). One would imagine that the entire sentence was spoken in Spanish, yet the "original" language is set apart by italics, a clear indication of foreign origins. West's translation renders the phrase entirely in Spanish with no change in typeset: "Bueno, mi amor, hace tiempo que pasaste la edad de las ilusiones" (García 37, West translation). The difference marks the original text as the reconstructed memory of a narrator who writes over the past with her English present without erasing the Spanish of previous generations. García's text is as much a de-facing as is West's translation. We could say that a translation into Spanish of an interlingual,[5] Latina text such as García's silences the dual linguistic register that the original deploys in its use of Spanish and English. Does that mean that these kinds of texts are untranslatable, that the Latina/o experience cannot be known outside its already heterogeneous linguistic parameters?

Consider what a Latina/o text does to English as it tries to convey a Spanish past by means of literal translation. Judith Ortiz Cofer's novel *The Line of the Sun* depicts a journey from Puerto Rico to New Jersey and a family saga that spans two generations, all of which is remembered by a young, first-person narrator, Marisol, who has lived in the United States all her life. From her U.S. perspective, she recounts the lives of those generations before her that were born in Puerto Rico, and Spanish is obviously their language even though the narrator remembers their experiences in English. In some instances we read an English phrase that is so obviously a literal translation of a Spanish colloquialism that it sounds as if the Spanish past is trying to speak through the English grammar. "Maybe I shouldn't be telling you this, but I'm going to kill that *son of a great bitch* one of these days," says Marisol's father, Rafael, as a young man in Puerto Rico who rebels against his abusive, alcoholic father (Ortiz Cofer 60, my emphasis). Ortiz Cofer attempts to convey the severity of a Spanish curse such as *"hijo de la gran puta"* with a literal translation, even though it sounds somewhat awkward in English. Her text demonstrates a yearning for Spanish, just as the young narrator, Marisol, yearns to retrace her family's story of migration to the United States. When Elena Olazagasti-Segovia translates Ortiz Cofer's novel into Spanish for the 1996 edition from Editorial de la Universidad de Puerto Rico, she easily returns Marisol's story back to the language of the first generation, so that the original phrase in English that carries the mark of a Spanish origin has been tentatively returned to that origin. The Spanish translation renders Rafael's curse as "Tal vez no debiera decirte esto, pero voy a matar a ese *hijo de la gran puta* uno de estos días" (61, my emphasis). What is lost here in this translation from English to Spanish, is the English text's own attempt to pay homage to a defaced Spanish that lies underneath its twisted English grammar. The structure of the novel, itself, still communicates the second-generation perspective of its narrator, but the Spanish language of the translation has betrayed the yearning that impels the English-speaking Marisol to write her story in the first place.

We find another narrative example of the Puerto Rican imagination that moves between languages in one of the more controversial, and least translatable, short stories to reproduce the Spanglish of U.S. Latinos. This story is not written by a Latina at all but by a Puerto Rican Islander, Ana Lydia Vega.[6] Her story "Pollito Chicken" parodies the bicultural consciousness of one Suzie Bermiúdez, who, although born in Puerto Rico and now living in New York, decides to vacation on the Island "a pesar de que no pasaba por el Barrio a pie ni bajo amenaza de ejecución por la Mafia, a pesar de que prefería mil veces perder un fabulous job antes que poner Puerto Rican en las applications de trabajo y morir de hambre por no coger el Welfare o los food stamps como todos esos lazy, dirty, no-good bums que eran sus compatriotas . . ." (Vega 75).

We have to assume that it is through Suzie's perspective that the previous tirade against Puerto Ricans is strung together. The comedy of this piece comes from the irony that even though Suzie prefers to dis-identify with her Puerto Rican compatriots, Spanish structures her insults even if they are in English. Suzie is determined to seduce an American tourist on her vacation, but to her dismay there are only young Puerto Rican men at the hotel pool on that particular afternoon. Although she tries to ignore the advances of the "native specimens" (78), after three piña coladas and many suggestive looks, Suzie decides to enlist the amorous services of the bartender. Recounting his sexual conquest later to his friends, the bartender tells how

> en el preciso instante en que las platinum-frosted fingernails se incrustaban passionately en su afro, desde los skyscrapers inalcanzables de una intra-uterine orgasm, los half-opened lips de Suzie Bermiúdez producían el sonoro mugido ancestral de:
>
> —¡VIVA PUELTO RICO LIBREEEEEEEEEEEEEEEE! (79)

Vega's story differs from Ortiz Cofer's novel because the former is written in a Spanish grammar that erupts with English words and phrases, implying that Suzie Bermiúdez's consciousness is essentially a Puerto Rican one that explodes through the Anglo-American façade in moments of explicit ecstasy. Her fatal flaw, which is the real target of Vega's ridicule, is that she forgets to acknowledge the ancestral language that undermines her assimilationist desires. On the other hand, Ortiz Cofer, like García, writes in an English that remembers Spanish even as it traces over it.

This kind of textual de-facing is much less a symptom of cultural and linguistic repression than it is a manifestation of what Marianne Hirsch calls "postmemory." In *Family Frames: Photography, Narrative and Postmemory,* Hirsch uses the term to describe the effect of family photographs on the children of Holocaust survivors. While the victims who experienced the terror of the Holocaust look at photographic images and construct a memory that is "directly connected to the past," the members of the second generation experience the trauma through "narratives that preceded their birth, whose own belated stories are evacuated by the stories of the previous generation shaped by traumatic events that can be neither understood nor recreated" (Hirsch 22). In art, photography, and literature, Hirsch argues that the "aesthetics of postmemory . . . is a diasporic aesthetics of temporal and spatial exile that needs simultaneously to (re)build and to mourn" (246). I find this term useful to describe the relation between García's text and the characters who have experienced the trauma of exile first hand, for their memories of the homeland are mediated by the pull of two languages and two cultures, what Gustavo Pérez Firmat has described as the condition of the

"1.5" generation of Cuban Americans.[7] For Constancia Agüero, her memories of the trauma of exile and migration are "directly connected to the past." Our reading of those memories, similar to Constancia's reading of her father's letter, rebuilds and mourns a trauma "that can be neither understood nor recreated." The narratives that precede this novel—this particular refraction of the past—exist as the de-faced Spanish of the English-language text.

Constancia Agüero devises her own scheme to piece together the past through her line of cosmetics, *Cuerpo de Cuba*. She sells the various emollients and lotions—*Cuello de Cuba, Senos de Cuba, Codos de Cuba, Muslos de Cuba*—with the slogan "Time is indifferent but you needn't be" to the Cuban women of Miami, who swear they feel more *cubana* after using these products (131–32). Constancia admits that she "is not immune from these sudden reveries herself" (132), even though she feels ostracized by the Miami Cubans and capitalizes on what she disparages as their relentless nostalgia. Constancia's memories of Cuba and her mother are very vague, but the application of her eye cream conjures up images of her family in Cuba, particularly the scene of her mother's burial. Although her cosmetics contain no preservatives, they function much in the same way as her ornithologist father's taxidermy—a rearrangement of skin that reproduces the appearance of a past life in death.

García's text is one step removed from that cosmetological and taxidermical mediation of memory. In an interview that accompanies the paperback edition of *The Agüero Sisters*, the unnamed interviewer asks, "You were born in Havana but moved with your family to New York when you were two. Do you have any memories that survive from those early years?" García answers succinctly, "None whatsoever." We can read her novel, then, as an example of postmemory because "its connection to its object or source is mediated not through recollection but through an imaginative investment and creation" (Hirsch 22). When we read that Constancia wakes up one morning to find her mother's face superimposed onto her own, we glimpse at the tragedy of a woman who has not reconciled herself with her memories and who is forced to return to Cuba and confront a past life revealed to have been a veneer of lies. When we look at García's language, with its numerous references to Latin American literature and its incorporation of Spanish words and phrases in an English-language text, we see the de-facing operations performed by postmemory. The novel is the representation of a trauma that the writer does not remember but cannot seem to forget.

How does Alan West's translation render this complex relation between language and memory into a text that is uniformly Spanish? It does not, indeed it cannot, fully reproduce the de-facing that a Latina text inscribes on language. This is not a shortcoming of this translation or of translation, in general. West achieves a partial return to the literary traditions that inform García's text through the necessary departures that his Spanish must take from the English original. We can compare the way West translates the following line in the "Prologue" to see how his language must necessarily find its own poetics:

> Then he carried his wife seventeen miles to the nearest village and began to tell his lies. (5)

> Luego cargó a su esposa treinta kilómetros hasta el próximo pueblo y comenzó a soltar sus mentiras. (4, West translation)

Aside from the obvious cultural conversion of miles into kilometers, the most interesting detail lies in the transformation of "to tell" into "soltar," which means to let loose, to let go or to let fly. West subtly refers to the many birds that appear throughout the novel with the use of this particular verb, but the word can also imply that the father's lies are the initial break with the past that follows Constancia into her exile. She returned to Cuba because she felt unmoored, untethered—*suelta*. Because West's translation returns to a Spanish that was never part of the original yet implicitly structured the characters' memories, his de-facing of the text refracts the postmemory of the second generation, namely, García, who had already written over the trauma of exile experienced by their parents. That postmemory becomes part of a new poetics that succeeds in conveying the experience of exile even as it writes over the experience of exile in language.

García's novel encapsulates so much of the Latina/o condition in the United States because it tells its story in English, an English that cannot exist without Spanish. Translating an interlingual text such as *The Agüero Sisters* only makes more acute the difficulty in translating any text. Suzanne Jill Levine says that "translation should be a critical act . . . creating doubt, posing questions to its reader, recontextualizing the ideology of the original text" (3). Is this not the task that many Latinas/os face when they look back on their countries of origin or when they rewrite the histories of exile and migration? García's novel is very critical of a notion of an "original" Cuba. The contentious versions of Cuba that exist simultaneously in Miami and on the Island construct their authenticity through narratives that forget more than they remember. West's translation, therefore, must refract into Spanish what was an English nostalgia for a silenced mother tongue. How does García represent a memory that is not hers? How does West translate a Spanish that was never really there? They de-face their origins, be they familial, national, or literary.

NOTES

1. The Miami-based magazine, *generation ñ*, has a somewhat regular column titled "Cubanamericanisms," by Bill Cruz, which includes such gems as

Bibaporrú for Vick's Vapor rub and *Tensén* for a Woolworth's or other five-and-ten stores. Similar to the oft-cited Spanglish particular to Chicanos and Puerto Ricans, Cubanamericanisms circulate within and among the various generations of Cuban exiles that have changed the cultural and linguistic landscape of Miami since the early Sixties.

2. See Larousse's *Gran Diccionario Español-Inglés* (Mexico: Ediciones Larousse, 1984).

3. I use this neologism to echo what Ricardo Ortiz, in "Café, Culpa and Capital: Nostalgic Addictions of Cuban Exile" (*The Yale Journal of Criticism* 10:1 [1997]: 63–84), has commented on the music of Cuban American singer, Albita Rodriguez, when he discusses her song, "Bolero para nostalgiar": "Recognizing that she speaks to a culture for whom 'nostalgia' operates grammatically less as a substantive and more as an infintive verbal form, Albita offers up a kind of tonic, if not an antidote for Cuban America's most profound psychic addiction" (73). That addiction is, I argue, the desire for a recovery from the slippage that occurs between language and memory.

4. In the same essay cited above, Ortiz also tells of how Cuban exiles in Miami perform the same toast every year: "next year in Havana" (63). Ortiz notes that such a gesture simultaneously promises return as it continually defers it.

5. Bruce-Novoa makes this argument in "Spanish-Language Loyalty and Literature," a chapter in his collection, *Retrospace* (Houston: Arte Público Press, 1990), 41–51. The interlingual text, unlike a bilingual text, is "a different code, one in which neither monolingual codes can stand alone and relate the same meaning. Translation becomes impossible, and purists from either language deny its viability" (49). Bruce-Novoa argues against linguistic purism and affirms Chicano literature's attempt to convey the border idiom often known as Spanglish. If we consider the role language plays in memory, we see that the interlingualism Bruce-Novoa describes represents the idiom of the here and now. Is it, however, an accurate representation of a monological past? It is precisely that "here and now" that invariably refracts the past, just as the target language of a translation de-faces the codes of the original.

6. Nicholasa Mohr, a prominent Nuyorican writer, has criticized Vega's portrayal of the U.S Latino experience in her essay, "Puerto Rican Writers in the United States, Puerto Rican Writers in Puerto Rico: A Separation Beyond Language," *The Americas Review* 15:2 (Summer 1987): 87–92.

7. Pérez Firmat adopts this term from sociologist Rubén Rumbaut. See Pérez Firmat's *Life on the Hyphen: The Cuban-American Way* (Austin: U of Texas P, 1994).

WORKS CITED

"Agüero." *Larousse: Gran Diccionario Español-Inglés*. Mexico: Ediciones Larousse, 1984.

Bruce-Novoa, Juan, ed. *Retrospace: Collected Essays on Chicano Literature.* Houston: Arte Público, 1990.

Carpentier, Alejo. *Los pasos perdidos*. 1953. Madrid: Alianza, 1996.

Derrida, Jacques. *The Ear of the Other*. Trans. Peggy Kamuf. Lincoln, NE: U Nebraska P, 1985.

García, Cristina. *The Agüero Sisters*. New York: Ballantine, 1997.

———. *Dreaming in Cuban*. New York: Ballantine, 1992.

———. *Las hermanas Agüero*. Trans. Alan West. New York: Random House, 1997.

Hirsch, Marianne. *Family Frames: Photography, Narrative, and Postmemory*. Cambridge: Harvard UP, 1997.

Lefevere, André. "Literary Theory and Translated Literature." *Dispositio* 7.19 (1982): 3–22.

Levine, Suzanne Jill. *The Subversive Scribe: Translating Latin American Fiction*. St. Paul, MN: Greywolf, 1991.

Mohr, Nicholasa. "Puerto Rican Writers in the United States, Puerto Rican Writers in Puerto Rico: A Separation Beyond Language." *The Americas Review* 15.2 (1987): 87–92.

Oritz, Ricardo L. "Café, Culpa, and Capital: Nostalgic Addictions in Cuban Exile." *The Yale Journal of Criticism* 10.1 (1997): 63–84.

Ortiz Cofer, Judith. *The Line of the Sun*. Athens, GA: U Georgia P, 1989.

———. *La línea del sol*. Trans. Elena Olazagasti-Segovia. San Juan, P.R.: Editorial de la Universidad de Puerto Rico: 1996.

Pérez Firmat, Gustavo. *Life on the Hyphen: The Cuban-American Way*. Austin: U Texas P, 1994.

Vega, Ana Lydia. "Pollito Chicken." *Vírgenes y mártires*. With Carmen Lugo Filippi. Río Piedras, PR: Antillana, 1988. 75–79.

Translation and Teaching:
The Dangers of Representing Latin America
for Students in the United States

Steven F. White

The purpose of this chapter is to stimulate discussion on the problematic issue of how Latin America is represented to English-speaking university students in the United States. I will focus on four areas: the availability of works by Latin American authors translated into English, the questionable paradigm of the "smooth" translation, how academics tend to teach Latin America to English-speaking students (especially in interdisciplinary programs) and, finally, the ways "first world" students often read "third world" literature in translation.

In terms of the U. S. publishing industry, there is very little interest in translated works. According to the 1999 *Bowker Annual,* of the 65,796 hard and trade paper titles published in the United States in 1997, only 1,458 (2.2 percent) were translations. Preliminary data for 1998 reflect a similar percentage. From 1993–98, according to the same source, there were an average of 146 translations from the Spanish language (Spain and Hispanic America) published each year in the English language (Ink 530, 532). By comparison, many other countries, much smaller than the United States, have a far higher percentage of translations in their total output of published titles: 6 percent in Japan, 10 percent in France, 14 percent in Hungary, 15 percent in Germany, and 25 percent in Italy (Venuti 88). Publishers quoted in related articles that appeared in *The Christian Science Monitor* and *Publishers Weekly* commented on how unprofitable translations are, how the United States is a very parochial country, and how presses that publish translations are often subsidized by a variety of grants, including funds from the government of the author's native country (see Lottman, Sappenfield, and Campbell). To get an approximate, nonscientific idea as to what percentage of the already small number of translated works published in the United States are works by Latin American authors, I consulted the July 2000 *Annotated Books Received* Supplement compiled by *Translation Review*. This listing consists of translated works published primarily between 1999–2000 by 125 publishers: a mix of large New York publishing houses, university presses, and small presses (including some in Canada and England). What follows is my own compilation of works by Latin American authors translated into English based on the categories established by the editors of *Translation Review*:

2 anthologies
2 reprints (one literary work, one biography)
0 Art and Architecture
2 Autobiography, Letters, Memoirs, Interviews
1 Biography
0 Cultural Studies
1 History and Politics
3 Literary Theory and Criticism
0 Natural History and Science
0 Philosophy and Religion
0 Reference
0 Social Sciences
0 Translation Studies

In terms of literary works written in languages from Latin America, there was one title translated from the French (a novel by a Haitian author); no titles of works by Brazilian authors translated from Portuguese; and fifteen titles by Hispanic American authors (which included two novels by the same author, one of which is an out-of-print classic) (Baity).[1] Granted, this listing compiled by *Translation Review*, the official publication of the preeminent American Literary Translators Association (ALTA), is incomplete in that publications in Agriculture, Business, Home Economics, Juveniles, Law, Medicine, Sports/Recreation, and Technology are outside its purview. The compilation, furthermore, in no way claims to be comprehensive or systematic despite the ample selection of translated works that it does include. No doubt some important works by Latin American authors in English translation have escaped their attention. Even so, if one scans the advertisements for new publications that appear in the programs for major conferences such as those sponsored by the Modern Language Association (MLA) and the Latin American Studies Association (LASA), it is readily apparent that the vast majority of works published on Latin America from all the disciplines are books written in English by U. S. academics.

This leads to an obvious troubling question: Who represents Latin America in the United States? In the *LASA Forum*, John D. French, from Duke University, in a very brief piece entitled "Translation: An Imperative for a Transnational World," says that "In the English-speaking world, Latin Americans are more often written about than read. As a result, the educated public in the United States continues to learn most of what it does know about the region from Latin Americanists who are themselves foreigners to the national realities they study" (French 44). As an effort to rectify this situation, Duke University established a publishing project called "Latin America—In Translation/En Traducción/Em Tradução" that has published a limited number of books since 1993 and plans to continue the series into the new millennium. Seven books over a seven-year period (with five titles planned for 2001–2002), representing works published throughout Latin America in the social sciences and humanities, is a praiseworthy contribution, but it is extremely modest given the nature of the imbalance. Over the last three decades, of course, a number of works of Latin American fiction and poetry in English translation have achieved a great deal of recognition. In a review essay that appeared in *Latin American Research Review,* Clifford E. Landers mentions the names of some two dozen Latin American authors whose names would be familiar not only to academic specialists but to many general readers as well. Landers says that "this roll, however striking, is tiny when compared with the many talented and original voices that are unlikely to be heard outside their native languages and their country of origin. It is perhaps inevitable in the economic scheme of things that even in their original languages, many works of merit never go beyond their initial limited printing." Landers goes on to discuss the radical inequalities that exist when it comes to the availability of English source materials in Latin American countries, where as many as 70–100 percent of the top ten best-selling books may be translations from English. According to Landers, "[w]hile the hemispheric net flow of capital in the past three decades has moved from the underdeveloped to the developed world, the stream of translated materials has also proceeded largely one way, but in the opposite direction" (Landers 254–55).

I would like to turn now to certain issues regarding the translation process itself and how it can influence the way Latin America is represented, and therefore taught, in the United States. Traditionally, translation has been considered the supremely laudable endeavor of the humanist, who builds bridges between cultures and makes known what was previously unknown. Currently, however, the discussions of translation have focused on the difficult issue of how texts from Latin America are recreated in the English language and subsequently made available for pedagogical purposes in the United States. Clayton Eshleman has defined what he calls "translational imperialism," the process by which "first world" translators work on texts by "third world" authors, reshaping the "raw material" of the "colonized" text in order to produce translations that lead the reader to believe that the foreign author is aping literary conventions of the United States (Eshleman 4). Even if one disagrees with Eshleman, students often need to be reminded that there is a text behind the text before them, one that is conceived in a language reflecting a world view that is not that of an English speaker. The act of translation, we might also inform our students, implies ideological choices and can also be considered an act of literary criticism given the need for interpretive, textual analysis. Many of our colleagues, too, unfortunately, especially those who work in the increasingly common interdisciplinary initiatives in cultural studies on U. S. college campuses, present translated texts in class as if they were written originally in English, assuming what Tejaswini Niranjana calls "an unproblematic notion of representation," ignoring the "historicity of translation" and how translation can "completely occlude the violence that accompanies the construction of the colonial subject" (Niranjana 2).

Again, even if one believes that the positions regarding translation taken by Eshleman and Niranjana are extreme, worst-case scenarios that do not reflect the modus operandi of translators in the United States, what sorts of assumptions underlie the goal of the translator who strives to make the translated work "sound like a book in English"? According to Edith Grossman, who translates the work of Gabriel García Márquez and who is one of a very select few in the United States who can earn a living by means of literary translation, "What is important is that the ideas and concepts are in the same tone as if the writer could speak in English" (Sappenfield 14). What does it mean when multilingual translators, who are engaged in the process of self-criticism, and monolingual editors and reviewers of translations, who are unable to enter into the dialogue between the translated text and the original, all speak of the translation solely in terms of "smoothness" and how easily the translation can be assimilated into literary and thematic traditions that already have shaped the English canon? Do translators apply the ostensibly aesthetic criterion for the creation of "readable" translations to the text-selection process with limiting or exclusionary results? In other words, if a particular, perhaps experimental or culturally different, work cannot be rendered in such a way as to give the appearance of having been written originally in English, should it, then, not be translated at all?

In light of these questions, consumers as well as creators of books, especially works that are used for the purposes of higher education, need to discover the advantages of not exempting themselves from issues related to translation. Teachers and students may feel compelled to ask why a certain work was translated into English at a particular time and to consider the translator, whose identity and motivations throughout the translation process might reveal significant insights into the original work. Publishers in the United States, who often lack a continually updated, systematic knowledge of Latin American literature, might understand the translator more fully as a mediator, an unofficial broker of literary power. The difficulties of this situation are clear, according to Rainer Schulte, who, in his article "Cross-Cultural Communication on the Information Highways" says that "the transplantation of works from other languages into English has never followed any clearly defined procedures or methods. Often, a book makes its way into English because a translator happens to meet an author or comes across a work by pure coincidence, which in many instances leads to the translation of a work whose literary quality or importance might be quite questionable" (Schulte 1). When, as the data clearly demonstrate, the number of published translations is severely limited, chance and the perseverance of a single translator can shape the knowledge of an entire country's literary production. An interesting example of this is the case of a Brazilian novelist, the sole author from his country in a recent listing of *Translation Review*: one translator negotiated contracts for the publication of two novels by this particular author.

Are there other, extraliterary, factors that affect which works of Latin American literature in translation will be translated, published, and available for pedagogical purposes? For example, what causes works from certain countries (post-1990 Nicaragua, for example) or even entire regions (Latin America, for example) suddenly to lose even their minimal presence in the literary landscape of the United States? Although these questions are difficult to answer, they do facilitate what might be called "translation awareness," an understanding that reading a translated text may entail recognizing asymmetrical power relationships, seeking explanations as to who translated a text (as well as when and why), and realizing that, yes, when it comes to literature in translation, the cliché is true: market forces in the United States play a dynamic role in the creation of more accurate definitions of terms equated with democratic ideals such as freedom of expression.

If, as many publishers agree, the United States is fundamentally an isolated, inward-looking country with little interest in what happens in literature beyond its borders, new kinds of internal inequalities undoubtedly will play a future role with regard to teaching and translation. Translations into English of works by Latin American authors may dwindle virtually to nonexistence as the market for works written in English by the long-ignored and marginalized U.S. Hispanic population continues to improve. Publishers and editors in the United States, who are generally monolingual and suspicious of the translation process in general and who are loath to remunerate and recognize the translator's efforts, may soon be able to eliminate the translator completely, or very nearly so. Authors such as Rudolfo Anaya, Sandra Cisneros, Cristina García, and Julia Alvarez, whose works are now big sellers, are American authors writing in English on American themes in keeping with American literary traditions (e.g., the immigrant experience). Of course, there still will be translations of Gabriel García Márquez, Carlos Fuentes, Mario Vargas Llosa, Isabel Allende, and a handful of other authors who have achieved international recognition. There also will be continued attempts to market Spanish-language books in the United

States in certain urban areas. But it will become increasingly more attractive for U. S. publishers to represent Latin America (for mass market audiences as well as academic programs exploring the theme of American cultural pluralism) by means of U. S. Latino/a authors writing in English who, not surprisingly, are often praised in reviews for their "lyric magical realism," a legacy of the Latin American "boom" novelists whose writing styles (readily available in English translation) they have assimilated.

Would it be preferable, then, to represent Latin America in the classroom by means of Anglo writers whose works are set in Latin America? In an article entitled "Mermaids and Other Fetishes: Images of Latin America," Geoffrey Fox mentions *A Flag for Sunrise* by Robert Stone, *Under the Volcano* by Malcolm Lowry, *The Power and the Glory* by Graham Greene, and *Imagining Argentina* by Lawrence Thornton as works seeming to hold that "human nature is universal and immutable." Fox goes on to say that "this view of the essential sameness of human beings, generally associated with a liberal political outlook, masks or ignores the true relations of power that shape personalities and make them capable of inflicting, resisting, submitting or enduring in particular ways. And, of course, if we cannot see these relations of power, we cannot act consciously to change them" (Fox 138). The issue, clearly, has to do with representation, the central theme of current debate in a wide range of academic disciplines: in other words, yes, let's study the photographs in Paul Strand's remarkable *Mexican Portfolio,* but in direct and continuous relation to the work of Mexican photographers such as Manuel Alvarez Bravo, Graciela Iturbide, and Maya Goded (Parada 93–102). The same case might be made for juxtaposing Thornton's work with Marta Traba's *Mothers and Shadows* (without ignoring this English translation of the original title *Conversación al sur*), the testimonies gathered in Ernesto Sabato's *Nunca más,* and Ricardo Piglia's brilliant novel *Artificial Respiration.* The kind of comparative study made possible by examining a work such as Juan Rulfo's *Pedro Páramo* in conjunction with Harriet Doerr's *Stones for Ibarra* might stimulate worthwhile discussions of issues regarding representation and the authority of the author.

It is by means of an analysis of power relations that many teachers choose to represent Latin America to their English-speaking U. S. students. In a remarkably frank, pragmatic, and self-critical article called "How First World Students Read Third World Literature," however, Leigh Binford and Wendy Hardin assess why their progressive, innovative strategies for presenting Third World literature to students in a U.S. university was largely a failure. Binford and Hardin team-taught an interdisciplinary course on Third World Literature, using authors such as Gabriel García Márquez, Manlio Argueta, Jorge Amado, Bessie Head, Nadine Gordimer, and others, from their vantage points as anthropologist and reading specialist. They planned to study literature from a socioeconomic perspective and culture through the lens of literary texts, with the idea of countering the segmentation of knowledge in U. S. academic institutions and challenging the interests of dominant culture "by privileging the representations of the dominated": Binford and Hardin hoped that "students would be encouraged to revise some of the preconceptions they inherit as members of the dominant culture" (Binford and Hardin 146–47). Unfortunately, the two professors found that, more often than not, their students "translated" the translated texts they were reading in an attempt to make the unfamiliar more familiar and in so doing defused the threatening ideological implications of the texts. According to Binford and Hardin, "[m]embers of the class employed a variety of reading strategies which ignored, selectively attended [to], or transfigured alternative voices with the result that pre-existing discourses were usually reconfirmed" (Binford and Hardin 147).

This brings me full circle to where I began, in that the commercial logic of the publishing world often reinforces a sensationalistic, stereotypical view of Latin America that mirrors U.S. students' perception of this region. The transformation of the titles of some works by Latin American authors that are widely used in universities in the United States illustrate this point perfectly: the Spanish title of Manlio Argueta's *Un día en la vida* emphasizes the common, everyday nature of the horror described in the novel (which serves to heighten this horrific reality), whereas the English translation *One Day of Life* makes everything melodramatic and removed from ordinary experience; the ambiguous, abstract, unwieldy poetry of Omar Cabezas's *La montaña es algo más que una inmensa estepa verde* becomes the Rambo-esque *Fire from the Mountain*. Similarly, *Me llamo Rigoberta Menchú y así me nació la conciencia*, which might be translated "My Name is Rigoberta Menchú, and This Is How My Political Awareness Was Born," or ". . . Came into Being" has a colloquial, simple, personal directness that is the exact opposite of the pretentious anthropological tone of *I . . . Rigoberta Menchú: An Indian Woman in Guatemala*. Would the mention of "political awareness" in the translated title have had a negative impact on the marketability of such a book in the United States at the time of its publication? Can one also imagine the opposite case, whereby a work by a Latin American author that has no overtly political theme would be deemed unmarketable in English translation?

Rigoberta Menchú's testimonial work has circulated widely in U.S. academic institutions, especially after Menchú won the Nobel Peace Prize during the same year of controversy surrounding the five hundredth anniversary of Columbus's arrival in the so-called New World. It provides a good example of how the issues of translation can be incorporated effectively in the classroom in a sophisticated way. As a woman, as a citizen of the Third World, and as a member of an ethnic minority, Menchú represents a triple marginalization as "subaltern." On the one hand, her current prominence as well as the availability of her work in English translation will enable indigenous peoples of Latin America to have a global voice. On the other hand, there are some well-known issues regarding how Menchú represents herself and speaks in the first person which might be raised with students when using this work in the classroom. In order to generate the text for *I . . . Rigoberta Menchú . . . ,* the First World academically-trained ethnographer Eliza-beth Burgos-Debray tapes the interview in France in the second lan-guage of the Third World activist-interviewee, chooses the questions that form the basis of the conversation, turns orality into written text, imposes the structure of a book (including epigraphs for individual chapters), then edits herself from the published text as if she (the inter-viewer) had never been present, and as if the format were not an extended interview. Is Rigoberta Menchú truly representing herself and her culture in the book that purports to contain her words verbatim, or is testimonial literature generated under these circumstances another example of an imperialist construct of a subject? Is the subsequent translation of the work into English by Ann Wright an added layer of mediation, expropriation, or domestication? In an extremely insightful chapter entitled "Translation as a Method for Cross-Cultural Teach-ing," which focuses on Menchú's narrative, Anuradha Dingwaney and Carol Maier believe that "a desirable goal in teaching and reading cross-cultural texts as an exercise involving translation is to nudge stu-dents/readers to occupy that space or tension where they are 'faithful' to the text at the same time as they acknowledge that their 'fidelity' is itself refracted through their ideological formations as 'subjects' in the first world" (Dingwaney and Maier 57). The authors conclude by say-ing that, despite a desire for invisibility on the part of certain ethnog-raphers, editors, and translators, the job of teachers and students is to call attention to mediating, underlying presences that are often barely discernible and to make this activity an important part of the pedagog-ical process: "[A] translator's visibility does not lessen the impact of immediacy of a story for its readers, but actually intensifies that imme-diacy by compounding an awareness of translation and bringing the act of mediation to light" (Dingwaney and Maier 59).[2]

What are some of the possible consequences of not adopting this kind of approach to teaching Latin American works in English transla-tion? In *The Scandals of Translation: Towards an Ethics of Difference,* Lawrence Venuti declares in no uncertain terms that "the repression of translation in the classroom conceals the inevitable inscription of British and American cultural values in the foreign text, yet simultaneously treats English as the transparent vehicle of universal truth, thus encour-aging a linguistic chauvinism, even a cultural nationalism" (Venuti 92).

Working toward ethical solutions in pedagogical strategies means posing a series of questions that will promote discussion of the need for greater "translation awareness" when we teach Latin American literature in English translation: Are market forces the sole explanation as to why so few works written by Latin American authors across the disciplines are available in English translation? What are the pedagogical implications of this paucity of translated material? Should both teacher and translator question the paradigm of the "smooth" translation and attempt to take student and reader closer to the original language of the author? What is "foreign" about the original text in relation to the translation and how might "foreignness" manifest itself in beneficial ways in the English version? If one accepts the desirability of locating a particular work in a social and historical context in the classroom, why shouldn't this process be taken a step farther by means of a discussion of the situatedness of the translation/translator? How should teachers and students seek ways to define their own cultural identities in relation to what Venuti calls "the text and culture of the translation" (Venuti 93)? Can students be taught to read texts translated into their first language with a translator's eye so that there might be a dialogue between translation and original text? Can analysis of Latin American literature highlight discussions of the translation itself by, as Venuti says, "calling attention to the multiple, polychronic forms that destabilize its unity and cloud over its seeming transparency" (Venuti 96)? And, finally: How might teachers of Latin American literature in translation change the ways they present classroom material so as not to reinforce their students' stereotypical perceptions of Latin America?

NOTES

1. A previous listing in *Translation Review: Annotated Books Received* included in vol. 5, no. 1 (July 1999), representing nearly 100 publishers, contains a similarly meager number of translations of works by Latin American authors published from 1998–1999: four anthologies (two of which are translations from the indigenous languages Quechua and Mapuche), three reprints (one of which is a Brazilian classic), two autobiographies, four literary works by Francophone Caribbean authors, no listing at all for the Portuguese language, thirteen literary works by Hispanic American authors, and no listings in other categories.

2. See also, Carey-Webb, Allen, ed. *Teaching and Testimony: Rigoberta Menchú and the North American Classroom* (New York: SUNY Press, 1996). A summary of the controversies in academia regarding Rigoberta Menchú that were generated by David Stoll's *I, Rigoberta Menchú and the Story of All Poor Guatemalans* (Boulder: Westview Press, 1999) can be found in Robin Wilson, "Anthropologist Challenges Veracity of Multicultural Icon," <http://chronicle.com/colloquy/99menchu/background.htm>.

WORKS CITED

Baity, Linda Sullivan, ed. *Translation Review: Annotated Books Received Supplement* 6.1: 2000.

Binford, Leigh, and Wendy Hardin. "How First World Students Read Third World Literature." *Translating Latin America: Culture as Text.* Ed.William Luis and Julio Rodríguez-Luis. Translation Perspectives VI. Binghamton, NY: Center for Research in Translation, SUNY Binghamton, 1991. 145–52.

Campbell, Kim. "U.S. Consumers Say 'Yes' to Books." *The Christian Science Monitor* (1995): 10.

Dingwaney, Anuradha and Carol Maier. "Translation as a Method for Cross-Cultural Teaching." *Understanding Others: Cultural and Cross-Cultural Studies and the Teaching of Literature.* Ed. Joseph Trimmer and Tilly Warnock. Urbana: National Council of Teachers of English, 1992. 47–62.

Eshleman, Clayton. "Addenda to A Note on Apprenticeship." *Translation Review* 20 (1986): 4–5.

Fox, Geoffrey. "Mermaids and Other Fetishes: Images of Latin America." *Translating Latin America: Culture as Text.* Ed. William Luis and Julio Rodríguez-Luis. Translation Perspectives VI. Binghamton, NY: Center for Research in Translation, SUNY Binghamton, 1991. 135–44.

French, John D. "Translation: An Imperative for a Transnational World." *LASA Forum* 28.1 (1997): 44–45.

Ink, Gary. "Book Title Output and Average Prices: 1997 Final and 1998 Preliminary Figures." *The Bowker Annual: Library and Book Trade Almanac.* New Providence, NJ: Bowker, 1999. 529–35.

Landers, Clifford E. "Latin America and Translation: Three Contributions to Knowing the Other." *Latin American Research Review* 30.3 (1995): 254–63.

Lottman, Herbert R. "One Notable Trade Imbalance: The Buying of Book Translations." *Publishers Weekly* (June 5, 1995): 12.

Niranjana, Tejaswini. *Siting Translation: History, Post-Structuralism, and the Colonial Context.* Berkeley and Los Angeles: University of California Press, 1992.

Parada, Esther. "Jewels, Native Fruits, and Ragged Merchandise: Imaging Latin America." Ed. Catherine Tedford. *Photographs at St. Lawrence University.* Canton, NY: St. Lawrence U, 2000.

Sappenfield, Mark. "Small, Specialized Publishers Fill Book-Translation Niche." *The Christian Science Monitor* (August 9, 1995): 14.

Schulte, Rainer. "Cross-Cultural Communication on the Information Highways." *Translation Review* 46 (1994): 1–2.

Venuti, Lawrence. *The Scandals of Translation: Towards an Ethics of Difference.* London and New York: Routledge, 1998.

Bibliography

TRANSLATION THEORY AND HISTORY

Baker, Mona, ed. *Routledge Encyclopedia of Translation Studies*. New York: Routledge, 1998.

Bassnett, Susan, and Harish Trivedi, eds. *Postcolonial Translation Theory*. New York: Routledge, 1999.

Berman, Antoine. *The Experience of the Foreign: Culture and Translation in Romantic Germany*. Trans. S. Heyvaert. Albany: SUNY P, 1992.

Bower, Lynne, Michael Cronin, Dorothy Kenny, and Jennifer Pearson. *Unity in Diversity? Current Trends in Translation Studies*. Manchester: St. Jerome, 1998.

Budick, Sanford, and Wolfgang Iser, eds. *The Translatability of Cultures. Figurations of the Space Between*. Stanford: Stanford UP, 1996.

Bush, Peter, and Kirsten Malmkjaer, eds. *Rimbaud's Rainbow: Literary Translation in Higher Education*. Amsterdam: John Benjamins, 1998.

Cheyfitz, Eric. *The Poetics of Imperialism: Translation and Colonialization from The Tempest to Tarzan*. Philadelphia: U PA P, 1997.

Classe, Olive, ed. *Encyclopedia of Literary Translation into English*. London and Chicago: Fitzroy Dearborn, 2000.

Derrida, Jacques. "What Is a Relevant Translation?" Trans. Lawrence Venuti. *Critical Inquiry* 27.2 (2001): 169–200.

D'Hulst, Lieven, and John Milton, eds. *Reconstructing Cultural Memory: Translation, Scripts, Literacy*. Vol. 7 of the Proceedings of the XVth Congress of the International Comparative Literature Association. Leiden 16–22 August 1997.

Dingwaney, Anuradha, and Carol Maier, eds. *Between Languages and Cultures: Translation and Cross-Cultural Texts*. Pittsburgh: U Pittsburgh P, 1995.

France, Peter, ed. *The Oxford Guide to Literature in English Translation*. Oxford: Oxford UP, 2000.

Gaddis Rose, Marilyn, ed. *Translation Horizons: Beyond the Boundaries of "Translation Spectrum." Translation Perspectives* IX (1996).

Gallego Roca, Miguel. *Traducción y literatura: los estudios literarios ante las obras traducidas*. Madrid: Jucar, 1994.

Gentzler, Edwin. *Contemporary Translation Theories*. New York: Routledge, 1993.

Graham, Joseph F., ed. *Difference in Translation*. Ithaca: Cornell UP, 1985.

Lefevere, André, ed. *Translation, History, Culture: A Sourcebook*. New York: Routledge, 1992.

——. *Translation, Rewriting, and the Manipulation of Literary Fame*. London: Routledge, 1992.

——, and Kenneth David Jackson, eds. *The Art and Science of Translation*. *Dispositio* 7 (1982).

Niranjana, Tejaswini, ed. *Siting Translation: History, Poststructuralism, and the Colonial Context*. Berkeley: U CA P, 1992.

Robinson, Douglas. *Translation and Empire: Postcolonial Theories Explained*. Manchester: St. Jerome, 1997.

——. *The Translator's Turn*. Baltimore: Johns Hopkins UP, 1991.

——. *Western Translation Theory: From Herodotus to Nietzsche*. Manchester: St. Jerome, 2001.

——. *What Is Translation? Centrifugal Theories, Critical Interventions*. Kent, OH: Kent State UP, 1997.

——. *Who Translates? Translator Subjectivities Beyond Reason*. Albany: SUNY P, 2001.

Schulte, Rainer, and John Biguenet, eds. *The Craft of Translation*. Chicago: U Chicago P, 1989.

Simon, Sherry. *Gender in Translation*. New York: Routledge, 1996.

Snell Hornby, Mary, Franz Pöchhacker, and Klaus Kaindl, eds. *Translation Studies: An Interdiscipline*. Amsterdam/Philadelphia: John Benjamins, 1992.

Steiner, George. *After Babel: Aspects of Language and Translation*. Oxford: Oxford UP, 1992.

Studies in the Humanities 22.1–2 (1995). Special issue "Translation and Culture."

Swann, Brian, ed. *On the Translation of Native American Literatures*. Washington, DC: Smithsonian, 1992.

Toury, Gideon. *Descriptive Translation Studies and Beyond*. Amsterdam: John Benjamins, 1995.

Venuti, Lawrence, ed. *Rethinking Translation: Discourse, Subjectivity, Ideology*. New York: Routledge, 1992.

——. *The Scandals of Translation: Towards an Ethics of Difference*. New York: Routledge, 1998.

——, ed. *The Translation Studies Reader*. New York: Routledge, 2000.

——. *The Translator's Invisibility: A History of Translation*. New York: Routledge, 1995.

Warren, Rosanna, ed. *The Art of Translation: Voices from the Field*. Boston: Northeastern UP, 1989.

BOOKS ON TRANSLATION AND LATIN AMERICAN WRITING

Aparicio, Frances. *Versiones, interpretaciones, creaciones: Instancias de la tra-ducción literaria en Hispanoamérica en el siglo veinte.* Gaithersburg, MD: Hispamérica, 1991.

Arrojo, Rosemary. *Tradução, desconstrução e psicanálise.* Rio de Janeiro: Imago, 1993.

Bradford, Lisa, ed. *Traducción como cultura.* Rosario, Argentina: Beatriz Viterbo, 1997.

Carbonell i Cortés, Ovidi. *Traducir al otro: Traducción, exotismo, poscolonial-ismo.* Cuenca: Universidad de Castilla-La Mancha, 1997.

Catelli, Nora, and Marietta Gargatagli, eds. *El tabaco que fumaba Plinio. Esce-nas de la traducción en España y América: relatos, leyes y reflexiones sobre los otros.* Barcelona: Serbal, 1998.

Felstiner, John. *Translating Neruda: The Way to Macchu Picchu.* Stanford: Stan-ford UP, 1980.

Jakfalvi-Leiva, Susana. *Traducción, escritura y violencia colonizadora: un estu-dio de la obra del Inca Garcilaso.* Syracuse: Maxwell School of Citizenship and Public Affairs, 1984.

Kristal, Efraín. *Invisible Work: Borges and Translation.* Nashville: Vanderbilt UP, 2002.

Levine, Suzanne Jill. *The Subversive Scribe. Translating Latin American Fiction.* St. Paul, MN: Graywolf, 1991.

Luis, William, and Julio Rodríguez-Luis, eds. *Translating Latin America: Cul-ture as Text. Translation Perspectives VI* (1991).

Milton, John. *O poder da tradução.* São Paulo: Ars Poetica, 1993.

———. *A Translation Model from Latin America: The Translation Theory and Practice of Augusto and Haroldo de Campos.* Lewiston: Mellen, 1996.

Payne, Johnny. *Conquest of the New Word: Experimental Fiction and Transla-tion in the Americas.* Austin: U TX P, 1993.

Paz, Octavio. *Traducción: literatura y literalidad.* Barcelona: Tusquets, 1980.

Pym, Anthony. *Negotiating the Frontier: Translators and Intercultures in His-panic History.* Manchester: St. Jerome, 2000.

Rostagno, Irene. *Searching for Recognition: The Promotion of Latin American Literature in the United States.* Westport: Greenwood, 1997.

Round, Nicholas G., ed. *Translation Studies in Hispanic Contexts. Bulletin of Hispanic Studies* 75.1 (1998).

Sammons, K. and J. Sherzer, eds. *Translating Native Latin American Verbal Art: Ethnopoetics and Ethnography of Speaking.* Washington: Smithsonian Institution, 2000.

Sarlo, Beatriz. *La máquina cultural: maestras, traductores y vanguardistas.* Buenos Aires: Ariel, 1998.

ARTICLES ON TRANSLATION AND LATIN AMERICAN WRITING

Alarcón, N. "Traddutora, Traditora: A Paradigmatic Figure of Chicana Feminism." *Cultural Critique* (Fall 1989): 57–87. Also *Dangerous Liaisons: Gender, Nation, and Postcolonial Perspectives.* Ed. Anne McClintock, Aamir Mufti, and Ella Shohat. Minneapolis: U MN P. 1997. 278–97.

Angulo, María-Elena. "Ideologeme of 'Mestizaje' and Search for Cultural Identity in *Bruna, Soroche y los tíos* by Alicia Yáñez Cossío." Luis and Rodríguez-Luis. 205–13.

Aparicio, Frances. "Cultural (Mis)Translations and Crossover Nightmares." In *Listening to Salsa. Gender, Latin Popular Music, and Puerto Rican Cultures.* Hanover: UP of New England, 1998, 104–17.

———. "Epistemología y traducción en la obra de Octavio Paz." *Hispanic Journal* 8.1 (1986): 157–67.

Arguedas, José María. "La novela y el problema de la expresión literaria en el Perú." *Mar del Sur, Revista Peruana de Cultura* 3.9 (1950): 66–72.

Averbach, Márgara. "Traducción de novelas y cuentos de autor indio." Bradford. 119–24.

Balderston, Daniel. "Huidobro and the Notion of Translatability." *Fragmentos* (Florianopolis, Brazil) 3.1 (1990): 59–74.

Bastin, Georges. "Latin American Tradition." *Routledge Encyclopedia of Translation Studies.* Ed. Mona Baker. New York and London: Routledge, 1998. 505–12.

Bellessi, Diana. "Género y traducción." Bradford. 93–98.

Belitt, Ben. "The Enigmatic Predicament: Some Parables of Kafka and Borges." *The Forgèd Feature. Toward a Poetics of Uncertainty.* New York: Fordham UP, 1995. 41–65.

———. "Memoir as Myth: The Odysseys of Pablo Neruda." *The Forgèd Feature. Toward a Poetics of Uncertainty.* New York: Fordham UP, 1995. 97–115.

———. "Revaluations: Pablo Neruda." *Adam's Dream: A Preface to Translation.* New York: Grove, 1978. 101–83.

———. "The Vanishing Original: Transvaluations." *The Forgèd Feature. Toward a Poetics of Uncertainty.* New York: Fordham UP, 1995. 142–74.

Berg, Mary C. "Rereading Fiction by 19th-Century Latin American Women Writers: Interpretation and the Translation of the Past into the Present." Luis and Rodríguez-Luis. 127–34.

Binford, Leigh, and Wendy Hardin. "How First World Students Read Third World Literature." Luis and Rodríguez-Luis. 145–52.

Bocchino, Adriana. "Escrituras del exilio y traducción." Bradford. 63–80.

Borges, Jorge Luis. "Las dos maneras de traducir." *Textos recobrados 1919–1929.* Buenos Aires: Emecé, 1997. 256–59.

———. "El enigma de Edward Fitzgerald." *Otras inquisiciones.* 1952. *Obras completas.* Buenos Aires: Emecé, 1974. 688–90.

———. "Sobre el *Vathek* de William Beckford." *Otras inquisiciones*. 1952. *Obras completas*. Buenos Aires: Emecé, 1974. 729–32.

———. "Los traductores de las 1001 Noches." *Historia de la eternidad*. 1936. *Obras completas*. Buenos Aires: Emecé, 1974. 397–413.

———. "Las versiones homéricas." *Discusión*. 1932. *Obras completas*. Buenos Aires: Emecé, 1974. 239–43.

———. "Word Music and Translation " *This Craft of Verse*. Cambridge: Harvard UP, 2000. 57–76.

Borinsky, Alicia. "On Translation and the Art of Repetition." *Dispositio* 7 (1982): 217–28.

Bradford, Lisa Rose. "La transculturación de los juegos de géneros: La pasión de Jeanette Winterson." Bradford. 47–62.

Braga-Pinto, César. "Translating, Meaning and the Community of Languages." *Studies in the Humanities* 22.1–2 (1995): 33–49.

Bravo, María Elena. "Borges traductor: el caso de *The Wild Palms* de William Faulkner." *Insula* 40.462 (1985): 11–12.

Bush, Peter. "Strawberry Flowers in Realms of Chocolate: The Training of Literary Translators." *The Changing Scene in World Languages: Issues and Challenges*. Ed. Marian B. Labrum. Amsterdam: Benjamins, 1997. 109–17.

———. "Translating Onetti for Anglo-Saxon Others." *Onetti and Others: Comparative Essays on a Major Figure in Latin American Literature*. Ed. Gustavo San Román. Albany: SUNY Press, 1999. 177–86.

Campos, Haroldo de. "Da tradução como criação e como crítica." *Tempo Brasileiro* 4–5 (1963): 164–81.

———. "De la traducción como creación y como crítica." Trans. Héctor Olea. *Quimera* 9–10 (1981): 30–37.

———. "Mephistofaustian Transluciferation: Contribution to the Semiotics of Poetic Translation." Trans. Gabriela-Suzanna Wilder. *Dispositio* 7 (1982): 181–87.

———. "Tradición, traducción, transculturación: Historiografía y ex-centricidad." Trans. Néstor Perlongher. *Filología* 22.2 (1987): 45–53.

Capobianco, Michael F., and Gloria S. Meléndez. "Translating a Poet's Prose: Amado Nervo's *El donador de almas*." Luis and Rodríguez-Luis. 343–48.

Caracciolo Trejo, E. "Octavio Paz, traductor." *Siglo XX/20th Century* 10.1–2 (1992): 195–209.

Castro-Klarén, Sara, and Héctor Campos. "Traducciones, Tirajes, Ventas y Estrellas: El 'Boom'." *Ideologies and Literature* 4.17 (1983): 319–38.

Céspedes, Diógenes. "Teoría de lo político, teoría de la traducción en Octavio Paz." *Cuadernos de Poética* 3.7 (1985): 58–91.

Colás, Santiago. "Translation and Postmodernism." Luis and Rodríguez-Luis. 99–112.

Cortázar, Julio. "Translate, traduire, tradurre: traducir." *Grandes Firmas. Antología de artículos hispanoamericanos y españoles*. Madrid: EFE, 1987. 66–68.

Costa, Walter Carlos. "Borges and Textual Quality in Translation." *Cadernos de Tradução* 1 (1996): 115–36.

———. "Borges Traductor de *Bartleby,* de Melville." *Fragmentos* 8.1 (1998): 89–96.

Courteau, Joanna. "The Clash of Cultures in *Policarpo Quaresma.*" Luis and Rodríguez-Luis. 259–66.

Danielson, David J. "Borges on Translation: Encoding the Cryptic Equation." *The Comparatist: Journal of the Southern Comparative Literature Association* 11 (May 1987): 76–85.

Delbecque, Nicole. "Traducir: El eterno dilema entre fidelidad reproductora y libertad creadora: de José Ortega y Gasset a Octavio Paz." *Review of Applied Linguistics* 97–98 (1992): 71–105.

Dornheim, Nicolás. "Una entrevista frente al espejo: las preguntas que me gustaría contestar sobre traducción literaria." Bradford. 125–32.

Dumitrescu, Domnita. "Traducción y geteroglosia en la obra de Octavio Paz." *Hispania* 78.2 (1995): 240–51.

Eckstrom, Margaret V. "Interpreting Ethnicity: Differing Views of Biculturalism in Arguedas, Carpentier, Castellanos, and Valle-Inclán." Luis and Rodríguez-Luis. 173–77.

Engelbert, Jo Anne. "But Is It English? English Poetic Idiom and the Translation of Neruda." *Across the Language Gap: Proceedings of the 28th Annual Conference of the American Translators Association* Oct. 8–11, 1987, Albuquerque, NM. Ed. Karl Kummer. Medford, NJ: Learned Information, 1987. 205–208.

Ette, Ottmar. "Mit Worten des Anderen. Die literarische Übersetzung als Herausforderung der Literaturwissenschaft." In *Horizont-Verschiebungen: Interkulturelles Verstehen und Heterogenität in der Romania. Festschrift für Karsten Garscha zum 60. Geburtsdag.* Ed. Claudius Armbruster and Karin Hopfe. Tübingen: Gunter Narr Verlag, 1998. 13–33.

Ferré, Rosario. "Destiny, Language, and Translation, or Ophelia Adrift on the C & O Canal." *Women's Writing in Latin America: An Anthology.* Eds. Sara Castro-Klarén, Sylvia Molloy and Beatriz Sarlo. Boulder, CO: Westview, 1991. 89–94.

Foster, David William. "La política de las traducciones del español en los Estados Unidos." Bradford. 141–54.

———. "The Politics of Spanish Language Translation in the United States." *Punto de Contacto* 4.2 (1995): 63–72.

Fox, Geoffrey. "Mermaids and Other Fetishes: Images of Latin America." Luis and Rodríguez-Luis. 135–44.

French, John D. "Translation: An Imperative for a Transnational World." *LASA Forum* 28.1 (1997): 44–45.

García Márquez, Gabriel. "Los pobres traductores buenos." *GGM: Notas de prensa (1980–1984).* Madrid: Mondadori, 1991. 290–92.

Hewitt, Julia Cuervo. "Voces africanas: Historia, folklore y transculturación en la narrativa hispana caribeña." Luis and Rodríguez-Luis. 223–34.

Hodgson, Irene B. "Effects of Translation on Interpretation and Reader Response in Some Recent Latin American Novels." Luis and Rodríguez-Luis. 309–16.

Howard, Matthew. "Stranger Than Ficción: The Unlikely Case of Jorge Luis Borges and the Translator Who Helped Bring His Work to America." *Lingua Franca* June/July 1997: 40–49.

Hunt, Lydia. "Heightened Access to Literary Texts through Comparison of SL and TL Versions: Cortázar's *Rayuela* and Rabassa's *Hopscotch*." Luis and Rodríguez-Luis. 325–36.

Hurley, Andrew. "What I Lost When I Translated Jorge Luis Borges." *Cadernos de Tradução* 4 (1999): 289–304.

Iglesia, Cristina. "La escritura de Victoria Ocampo: malestar, destierro y traducción." *Feminaria* 8.15 (1995): 4–6.

Iriarte, Fabián O. "T.S. Eliot en la Argentina: 1930–1990." Bradford. 25–46.

Jackson, Kenneth David. "The Pleasure of Subverting the Text: Oswald de Andrade's *Seraphim Gross Pointe*." *Dispositio* 7 (1982): 203–208.

Johnson, David E. "The Time of Translation: The Border of American Literature." In *Border Theory: The Limits of Cultural Politics*. Eds. Scott Michaelsen and David E. Johnson. Minneapolis: U MN P, 1997. 129–65.

Kelley, Alita. "Conveying a World: The Andean Text as Translation, and Translation of the Andean Text." Round. 69–82.

Klor de Alva, J. Jorge. "Language, Politics, and Translation: Colonial Discourse and Classical Nahuatl in New Spain." R. Warren. 143–62.

Kutzinski, Vera M. "Turbulence and Noise: Translating Nicolás Guillén's *El diario que a diario*." Luis and Rodríguez-Luis. 241–48.

Laabs, Klaus. "Traducir a Reinaldo Arenas." *Apuntes Postmodernos/Postmodern Notes* (Miami) 6.1 (1995): 53–55.

Landers, Clifford E. "Latin America and Translation: Three Contributions to Knowing the Other." *Latin American Research Review* 30.3 (1995): 254–63.

———. "The Nocturnal World of Marcos Rey." Luis and Rodríguez-Luis. 267–84.

Levine, Suzanne Jill. "La escritura como traducción: *Tres tristes tigres* y una *Cobra*." *Revista Iberoamericana* 92–93 (1975): 557–67.

———. "From 'Little Painted Lips' to *Heartbreak Tango*." R. Warren. 30–46.

———. "Translating Bioy Casares' 'Flies and Spiders.'" Luis and Rodríguez-Luis. 45–55.

———. "Translation as (Sub)Version: On Translating *Infante's Inferno*." In *Rethinking Translation: Discourse, Subjectivity, Ideology*. Ed. Lawrence Venuti. New York: Routledge, 1992. 75–85.

Levinson, Brett. "Translating Erasure: The True Story of Lezama's 'Eras Imaginarias.'" Luis and Rodríguez-Luis. 79–86.

Lima Costa, Claudia de. "Being Here and Writing There: Gender and the Politics of Translation in a Brazilian Landscape." *Signs* 25.3 (2000): 727–60.

Longland, Jean R. "On Translating Haroldo de Campos." *Dispositio* 7 (1982): 189–202.

Louis, Anne Marie. "La traduction selon Jorge Luis Borges." *Poétique: Revue de Théorie et d'Analyse Littéraire* 107.27 (Sept. 1996): 289–300.

Luis, William. "Culture as Text: The Cuban/Caribbean Connection." Luis and Rodríguez-Luis. 7–21.

MacAdam, Alfred J. "Rebirth of a Novel." Luis and Rodríguez-Luis. 337–42.

———. "Translation as Metaphor: Three Versions of Borges." *MLN* 90 (1975): 747–54.

Maier, Carol. "Notes after Words: Looking Forward Retrospectively at Translation and (Hispanic and Luso-Brazilian) Feminist Criticism." *Cultural and Historical Grounding for Hispanic and Luso-Brazilian Feminist Literary Criticism.* Ed. Hernán Vidal. Minneapolis: Institutute for the Study of Ideology and Literature, 1989. 625–53.

Magalhães, Célia. "Tradução e Transculturação: A Teoria Monstruosa de Haroldo de Campos." *Cadernos de Tradução* 3 (1998): 139–56.

Martin-Ogunsola, Dellita L. "Translation as a Poetic Experience/Experiment: The Short Fiction of Quince Duncan." *Afro-Hispanic Review* 10.3 (1991): 42–50.

Martínez-Echazabal, Lourdes. "Testimonial Narratives: Translating Culture While Narrowing the Genre Gap." Luis and Rodríguez-Luis. 57–66.

Martínez-San Miguel, Yolanda. "*Balún canán* y la perspectiva femenina como traductora/traidora de la historia." *Revista de Estudios Hispánicos* 22 (1995): 165–83.

———. "Bitextualidad y bilingüismo: reflexiones sobre el lenguaje en la escritura latina contemporánea." *Centro Journal* 12.1 (2000): 19–34.

Matamoro, Blas. "Metáfora y traducción." *Cuadernos Hispanoamericanos* 505–507 (1992): 425–35.

Merrim, Stephanie. "In the Wake of the Word: Translating Guimarães Rosa." *Dispositio* 7 (1982): 209–16.

Milton, John. "'Make Me Macho. Make Me Gaucho. Make Me Skinny': Jorge Luis Borges' Desire to Lose Himself in Translation." *Cadernos de Tradução* 4 (1999): 87–98.

———. "Translation Theory in Brazil." Round. 123–36.

Molloy, Sylvia. "Lost in Translation: Borges, the Western Tradition, and Fictions of Latin America." *Borges and Europe Revisited.* Ed. Evelyn Fishburn. London: Institute of Latin American Studies, University of London, 1998. 8–20.

Montezanti, Miguel Angel. "Traducción y pluralismo cultural." Bradford. 155–66.

Munday, Jeremy. "The Caribbean Conquers the World? An Analysis of the Reception of García Márquez in English Translation." Round. 137–44.

Nobrega, Thelma-Medice. "Haroldo de Campos, José Paulo Paes e Paulo Vizioli Falam sobre Tradução." *Trabalhos em Linguística Aplicada* 11 (1988): 53–65.

Nunn, Frederick. "The Latin American 'New Novel' in Translation: Archival Source for the Dialogue Between Literature and History." Luis and Rodríguez-Luis. 67–78.

Offutt, Leslie S. "Indian Texts in a Spanish Context: The Nahuatl Wills of San Esteban de Nueva Tlaxcala." Luis and Rodríguez-Luis. 153–64.

Oliveira Tavares de Lyra, Regina Maria de. "Explicar é preciso? Notas de Traductor: Quando, Como e Onde." *Fragmentos* 8.1 (1998): 73–88.

Ortiz, Fernando. "El traductor de Humboldt en la historia de Cuba." *Ensayo político sobre la Isla de Cuba by Alejandro de Humboldt*. Havana: Publicaciones del Archivo Nacional de Cuba, 1996. 395–85.

Pastermerlo, Sergio. "Borges y la traducción." On website from Borges Center in Denmark: *www.hum.au.dk/romansk/borges/bsol/pastorml.htm*

Peden, Margaret Sayers. "A Conversation on Translation with Margaret Sayers Peden." *Translation Perspectives* IV (1986–87): 142–56.

Pera, Cristóbal. "'Three Trapped Tigers' or Literature as Translation." Luis and Rodríguez-Luis. 249–58.

Porrúa, Ana. "Leónidas Lamborghini: la máquina de traducir." Bradford. 81–92.

Quiroga, José. "Translating Vowels and the Defeat of Sounds." Luis and Rodríguez-Luis. 317–24.

Rabassa, Clementine C. "Politics and Religion: Burton's Translation of *O Uraguai*." Luis and Rodríguez-Luis. 285–93.

Rabassa, Gregory. "No Two Snowflakes Are Alike: Translation as Metaphor." Schulte and Biguenet. 1–12.

———. "Translation: A Matter of Choice." *Across the Language Gap: Proceedings of the 28th Annual Conference of the American Translators Association* Oct. 8–11, 1987, Albuquerque, NM. Ed. Karl Kummer. Medford, NJ: Learned Information, 1987. 11–16.

———. "Words Cannot Express . . . The Translation of Cultures." Gaddis Rose. 183–92.

Ramos Orea, Tomás. "The Poetic Translation of Translation: Reflections and Findings." *Meta* 37.3 (1992): 482–86.

Reyes, Alfonso. "De la traducción." *Teorías de la traducción. Antología de textos*. Ed. Dámaso López García. Cuenca: Ediciones de la Universidad de Castilla-La Mancha, 1996. 447–59.

Reyes, Rogelio. "The Translation of Interlingual Texts: A Chicano Example." Luis and Rodríguez-Luis. 301–308.

Ríos, Alicia. "La idea de nación y cultura nacional en las primeras constituciones venezolanas." Luis and Rodríguez-Luis. 235–40.

Ríos, Julián, ed. "Traducción/Transcreación" section in *Quimera* 9–10 (1981): 30–43.

Rodríguez Espinoza, Marcos. "La traducción como forma de exilio." Round. 83–94.

Rodríguez-Luis, Julio. "Introduction: Translating Latin America." Luis and Rodríguez-Luis. 1–6.

Romano-Sued, Susana. "Borges y la ficción como crítica: ficción, abismo y meta-textualidad." Bradford. 167–84.

Saldanha de Brito, Ana. "Traduzir ou não traduzir? Notas explicativas em 'Longo Caminho para a Liberdade' e 'Um Mês e um Dia: Diário de uma Detenção.'" Round. 159–73.

Salmón, Josefa. "Etnicidad y nacionalismo en el discurso indigenista peruano y boliviano de principios de siglo." Luis and Rodríguez-Luis. 179–84.

Sánchez, Luis Rafael. "La literatura como traducción de una cultura." Luis and Rodríguez-Luis. 23–34.

Sanjinés, Javier C. "From Domitila to 'los relocalizados': An Essay on Margin-ality in Bolivia." Luis and Rodríguez-Luis. 185–96.

Schwartz, Marcy E. "Cortázar's Plural Parole: Multilingual Shifts in the Short Fiction." *Romance Notes* 36.2 (1995): 331–38.

———. "Tradition and Treason: Sacred Translation in Two Stories by Borges and Chekhov." *Canadian Review of Comparative Literature* 23.4 (1996): 1085–95.

Seager, Dennis L. "Translating Bogotá to the Jungle: The Loss of Culture (?)" Luis and Rodríguez-Luis. 197–204.

Simas, Rosa. "'Ripples,' 'Una Rueda Giratoria,' and 'A Espiral e o Quadrado' (Circularity in Three Twentieth-Century Novels of the Americas.'" Luis and Rodríguez-Luis. 87–98.

Sommer, Doris. "Cortez in the Courts." *Proceed with Caution, When Engaged by Minority Writing in the Americas.* Cambridge: Harvard UP, 1999. 92–112.

Stavans, Ilan. "Translation and Identity." *Prospero's Mirror: A Translators' Portfolio of Latin American Short Fiction.* Ed. Ilan Stavans. Willimantic, CT: Curbstone, 1998.

Terra, Paulo Octaviano. "Translanco: Uma projeção de transposição espacio-temporal ou quando os astros trocam brilhos no espaco circular." *Suplemento Literario* (Minas Gerais) 23.1130 (1989): 8–10.

Tittler, Jonathan. "Contemporary Spanish American Fiction in English: Who is Translating Whom?" *Journal of Iberian and Latin American Studies* 4.1 (1998): 91–104.

———. "Translating Translation: Manuel Zapata Olivella's *Chambacú*." Luis and Rodríguez-Luis. 295–300.

Vasconcellos, Maria Lúcia. "Focus: the Effects of the Translator's Choices." *Fragmentos* 7.2 (1998): 73–84.

Vélez, Diana. "Introduction." *Reclaiming Medusa: Short Stories by Contempo-rary Puerto Rican Women.* Ed. Diana Vélez. San Francisco: Spinster/Aunt Lute, 1988. 1–22.

Vieira, Else Ribeiro Pires. "A Postmodern Translational Aesthetics in Brazil." Snell Hornby. 65–72.

———. "Liberating Calibans: Readings of *Antropofagia* and Haroldo de Cam-pos' Poetics of Transcreation." Bassnett and Trivedi. 95–113.

———. "Towards a Minor Translation." *Inequality and Difference in Hispanic and Latin American Cultures*. Ed. Bernard McQuirk and Mark I. Millington. Lewiston, NY: Edwin Mellen, 1995. 141–52.

Villanueva, Tino. "Brief History of Bilingualism in Poetry." *The Multilingual Anthology of American Literature. A Reader of Original Texts with English Translations*. New York: NY UP, 2000. 693–710.

Villanueva-Collado, Alfredo. "Gender Ideology and Spanish American Critical Practice: José Asunción Silva's Case." Luis and Rodríguez-Luis. 113 26.

Villoro, Juan. "El traductor." *Efectos personales*. Mexico: Era, 2000. 94–102.

Waisman, Sergio. "Ethics and Aesthetics North and South: Translation in the Work of Ricardo Piglia." *Modern Language Quarterly* 62.3 (2001): 259–83.

Wald, Miguel. "Traductores: atrapados por su destino." Bradford. 111–18.

White, Steven F. "Translation in Nicaraguan Poetry as a Literary Weapon Against Imperialism." Luis and Rodríguez-Luis. 165–72.

Willson, Patricia. "Traductores en *Sur*: teoría y práctica." Bradford. 133–40.

———. "La traducción literaria en la Argentina: las editoriales Sur y Losada en la década del treinta." *Actas del II Congreso Latinoamericano de Traducción e Interpretación*, 23–25 April 1998. Buenos Aires: Colegio de Traductores Públicos de Buenos Aires.

———. "La fundación vanguardista de la traducción." *Espacios* 25 (1999).

———. "Traducir lo nuevo." *Lenguas Vivas* 1 (2000–2001): 4–9.

———. "Estudios de traducción: una nueva antología" (review). *Lenguas Vivas* 1 (2000–2001): 118–19.

Wilson, Jason. "Tradición y traducción: Acerca de las relaciones de Octavio Paz con la poesía anglosajona." *Insula* 46.532–33 (1991): 34–35.

Contributors

Daniel Balderston is professor and chair of the Department of Spanish and Portuguese at the University of Iowa. Author of several books on Borges and editor of books on the historical novel, the short story, and sexuality studies in Latin America, he is also an active translator of fiction by such authors as José Bianco, Silvina Ocampo, Sylvia Molloy, Juan Carlos Onetti, and Ricardo Piglia.

Diana Bellessi is an Argentine poet, activist, and critic. She collaborated with Ursula LeGuin on a project on women's writing across cultures and languages. She is also the editor and translator of a major volume of women's poetry from the United States, published in Venezuela.

Jorge Luis Borges (1899–1986) was an Argentine poet, short story writer, and essayist. Some of his earliest publications in the 1920s were translations of German expressionists and of a fragment of Joyce's *Ulysses*, and he went on to become an important translator into Spanish of works by Faulkner, Whitman, Kafka, and Woolf. His essays on translation are among the most influential to emerge from Latin America.

Julio Cortázar (1914–1984) was an Argentine novelist and short story writer who resided in Paris for the last thirty years of his life. Best known for his experimental novels *Rayuela (Hopscotch)* and *62, A Model Kit,* he also translated the complete short fiction of Edgar Allan Poe into Spanish.

Walter Carlos Costa teaches at the Universidade Federal de Santa Catarina in Florianopolis, Brazil. He has translated and written extensively on translation, focusing on Borges, and is one of the editors of the journal *Cadernos de Tradução.*

Junot Díaz is a Dominican-American writer who teaches creative writing at Syracuse University. He is the author of a collection of short stories, *Drown,* that has been translated into Spanish and fourteen other languages.

Ariel Dorfman is a Chilean human rights activist and author. His numerous books, including *The Empire's Old Clothes, The Last Song of*

Manuel Sendero, Mascara, Last Waltz in Santiago and Other Poems of Exile and Disappearance, and the award winning play *Death and the Maiden,* have been translated into more than thirty languages. His latest book is *Heading South, Looking North: A Bilingual Journey* (1998). Mr. Dorfman is the Walter Hines Page Research Professor at Duke University.

John Felstiner teaches at Stanford University. His book *Translating Neruda: The Way to Macchu Picchu* received the Commonwealth Club Gold Medal, and his Neruda translations won the British Comparative Literature Association's first prize. His book *Paul Celan: Poet, Survivor, Jew* won the Truman Capote award for literary criticism.

Rosario Ferré from Puerto Rico is the author of numerous books in a variety of genres including the essay, the novel, poetry, short stories, and children's literature. She has been translated into English and German. She has received prestigious literary prizes such as the Liberatur Prix in 1992 for the German translation of her novel *Maldito amor,* and the Critic's Choice Award in 1995 for her novel *The House on the Lagoon.*

Luisa Futoransky, Argentine poet, novelist, and essayist, resides in Paris. She is the author of three novels, two book-length essays, and more than eight books of poetry, and her work has been translated into English, French, and German. She has been the recipient of prestigious awards and fellowships such as the French Chevalier des Arts et des Lettres and a grant from the Guggenheim Foundation.

Cristina García is a Cuban-American journalist and writer and one of the most renowned Hispanic writers who works in English. She is the author of two novels, *Dreaming in Cuban* and *The Agüero Sisters.* She resides in California.

Gabriel García Márquez is a Colombian novelist, scriptwriter, and journalist. Winner of the Nobel Prize for Literature in 1982, he is best known for the best-selling novel *Cien años de soledad* (One Hundred Years of Solitude), published in Spanish in 1967 and in dozens of other languages in subsequent years. A recent work is *Noticias de un secuestro* (News of a Kidnapping).

Rolando Hinojosa-Smith, one of the best known Chicano writers, is the author of *The Klail City Death Trip Series.* Theses on his work have appeared in Germany, Italy, the Netherlands, Spain, and Sweden. He teaches at the University of Texas at Austin.

James Hoggard is the author of fourteen books, including five collections of translations of poems from Spanish. His most recent collection of translations is *Stolen Verses and Other Poems by Oscar Hahn* (Northwestern UP, 2000). The winner of numerous awards, he is the McMurtry Distinguished Professor of English at Midwestern State University in Wichita Falls, Texas, and is the poet laureate of Texas.

Tomás Eloy Martínez, Argentine novelist, journalist, and script writer, is Distinguished Professor and director of the Latin American Studies program at Rutgers University. His novels include *La novela de Perón* and *Santa Evita,* and he has been translated into many languages. He is the recipient of the 2002 Alfaguara literary prize for his recent novel *El vuelo de la reina.*

Suzanne Jill Levine, widely published translator, teaches at the University of California, Santa Barbara. She has translated novelists such as Guillermo Cabrera Infante and Manuel Puig and is the author of *The Subversive Scribe: Translating Latin American Fiction* (Graywolf, 1991).

Gerald Martin teaches at the University of Pittsburgh. He is the author of *Journeys into the Labyrinth* (Verso), and of sections of the *Cambridge History of Latin America* on culture and literature. He is currently working on a biography of Gabriel García Márquez.

Francine Masiello teaches at the University of California, Berkeley, and is the author of *Lenguaje e ideología* (Hachette), *La mujer y el espacio público* (Feminaria), *Between Civilization and Barbarism: Women, Nation and Literary Culture in Modern Argentina* (U Nebraska P), and *The Art of Transition* (Duke UP, 2001).

María Eugenia Mudrovcic teaches at Michigan State University. She is the author of *Mundo Nuevo: Cultura y Guerra Fría en la década del 60* (1997), and is currently working on a book about Latin American literary memoirs.

Edmundo Paz-Soldán teaches in the department of Romance Studies at Cornell University. He is the author of three novels and three books of short stories, and was awarded the Juan Rulfo Short Story Award (1997). He is co-editor with Debra Castillo of the book *Latin American Literature and Mass Media* (Hispanic Issues/Garland, 2000).

Cristina Peri Rossi is an Uruguayan novelist, poet, and short story writer who resides in Spain. She is the author of the novels *Solitario de amor* and *La nave de los locos,* and her work has been translated into English and several other languages.

Ricardo Piglia is an Argentine novelist who teaches at Princeton. His best known novel is *Respiración artificial,* which has been translated into English (Duke) as has his novel *La ciudad ausente* (Duke) and a book of short fiction, *Assumed Name* (Latin American Literary Review Press).

Nélida Piñon, Brazilian novelist and short story writer who has been president of the Brazilian Academy of Letters, teaches at the University of Miami. She has been awarded numerous honors and literary prizes. Her novels, including *The Republic of Dreams*, have been translated into Spanish, French, English, Polish, German, Italian, and Russian.

José Quiroga teaches at Emory University, and is the author of *Understanding Octavio Paz* (South Carolina UP) and *Tropics of Desire* (New York UP).

Gregory Rabassa, notable translator of authors such as Julio Cortázar and Jorge Amado, teaches at Queens College and the CUNY Graduate Center.

Israel Reyes teaches at Dartmouth College and specializes in U.S. Latino and Latin American literatures. He has published on Puerto Rican fiction and cultural studies in academia.

Margaret Sayers Peden, professor emerita at the University of Missouri, is well-known as a translator of Latin American literature, from Sor Juana Inés de la Cruz to Carlos Fuentes.

Marcy E. Schwartz teaches at Rutgers University. She is the author of *Writing Paris: Urban Topographies of Desire in Contemporary Latin American Fiction* (SUNY Press, 1999), and is currently working on a book about the representation of urban space in Latin American writing.

Maarten Steenmeijer teaches Latin American Studies at the University of Nijmegen, Holland. He has translated extensively from Spanish American literature into Dutch, and is the author of *De Spaanse en Spaans-Amerikaanse literatuur in Nederland 1946–1985* and *Bibliografía de las traducciones de la literatura española e hispanoamericana al holandés 1946–1990*.

Vicky Unruh teaches at the University of Kansas and is the author of *Latin American Vanguards: The Art of Contentious Encounters* (U of California P). She is currently writing a book on Latin American women writers of the 1920s and 1930s.

Else Ribeiro Pires Vieira teaches at the Federal University of Minas Gerais, Brazil. Her most recent publication, the special issue of *Inter-*

ventions: The International Journal of Postcolonial Studies (Routledge), focuses on the quincentenary of the discovery of Brazil. She is also the author of *Teorizando e Contextualizando a Tradução* (1996), the editor of *Transculturalidades* (forthcoming) and is finishing a book on cultural translation for St. Jerome Press.

Eliot Weinberger's essays are collected in *Works on Paper, Outside Stories,* and *Karmic Traces.* His many translations include works by Octavio Paz, Vicente Huidobro, Xavier Villaurrutia, and Bei Dao. His translations of Jorge Luis Borges received the National Book Critics Circle prize for criticism and he was also awarded the Order of the Aztec Eagle by the government of Mexico.

Steven F. White teaches at St. Lawrence University. He has edited and translated poetry anthologies by writers from Nicaragua, Chile, and Brazil. He has also published several books of poetry and a critical study of the Nicaraguan avant-garde.

Index

Aira, César, 217
Aksyonov, Vassily, 34
Alarcón, Francisco, 9
Alegría, Ciro, 131, 146
Algarín, Miguel, 9
Allende, Isabel, 34, 239
Alvarez, Julia, 8, 51, 239
Amado, Jorge, 131, 132, 138, 240
Anderson, Danny, 201, 202
Antelo, Raúl, 4
Anzaldúa, Gloria, 9
Arciniegas, Germán, 132
Arguedas, Alcides, 170–181
Arguedas, José María, 5–6, 148, 149, 151, 172, 180n 8
Argueta, Manlio, 240, 241
Arreola, Juan José, 107, 191
Arrigucci, Davi, 4
Arrowsmith, William, 79
Ashcroft, William, 3
Asturias, Miguel Angel, 139, 144, 148, 149, 151, 153n 4
Azuela, Mariano, 146

Babel, 6, 9, 10n 3, 74
Bakhtin, Mikhail, 173
Balderston, Daniel, 5, 6, 64, 183, 189, 192n 2
Barthes, Roland, 39
Baudelaire, Charles, 80, 95, 98n 1, 120, 126n 5, 182
Beckett, Samuel, 24, 31, 65
Bellessi, Diana, 216
Benjamin, Walter, 26, 98n 1, 119, 168, 186, 191, 199, 200
Berman, Antoine, 192n 1
Bhabha, Homi, 3, 199, 201
Bianciotti, Héctor, 2, 31, 213
Bioy Casares, Adolfo, 62
Blake, William, 205

Blest Gana, Alberto, 131
Bly, Robert, 79
Braga-Pinto, César, 2
Bolívar, Simón, 40
Bombal, María Luisa, 131
"Boom," 8, 144–155, 129–143, 240
Borges, Jorge Luis, 2, 3, 4, 5, 9, 21, 22, 61, 62, 65, 67, 87, 101, 113, 114, 136–137, 144, 145–146, 148, 149, 151, 157, 182–193, 205
Bourdieu, Pierre, 131, 139, 180n 9
Bruce-Novoa, Juan, 8, 233n 5
Brushwood, John, 201
Burgos, Elizabeth, 7, 242

Cabrera Infante, Guillermo, 92–99, 139
Caillois, Roger, 145
Calvino, Italo, 61
Campo, Vera Mascarenhas do, 4
Campos, Augusto de, 191, 206, 209, 210
Campos, Haroldo de, 3, 4–5, 168, 191
Camus, Albert, 23
Cândido, Antonio, 4
Carpentier, Alejo, 35, 36, 132, 139, 144, 146, 149, 151, 226, 228
Carroll, Lewis, 189
Castillo, Debra, 202n 3
Castillo, José Guillermo, 135
Céline, Louis-Ferdinand, 63
Center for Inter-American Relations, 129–130, 132, 134–141
Cervantes, Miguel de, 16, 21, 77, 86, 98n 2, 156, 182, 185, 188, 189
Chamoiseau, Patrick, 42, 44
Christ, Ronald, 129, 137, 138, 140n 8, 141n 13
Cisneros, Sandra, 8, 44, 239

Clifford, James, 1, 9, 179n 5
Coleman, Alexander, 135
Conrad, Joseph, 24, 31, 61, 65
Cornejo Polar, Antonio, 175, 179n 4
Cortázar, Julio, 3, 8, 9, 21–22, 31, 62, 85, 133, 136, 144, 148, 149, 151
Costa, Walter Carlos, 5
Costa du Rels, Adolfo, 132
Cruz, Sor Juana Inés de la, 36, 75, 77, 78–79, 81, 82
Cunha, Euclides da, 38

Dante, 5, 59, 66, 92–94, 98n 5, 99n 6
Darío, Rubén, 217
De Man, Paul, 26
Derrida, Jacques, 226
Díaz, Junot, 8, 42–44
Dingwaney, Anuradha, 242
Donne, John, 187, 205, 206–208, 210
Donoso, José, 10n 3, 130, 138, 140nn. 6, 7, 148, 149, 151
Dostoevsky, Teodor, 62, 117
Drummond de Andrade, Carlos, 209–210

Echeverría, Esteban, 64
Eco, Umberto, 98n 5
Eliot, T. S., 125, 204
Eshleman, Clayton, 237, 238

Faulkner, William, 62, 137
Felstiner, John, 5
Ferré, Rosario, 9, 46
Fitzgerald, Edward, 186–187, 191
Flaubert, Gustave, 187
Forero, Cristina. See María Moreno
Franco, Jean, 216
Freyre, Gilberto, 131
Fuentes, Carlos, 8, 34, 35, 61, 72, 76, 80–81, 82, 90, 93, 107, 140n 6, 144, 148, 149, 151, 239
Futoransky, Luisa, 10n 3, 213–215

Gallegos, Rómulo, 146, 171
Gambaro, Griselda, 215, 216, 219
García Canclini, Néstor, 138
García, Cristina, 8, 10n 3, 44, 224–234

García Márquez, Gabriel, 8, 9, 34, 135, 115, 138, 144, 148, 149, 151, 152, 153n 5, 156–163, 238, 239, 240
Garcilaso de la Vega, Inca, 2, 168
Gelman, Juan, 217
Gide, André, 21, 120
Giovanni, Norman Thomas di, 61, 189, 190
Goethe, Johann Wolfgang von, 116
Goldberg, Isaac, 131
Gombrowicz, Witold, 31
Góngora, Luis de, 34, 36
Grossman, Edith, 160, 238
Guebel, Daniel, 217
Gugelberger, Georg, 7
Guillén, Nicolás, 10n 1
Güiraldes, Ricardo, 146
Guzmán, Martín Luis, 131

Hahn, Oscar, 101–103
Harss, Luis, 134, 136
Hernández, José, 90
Hijuelos, Oscar, 44
Hinojosa-Smith, Rolando, 8, 9
Homer, 5, 15–20, 92, 100, 111, 118, 185
Huidobro, Vicente, 6, 164–169, 182

Icaza, Jorge, 147
Inter-American Foundation for the Arts, 133–135

Jackson, Richard, 10n 1
James, Henry, 189
Jameson, Fredric, 99n 9
Johnson, David, 9
Joyce, James, 24, 31, 61, 65, 86, 93, 120, 126n 5, 137

Kafka, Franz, 31, 109, 118, 187, 189
King, John, 5, 146
Klor de Alva, J. Jorge, 10n 2

Lane, Helen, 52, 53, 61, 130
Lautréamont, Comte de, 2
Lefevere, André, 226
Leibnitz, Gottfried Wilhelm Freiherr von, 40

León-Portilla, Miguel, 107
Leopardi, Giacomo, 23
Levine, Suzanne Jill, 227, 232
Lewis, Marvin, 10n 1
Lezama Lima, José, 24, 25, 36, 93, 182, 184
Lispector, Clarice, 40, 58, 184

Machado de Assis, 183, 184, 191, 192n 3
Maier, Carol, 242
Mallea, Eduardo, 131
Malraux, André, 23
Martin, Gerald, 141n 10
Martínez-San Miguel, Yolanda, 8
Marvell, Andrew, 208–209
Masiello, Francine, 7
Matto de Turner, Clorinda, 172
Melo Neto, João Cabral de, 191, 209, 210
Menchú, Rigoberta, 7, 241–242
Merwin, W. S., 79
Mignolo, Walter, 3, 10n 2
Mohr, Nicholasa, 51, 233n 6
Molloy, Sylvia, 5, 139, 146, 147
Moreno, María, 215, 219–222
Moro, César, 2
Morse, Richard, 35
Moya Pons, Frank, 43
Mudrovcic, María Eugenia, 8, 152
Mundo Nuevo, 141n 9

Nabokov, Vladimir, 31, 32, 34, 61, 65
Negroni, María, 215, 219
Neruda, Pablo, 5, 73, 76–77, 78–80, 119–126, 83n 2, 98–99n 5, 105, 107, 119–126, 168
Nietzsche, Friedrich Wilhelm, 65
Niranjana, Tejaswini, 238

Ocampo, Victoria, 2, 5, 145, 220
Onís, Harriet de, 132
Ortega y Gasset, José, 38, 86
Ortiz Cofer, Judith, 229, 230
Ortiz, Fernando, 38
Ortiz, Ricardo, 233n 3

Palés Matos, Luis, 165
Palma, Ricardo, 131

Parra, Nicanor, 134, 140n 6
Paz, Octavio, 3, 6–7, 75, 99n 9, 101, 104, 107, 108, 118, 119, 227–228
Paz Soldán, Edmundo, 7
Pérez Firmat, Gustavo, 51, 230–231, 233n 7
Peri Rossi, Cristina, 10n 3
Pezzoni, Enrique, 62
Piglia, Ricardo, 240
Piñón, Nélida, 36, 40
Poe, Edgar Allan, 62, 80, 182
Poma de Ayala, Guaman, 2
Ponge, Francis, 22
Poniatowska, Elena, 107
Pound, Ezra, 108–109, 112, 119, 191
Prescott, Laurence, 10n 1
Proust, Marcel, 23, 92, 118, 182
Puga, María Luisa, 194–203
Pushkin, Alexander, 62, 84, 85

Quixote. See Cervantes

Rabassa, Gregory, 25, 53, 135, 158, 159, 160
Rama, Angel, 4, 138, 178
Reid, Alastair, 135
Reyes, Alfonso, 4, 5, 91, 131, 192n 5
Reyes, Israel, 8
Rimbaud, Arthur, 111
Rivera, José Eustasio, 147, 171, 180n 14
Rivera, Tomás, 50
Roa Bastos, Augusto, 6, 61
Rodríguez Monegal, Emir, 4, 130, 134, 135, 136, 137, 139, 140n6; 141nn. 9, 13, 147, 189, 192n 5
Roffé, Mercedes, 216
Rosa, João Guimarães, 4–5, 36, 131, 183
Rukeyser, Muriel, 29
Rulfo, Juan, 61, 191, 107, 140 n 6, 146, 148, 149, 151, 240
Rushdie, Salman, 117–118, 201
Ruskin, John, 23, 182

Sabato, Ernesto, 129, 130, 132, 139, 146, 240
Saer, Juan José, 213, 214, 222
Safranchik, Graciela, 215, 217–219

Saint-Exupéry, Antoine, 23
Santa Cruz, Nicomedes, 10n 1
Sarduy, Severo, 139
Sarlo, Beatriz, 1, 5
Sarmiento, Domingo Faustino, 64
Sartre, Jean Paul, 23
Saussure, Ferdinand de, 164
Schulte, Rainer, 238–239
Schwartz, Jorge, 4
Schwartz, Marcy, 3
Semprún, Jorge, 24
Shakespeare, William, 100, 104, 120, 121, 122, 123, 157, 182, 183, 187, 188, 189, 206, 217, 218, 222n 1
Sigüenza y Góngora, Carlos, 36
Simon, John, 135
Simon, Sherry, 196, 197, 199
Soto, Gary, 51
Spivak, Gayatri, 196
Steenmeijer, Maarten, 8
Steiner, George, 32, 34, 38
Strand, Mark, 135
Suárez Carreño, José, 132
Suárez, Virgil, 51
Supervielle, Jules, 2
Sur, 5, 145, 147

Tiffin, Helen, 3
Tolstoy, Leo, 62, 67

Torres Saillant, Silvio, 43
Traba, Marta, 140n 6

Ugarte, Manuel, 131
U.S. Latino/a literature, 8–9, 32–41, 42–44, 45–48, 49–51, 107, 224–234, 239–240

Vallejo, César, 61, 121, 165, 166
Vargas Llosa, Mario, 8, 144, 148, 149, 151, 153nn. 2, 5, 168, 190–191, 239
Vega, Ana Lydia, 229–230
Veloso, Caetano, 206
Venuti, Lawrence, 186, 192, 235, 242–243
Vieira, Elsa Ribeiro Pires, 4
Virgil, 95

Waisman, Sergio, 64
Weinberger, Eliot, 164, 166, 167, 168, 169
West, Alan, 224, 227, 231–232
White, Steven, 7, 8
Whitman, Walt, 120 122, 123, 126nn. 5, 13, 188, 189
Woolf, Virginia, 62, 67

Yourcenar, Marguerite, 21, 62